Airships in International Affairs, 1890–1940

Airships in International Affairs, 1890–1940

John Duggan
Management Consultant specializing in Oil Industry Economics

and

Henry Cord Meyer
Research Professor Emeritus
University of California
Irvine

First published 2001 by
PALGRAVE
Houndmills, Basingstoke, Hampshire RG21 6XS and
175 Fifth Avenue, New York, N. Y. 10010
Companies and representatives throughout the world

PALGRAVE is the new global academic imprint of
St. Martin's Press LLC Scholarly and Reference Division and
Palgrave Publishers Ltd (formerly Macmillan Press Ltd).

ISBN 0–333–75128–0

This book is printed on paper suitable for recycling and
made from fully managed and sustained forest sources.

A catalogue record for this book is available
from the British Library.

Library of Congress Cataloging-in-Publication Data
Duggan, John, 1932–
    Airships in international affairs, 1890–1940 / John Duggan,
    Henry Cord Meyer.
        p. cm.
    Includes bibliographical references and index.
    ISBN 0–333–75128–0
        1. Airships—History. 2. International relations. 3. Airships–
    –Political aspects. I. Meyer, Henry Cord, 1913– II. Title.

    TL651 .D74 2001
    629.133'24'0943—dc21
                                                        2001021885

10   9   8   7   6   5   4   3   2   1
10 09 08 07 06 05 04 03 02 01

Printed and bound in Great Britain by
Antony Rowe Ltd, Chippenham, Wiltshire

Remembering these earlier analysts of airship wonder

Hugo Eckener
Guy Hartcup
Hans G. Knäusel
Sir Peter G. Masefield
Douglas H. Robinson
Richard K. Smith

We are borne on their shoulders

Contents

List of Illustrations*

* Where no credit is given, the illustration is in the private collection of one of the authors.

Acknowledgements

After a generation of research and consultation it is a pleasure to express our appreciation for all the enlightenment and assistance we have received from nearly a hundred institutions and individuals scattered over four continents that were touched by the wonder of airship promise and operations. On various occasions our research has taken us over much of the United States, within Britain and Germany, and to Australia and Brazil. In our endeavors we have enjoyed friendly reception, generous hospitality and liberal cooperation. For all these gifts and aid we are deeply grateful.

Since historians usually turn first of all to documentation, let us begin by listing these basic institutions to which we are indebted, together with particularly helpful individuals: the archives of the Zeppelin Museum, Friedrichshafen (Dr Wolfgang Meighörner and Barbara Waibel); the National Archives, Washington, DC; the National Air and Space Museum, Washington, DC (Ms Catherine D. Scott); the Public Record Office, London, Chancery Lane and Kew; the Bundesarchiv, Koblenz (Drs Vogel and Montfort); the Political Archives, German Foreign Ministry, Bonn (Drs Weinandy and Keipert). Equally significant are the archives of several business firms: the Goodyear Tire and Rubber Company, Akron, OH (Mmes Marjory Garman, Cecile R. Norman, and Mary E. Maley); further documentation of the Goodyear-Zeppelin era deposited with the archives of the University of Akron (Dr John V. Miller); personal and business archives of Johann Schütte, Stadtmuseum and Stadtarchiv, Oldenburg (Drs J. Friedrich Jahn and Dorothea Halland); HAPAG-LLOYD archives, Hamburg (Rolf Fink); and Lufthansa archives, Cologne (Dr Werner E. Bittner).

Personal archives and collections of papers constitute the next stratum of documentation: Papers of Garland Fulton, Naval Historical Foundation, Washington Navy Yard, Washington, DC (H. A. Vadnais, Jr); Scott E. Peck Papers, Chula Vista, CA; Douglas H. Robinson Collection, Pennington, NJ; Hallett Everett Cole Airship Collection, University of Oregon, Eugene, OR; Papers of F. W. (Willy) von Meister, Peapack, NJ; Barnes Wallis Papers, the Science Library, London; Eckener Papers with Mrs Lotte Simon-Eckener, Konstanz; Dr Uwe Eckener Archives, Konstanz; Captain Hans von Schiller Archives, Tübingen (Mrs Elisabeth Pletsch); Friedrichshafen Rathaus Archives

(Messrs Scharpf and Buhl); Airship History Collection of Max Schorn, Friedrichshafen; and the two very important private airship history archives of the late Alfred F. Weber, Karlsruhe, and Werner Strumann, Münster/Westfalen.

We have enjoyed the resources and services of the Library of Congress, the New York Public Library, the British Museum, the Royal Aeronautical Society (A. W. L. Naylor), the Imperial War Museum, the Deutsches Museum (Munich) and the Hoover Institution (Stanford University, CA).

Without the interviews that Meyer was privileged to have with a number of the survivors of the airship era between 1972 and 1985, significant data and insights would not have been available for posterity. He is particularly indebted to Captain Garland Fulton, USN; Vice-Admiral Charles E. Rosendahl, USN; Vice-Admiral Thomas (Tex) G. W. Settle, USN; Rear-Admiral Scott E. Peck, USN; F. W. (Willy) von Meister; Thomas A. Knowles (Goodyear Aerospace); George H. Lewis (Goodyear-Zeppelin); Captain Clarence (Dutch) Schildhauer (DO-X & PanAm); Lord Kings-Norton; Sir Barnes Wallis; Captain George F. Meager; Crispin Rope; Mrs Lotte Simon-Eckener; Captain Heinrich Bauer; Captain Albert Sammt; Captain Hans von Schiller; Erich Hilligardt; German Zettel; and Klaus F. Pruss.

Duggan expresses appreciation to Manfred Bauer; E. Bowen; R. H. A. Carter; Sir Edward Fennesy; Oskar Fink; Cheryl Ganz; Jenny Hammerton; Admiral C. B. Higgins, RN; Georg Holl; Sidney Jefferson; R. V. Jones; Aleyn R. Jordan; Thomas Kass; Peter Kleinheins; Lis Koetter; Erwin Kube; Colin Latham; Jean-Pierre Lauwers; Manfred Lösemann; John Mellberg; Mildred Moering; J. Neil; Heinz Oberdrevemann; Peter Rickenback; Larry Sall; Heike Vogel; Barbara Waibel; and Nick Walmsley. We both wish to acknowledge how greatly indebted we are to our copy editor Anne Rafique for her dedication in reviewing and enhancing the text of this book. Finally, we should like to say how much we appreciate the interest and guidance of our commissioning editor Luciana O'Flaherty at Palgrave.

For further data we are indebted to Peter W. Brooks; Geoffrey A. Chamberlain; Barry Countryman; Prof. Clive Foss; Stephen V. Gallup; Hans G. Knäusel; Sir Peter G. Masefield; John Provan; Werner Rau; Douglas H. Robinson; K. H. Royter; Richard K. Smith; Heinz Steude; Rolf Striedacher; Prof. William F. Trimble; A. D. Topping; and officers of the Lighter-than-Air Society (Akron, OH); and Heinz M. Wronsky.

Each of the following individuals has made special contributions to our work over the years: Guy Hartcup; Prof. Robin Higham; Rolf xii *Acknowledgements*

Italiaander; Prof. J. E. Morpurgo; Werner Strumann; Gordon Vaeth; Lord Ventry; and Hepburn Walker, Jr.

We are especially indebted to the staffs of the Zeppelin Museum at Friedrichshafen and of the Interlibrary Loan section of the Library at the University of California at Irvine, CA. Other valuable assistance has come to us in manuscript preparation from the courtesies of Prof. Maria C. Pantella and Ms Beth E. Shanor of the Thesaurus Linguae Graecae at UCI. And we greatly appreciate the painstaking care of our computer text processor, Dr John Miller.

Further, Meyer expresses thanks to the Research-Travel Committee, School of Humanities, University of California at Irvine for various periodic grants of financial assistance over the years for travel to foreign research and consultation sites and for textual preparation of this book.

And finally, we both wish to acknowledge how much our work has benefited from the support, advice and meticulous textual scrutiny of Mrs Gisela Woodward.

All these institutions and individuals have given us their generous assistance; any textual errors that may persist are our own responsibility.

J. D. & H. C. M.

The Airships

Germany

Gross-Bassenach   Semi-rigids, built by the Prussian Airship Battalion

Parseval   Non-rigids. Army use

Schütte-Lanz   Rigids

SL1   German Army
SL2   German Army

Zeppelin
(Works Numbers)

LZ1	The first Zeppelin. First ascent 02.07.1900
LZ2	First flight 1905. Forced landing on second flight – dismantled
LZ3	First flight 1906. Purchased by German Army in 1908 as ZI
LZ4	Burned at Echterdingen 05.08.1908
LZ5	Purchased by German Army as ZII
LZ6	Operated by DELAG
LZ10	DELAG ship *Schwaben*
LZ11	DELAG ship *Viktoria Luise*
LZ12	German Army ZIII
LZ13	DELAG ship *Hansa*
LZ14	Naval L1. Lost in storm over Heligoland 09.09.1913 – 14 dead
LZ15	German Army *Ersatz* ZI
LZ16	German Army ZIV. Emergency landing at Lunéville, France in 1913
LZ17	DELAG ship *Sachsen*
LZ18	Naval L2. Burned in air at Johannisthal 10.07.1913 – 28 dead
LZ76	Naval L33. Forced down over England – model for Britain's R33 and R34
LZ96	Naval L49. Forced landing in France 20.10.1917
LZ104	Naval L59. Flight to Africa covering 4200 miles in 95 hours (1917)
LZ113	Surrendered to Great Britain. Dismantled in 1923
LZ114	Naval L72, surrendered to France in 1920 as *Dixmude* – crashed 1923

LZ120   *Bodensee* surrendered to Italy as *Esperia*. Dismantled 1928
LZ121   *Nordstern* surrendered to France as *Méditerranée*. Dismantled
        1926
LZ125   Not built. Negotiations with US Army's Colonel Hensley,
        1919–20
LZ126   Transferred to US where it became ZR3, later named *Los
        Angeles*
LZ127   *Graf Zeppelin* (1928–40). Round-the-World Flight 1929
LZ128   Not built. Designed as a hydrogen ship, but development
        aborted as a result of the R101 hydrogen fire
LZ129   *Hindenburg* (1936–7). First North American service
LZ130   *Graf Zeppelin II* (1938–40). Used for radio and radar espionage

Great Britain

No. 23
No. 32 Wooden-framed. Demonstration flight (with R33) over
        Amsterdam 1919
R33   Epic flight over the North Sea (1925), after breaking away
        from a mooring mast
R34   Built by William Beardmore & Co. Ltd and based on the
        design of the captured German LZ33. First airship to cross the
        Atlantic in both directions (1919)
R38   Became US airship ZR2. Broke up in the air during trials over
        Hull (1921)
R80   Built by Vickers (1920–1). Used only as a trial ship. Designed
        by Barnes Wallis
R100   Built by Vickers. Flew to Canada and back (1930). Designed
        by Barnes Wallis
R101   Built at HM Airship Works. Crashed in France on way to
        India (1930)

Italy

N1   Sold to Norway, as *Norge*. First airship to fly over the North
        Pole
N4   *Italia*. Crashed in the Arctic (1928)

United States

Roma	Army non-rigid airship, purchased by US Army from Italy (1921–2)
ZR1	*Shenandoah* (1923–5). Copy of the German LZ49 – Naval L49). Crashed 1925
ZR2	Built as British R38. Purchased by US. Crashed during trials over Hull 1921
ZR3	Built as German LZ126: to US as war 'reparations' ship. Named *Los Angeles*
ZRS4	*Akron*. Built by Goodyear as a US Navy 'Scout'. Crashed 1933 – 73 dead
ZRS5	*Macon*. Built by Goodyear as a US Navy 'Scout'. Crashed 1935 – 81 survivors

Airship Personalities

France

Commander Jean du Plessis de Grenédan — Major advocate of naval airships. Captain of the *Dixmude*

Germany

Nikolaus Bassenach — Engineer. Responsible for development of the Gross-Bassenach semi rigid 'M' ships used by German army

Dr Carl Berg — Industrialist, manufacturer and supplier of aluminium

Captain Walter Bruns — First World War Zeppelin commander. Leading member of Aeroarctic

Alfred Colsman — Managing Director of the Luftschiffbau Zeppelin GmbH, responsible for the successful business development of the Zeppelin companies

Dr Ludwig Dürr — Chief Designer, Luftschiffbau Zeppelin GmbH

Theodor Kober — Designer, pioneer zeppelins

Dr Hugo Eckener — Airship captain, Chairman of the Luftschiffbau Zeppelin and DZR

Major Hans Gross — Head of Prussian Airship Battalion. Developed Gross-Bassenach semi-rigid 'M' ships used by the German army

Ernst A. Lehmann — Zeppelin captain. DZR Director. Zeppelin experience since 1916

Major August von Parseval — Designer of the Parseval non-rigids, used by the army and exported to Austria, Great Britain, Japan and Russia

Dr Johann Schütte — Developer of the Schütte-Lanz rigid airships bought by German Army and Navy

David Schwarz — Builder of the first aluminium airship and first rigid to ascend (1897)

Captain Hans Bartsch von Sigsfeld	Developer of observation balloons for German army
Karl Wölfert	Built pioneer airship *Deutschland* (crashed 1896)
Count Ferdinand von Zeppelin	Inventor and developer of the rigid zeppelin airships

Great Britain

Commander Dennistoun Burney	Advocate of Imperial Airship Service
Sir Sefton Brancker	Director of Civil Aviation
Christopher Bullock	Permanent Secretary to Secretary of State for Air
Constructor-Commander Charles I. R. Campbell	Manager, Royal Airship Works. Chief Designer, R38
Wing Commander R. B. Colmore	Royal Air Force. Director of Airship Development
Harold Roxbee Cox	Chief Calculator, R101
Air Vice Marshall Hugh Dowding	Royal Air Force. Air Member for Supply & Research
Commodore E. M. Maitland	Air Ministry Director of Airships
Group Captain P. F. N. Fellows	Director of Airship Development
Brigadier E. A. D. Masterman	Pre-First World War airship captain. Head of Inter-Allied Control Commission
Flight Lieutenant J. E. M. Pritchard	Officer i/c R38 Trials. Air Ministry instrumentation expert
Squadron Leader Michael Rope	Designer. Innovative work on R101
Major G. Herbert Scott	Captain of the R34 on its transatlantic flight in 1919 and of the R100 on her flight to Canada in 1930. Assistant Director of Airship Development – Flying and Training
Lieutenant Colonel Vincent C. Richmond	Assistant Director of Airship Development – Technical. Chief Designer of the R101
Lord Thomson of Cardington	Secretary of State for Air
General Sir Hugh Trenchard	Founder of the Royal Air Force

Barnes Wallis	Engineer and inventor. Airship design for Vickers, including responsibility for R80 and R100

Italy

General Umberto Nobile	Airship designer. Captain of the *Norge* and *Italia*. Moved to the USSR to help develop airships

United States

Dr Karl Arnstein	Chief Designer in Friedrichshafen. Transferred to Goodyear and responsible for the design and helped build the *Akron* and *Macon*. Prepared designs for Goodyear commercial airships
Major Harold Geiger	US Army representative at Friedrichshafen
Colonel William M. Hensley	US Army. Negotiated to buy the LZ125
Dr Jerome C. Hunsaker	US Navy. Vice-president Goodyear-Zeppelin and responsible for commercial airship development
Rear Admiral Ernest J. King	US Navy. Advocate of carrier-borne aviation. Succeeded Moffett as Chief of Bureau of Aeronautics in 1933
Lieutenant Commander Zachary Lansdowne	US Navy. Captain of the *Shenandoah*. Died in crash
Paul W. Litchfield	Chairman, Goodyear-Zeppelin. CEO, Goodyear Tire & Rubber Co.
W. F. (Willy) von Meister	Luftschiffbau representative in USA. DZR Vice-President 1936–7
Brigadier General William Mitchell	Commander of US Army Flying Corps in France in First World War. Determined advocate of US Army aeronautical development and foe of naval airships
Admiral William A. Moffett	US Navy. Head of Naval Bureau of Aeronautics. Died in *Akron* crash 1933
Commander Charles E. Rosendahl	US Navy. Captain of *Los Angeles*. Lakehurst commander, 1937

| Harry Vissering | Businessman and engineer. 'Godfather' to Goodyear-Zeppelin and director of the company |
| Commander Ralph D. Weyerbacher | Designer and builder of the US Navy's ZR1 *Shenandoah* |

Introduction: Technology and the Human Psyche

This study examines the startling impact of a unique modern technological construction on the human psyche, together with its accompanying opportunities for political manipulation. Here are interwoven two very different but fundamental aspects of human endeavour. Technology is the logical offspring of scientific study. It proceeds from formulated study towards reasoned practical ends. Politics, by contrast, is not a science to be examined; it is an art to be learned. Bismarck once wrote succinctly: 'The practitioner of politics seeks power, either for ideological or egotistical support of other causes, or for its own sake, in order to relish the prestige which it bestows'.[1] Technology has always been linked with power-seeking, from the great affairs of state to the smallest individual circumstances of one human being pursuing advantage over another. The entire spectrum of this behaviour came into play with the developing technology of the rigid airship between 1890 and 1940. Before beginning with the outlines of that remarkable half-century of lighter-than-air evolution, three basic phenomena of that era require introductory attention.

   The first of these aspects is the wide spectrum of psychological responses to the wondrous skyships – from initial individual perceptive excitement, through moments of perplexity or fear, to the enthusiasm of crowd behaviour. Second is the significant intensification of these varied reactions resulting from the fact that relatively very few rigid airships were built and flown between 1900 and 1939, as compared to the widespread public awareness of their alleged promise, their celebrated accomplishments, and their dramatic failures. Third was the intrusion of politics, as seen in the efforts of some individuals and various groups to direct the designing, building, and flying of rigid airships toward personal or group objectives not basically inherent in the conceptualization or purposes of airship development per se. Here the behaviour of some established institutional bureaucracies occasionally influenced these political directions of airship technology. And here especially flourished the business and governmental agencies that propagandized the promise and performance of the impressive sky giants. Their focused efforts to manoeuvre the random sensationalism of popular journalism and film further energized the public zeppelin enthusiasm in Germany and 'zeppelin fever' in America. Intermittently also these popular media delivered abrupt negative blows to that positive enthusiasm, when the obverse of a coin of airship expectations and successes suddenly flipped to the reverse of their spectacular disasters. Seldom has a product of technological inspiration and fulfilment held so much of human fascination in suspense, together with a gradually increasing latent sense of imminent dread. Seldom before did such opportunities appear for the political manipulation of technology.

Quite fundamental to the recent popular appeal of the airship is the well-known penchant of humankind to express wonder or fear in the presence of nature's great manifestations – soaring peaks, deep chasms, magnificent vistas, violent storms, and natural catastrophes. This latent megalomaniac response of the human psyche has repeatedly expressed itself through time, from admiration of the seven wonders of the ancient world, by way of the towering Gothic cathedrals, to the palatial establishments of modern royalty. All these were more than testimonies to the creative genius of their designers and builders. Pre-eminently these structures celebrated the organizations or powerful men who ordained their construction and who made their political statements by direct identification with these technological accomplishments. Beginning in the early modern era, movement (and then speed) were added to the generic attractiveness of gigantism. These elements appeared first at sea, from the dimensions of the Great Armada, by way of the towering men-of-war that clashed at Trafalgar, to the tall-masted swiftness of American clipper ships. With railways came the moving technological wonders on land, with successively larger and faster locomotives and their trains. Here technology displayed the power and roar of their engines, the capacity and luxury of their cars, and new dimensions of empire-building in the Trans-Siberian, Cape-to-Cairo, and Berlin-to-Baghdad railways. These impressive constructions raised a few individuals to prominence, excited the peoples of their respective nations, and aroused various apprehensions about their implications for international politics and war. Count Witte of Imperial Russia, Cecil Rhodes of African fame, and Kaiser Wilhelm II of

German technological prowess: all manoeuvred, or were perceived as politically manipulating, these wondrous technological achievements.

Simultaneously, iron and steam also went to sea, reaching their apogee of naval might in the great grey line of Dreadnoughts that expressed the power of maritime empires. Concurrently there also developed the intense commercial rivalry of the northwest European nations, each seeking to exceed the other in the size, speed, and luxury of its respective entry in the race for the mythical Blue Riband of the North Atlantic. Dreadnoughts and liners alike were heavily subsidized by their political masters to assert national achievement and superiority in their engineering accomplishments. Into this era of technological competition for military advantage, commercial fame, and propaganda for national prestige came the first ascent of LZ1 on 2 July 1900.

The German rigid airship overcame most of its teething problems in the pre-war decade. Here it vied for attention in the burgeoning public enthusiasm for all aviation: free balloons, airplanes, and three types of dirigibles. And the zeppelin exceeded them all in attractive popularity. It was unique in carrying skyward the continuing thrust of gigantism, the promise of speed, and intimations of luxury. An ethereal quality of the new engineering overrode these baser elements. Nothing bound this great structure to earth except the expertise of its aeronauts to ascend and descend in relation to their terrestrial homes. Unlike the locomotive, the ocean liner, and the newly-arriving racing car, the rigid airship initially was a vehicle of surprise. No rails directed the course of its passage. No coastlines delimited its points of departure and arrival. Effortlessly it moved above its onlookers, seeming to convey the yearnings and hopes of the crowds below for new opportunities and new experiences. For six years before the outbreak of World War I, the cry, 'Zeppelin kommt!', brought the Germans out into the streets and onto the rooftops to enjoy and cheer this new pride of the *Vaterland*, until military needs coloured the airship battle grey and directed its voyaging secretively out over enemy seas and lands.

The people of Imperial Germany, both as individuals and in crowds, already experienced the full range of emotional response to the airship that would generally characterize popular perceptions worldwide between the wars. Thus were heard the praises: 'Her torpedo shaped silver hull agleam in the sun';[2] 'looking like a huge silver fish floating through the brilliant sky';[3] 'the sun transfiguring her grey hull until it seemed to be carved of alabaster, [the zeppelin] was a romantic phantom coming out of the dawn'.[4] Although various perceptual meanings were assigned to the airship phenomenon between the wars – in variations of viewers' places, times, and broader understandings of airship hazards – there were clearly defined psychological constancies of airship observation: its lightness, brightness, shape, colour, and ethereal appeal. These qualities were as evident in May 1937, when the *Hindenburg* made her last flight over Manhattan, as they had been in August 1908, when Count Zeppelin made his first long-distance flight down the Rhine river valley.[5]

Let us explore further some of the general psychological explanations that account for the unique impact of the rigid airship upon humankind during the generation of skyship awareness. These reactions can be conveniently sorted into three subgroups. First were the individual reactions of a positive and unthreatening quality: wonder, amazement, and admiration. These qualities easily escalated into excitement and sensationalism. This brighter side of the human psyche had its shadowed obverse. Here the individual airship observers wrestled with more troubling dimensions of their responses: uncanniness and incongruity, sexuality, apprehension and some instances of terror. A third major psychological reaction occurred in the special circumstances and behaviour of mostly friendly crowds. Of course, few of all these psychological airship perceptions took place in singular behavioural isolation. Mostly both the individual and crowd reactions manifested various combinations of behaviour.

Beginning with the first group of reactions, benign and positive, there was the wonder of the observer, possibly questioning, usually marvelling. In terms of humanistic psychology, the individual usually brought a richness of mind and consciousness to experience the wonder of a heavenly technological apparition. Possibly there were elements of a cognition of being, where the 'object tends to be seen as a whole, as a complete unit, detached from relations, from possible usefulness, from expediency and from purpose'.[6] Even in 1975, in presence of the comparatively unspectacular Goodyear blimp, an observer paused to watch and follow the ship because he found it wondrous in its dignified and unswerving majesty. Such circumstances suggest perception with an innocent eye, together with a brief moment of an altered state of consciousness.[7]

Amazement and admiration both derived from the sense of wonder. Although psychologists identify a so-called familiarization effect, this circumstance had only partially occurred by 1937. True, various journalists sent to report on the arrival of the *Hindenburg* at Lakehurst on 6 May 1937 had retreated to a nearby bar for conviviality, leaving only

Herbert Morrison to make his world-shaking radio broadcast of the disaster. The next day, however, the *New York Times* reported how people had earlier gazed in admiration: 'From windows, rooftops, sidewalks, fire escapes, and other points of vantage they viewed the giant airliner as the ship, its motors roaring and swastikas gleaming passed over the city.'[8] A decade earlier, Dr Hugo Eckener, himself trained by Wilhelm Wundt in behavioural psychology, had delayed the arrival of the *Graf Zeppelin* over San Francisco on 25 August 1929 in order to arrive near sunset over the Golden Gate – all for maximum viewer effect.[9] Comparably, a year later a writer for the *Canadian Forum* rhapsodized:

> On her western course she [R100] passed by low at night, vast, majestic, gold-washed by the moonlight against a serene dark sky, her lights as steady and assuring as those of a liner at sea, the drone of her engines implicit of her conscious power. On her return we saw her in the pride of day, as much at home in her element and as beautiful as a full-rigged ship on blue water. A sight to lift a man's heart.[10]

This was only one of many poetic tributes to the wonder of the airship. Psychologically, for many an individual the airship was more than poetry. It represented anticipation of pleasure and of wish-fulfilment. More than the appeal of a passing train or departing liner, the airship responded to that human yearning to soar and to be free. Its lingering majestic movement gave more promise of realizing that yearning than the spasmodic hop-skip of most airplanes that most people experienced. Eckener himself wrote of his conviction that the measured movement of the zeppelin calmed and satisfied the human spirit, that its arrival from a great distance and passing as a silver shadow fortified hopes for earthly peace, good fortune, and prosperity.[11] Psychiatrist Douglas H. Robinson has put it very suggestively:

> The rigid airship in a feminist guise suggests the ultimate in emotional security: life in the womb ... How we long to recreate this oasis of primal security! ... With her belly filled with happy children, flying aboard the rigid airship was going back to the security of the womb – back to before birth – with the advantage that one could see outside, and curiosity was satisfied.[12]

Beyond these contemplative moods, the airship very early produced also escalating individual reactions, from admiration, by way of excitement, to sensationalism. These phenomenological perceptions – experiences exaggerating reality onto some greater kind of appearance – had both positive and negative aspects.[13] Seen positively, this phenomenology expressed itself in exaggerated nationalism, in the endowment of airships with claims to cultural superiority and national prestige. This was the case with most Germans, from their national deification of the aeronaut Count and his zeppelin from 1908 onwards, until the end of the airship era. The accumulation and expression of prestige was easily derived from an object that assumed significance by affirmation, repetition, and emotional contagion and sought to dominate the mind and psyche of the viewer.[14] In this respect the US Navy used the airship both as a fleet scout and as a means to enhance the image of that service in national affairs. Seen negatively, this phenomenology enhanced French anti-Germanism and always left something of a pall on British airship perceptions, where the memories of the emotionally disturbing wartime zeppelin raids never fully left the public psyche. The relatively small band of enthusiasts for Britain's Imperial Airship Scheme of the 1920s could, however, still develop a thrust towards prestige and excitement. One of its historians has written:

> It was an aspiration on the frontiers of knowledge, which, like others since, gathers zest – and with zest, momentum – until it became a dominant force at Cardington, in Whitehall, and most of all among those who had dreamed dreams and seen visions of close-knit Commonwealth communications, twenty years before they became a reality. So, the flight to India became a quest for a new Holy Grail to be pursued even unto death.[15]

The disaster which that British quest produced in late 1930 gave impetus to erosion of the promise of rigid airships. During the interwar years, the public image of the skyships was gradually darkened as their accidents alternated with their achievements, finally reaching a crescendo at Lakehurst in 1937. Forty years thereafter, a popular sports writer quipped, 'Joe reacted as if they wanted to put him on the last flight of the *Hindenburg*: he was an unconscientious objector.'[16] And the Disney Studios, then advertising their film *Island in the Sky*, pictured an airship burning in the heavens – an up-to-date Grimm fairy tale. Except for the German people, by 1938–9 general admiration for the airship was gone. Its image was blighted and sensation served mostly its detractors.

For the previous forty years, however, the rigid dirigible had had its undeniably attractive influence upon humankind. What were some of its other more disquieting psychological impacts even while it was generally more positively received? Contemporary news accounts of an airship in flight often imparted a sense of incongruity. There were references to 'a flying battleship' passing in review, 'the largest dirigible greeting the largest building [in the world]'.[17] Other accounts described 'army and navy planes whirring and circling about her like little flies', or seeing the ZR3 'fleeing past the Woolworth Tower, her silver length and the tower itself forming a cross against the background of the sky'.[18] Seeing a moving skyborne object of that size inevitably suggested a weight that should properly fall. Most viewers were likely to be prepared for what they saw, but there was still the residual psychological effect of a well-established expectation resulting in a sense of wrongness. This circumstance forced the viewers to question that previous expectation. The result was a momentary sense of mental dislocation[19] – and thus the greater influence of the airship in demanding viewer attention. Psycho-historian Peter Loewenberg described the phenomenon plainly:

> Incongruity: the notion that something that *size* floats and moves effortlessly through the heavens carrying one's fellow man – we experience this as uncanny, i.e., 'By God, it is true that massive weighty objects can fly, just as I always believed they could as a child until reason made me wiser!' I think this may help explain the "normal" person's wonder, excitement, and gawking. Freud describes the Uncanny as arising thus: 'as soon as something *actually happens* in our lives which seems to confirm the old, discarded beliefs, we get a feeling of the Uncanny'.[20]

Given human responses to all massive constructions, of whatever degree and kind, this intermixture of wonder with uneasiness was uniquely peculiar to perception of the rigid airship, and thus made the experience all the more noteworthy and attractive.

In another area of psychological uneasiness is the touted Freudian significance of the rigid airship. Robinson directly comes to grips with this matter:

> Freud started the whole idea [of sexual explanations of the emotional appeal of rigid airships] in the year 1900, when he wrote in *The Interpretation of Dreams*: 'As a very recent symbol of the male

organ may I mention the airship, whose employment is justified by its relation to flying, and also occasionally by its form'. I cannot consider that Freud was qualified to speak with authority, for he knew nothing of flying and I do not believe that he ever flew as a passenger. Freud thought of sex in terms of anatomy, and the male was inherently superior; thus the airship was a phallic symbol. If he had ever hung around an airport, he would have discovered that aircraft are feminized in the speech and thought of those who fly – even treated as a love object.[21]

However individuals worldwide may have enjoyed or suppressed such sexual fantasies in their airship viewing, Germans got little reliable guidance from the usages in their own language. Generically speaking, airships of any kind are neuter, *das Luftschiff*. *Der Zeppelin*, of course, is masculine. Yet some Germans of the mid-thirties wrote or spoke of *die Hindenburg* – feminine, a carry-over from nautical terminology. Be that as it may, the rigid airship, as compared to airplanes, could apparently stimulate deeper and ambiguous recesses of the human psyche.

If there was some confusion in these sexual perceptions of the dirigible, there is clear evidence in instances not confined to one nation or one time that the rigid airship could provoke apprehension and terror. Some elderly Germans have recounted childhood memories of fright at the huge, roaring objects hovering overhead. Albert Speer spent his childhood in Mannheim, not far from the Schütte-Lanz airship works. He visited there and knew some of the crews. After one such visit he had recurring nightmares of an airship world going up in flames.[22] For the English, French, and Belgians the zeppelin was the terror instrument of indiscriminate civilian bombardment. The German raids over London and eastern England exceeded anything previous in British wartime experience. The memories of darkened cities, searchlights piercing the black night sky, and the noise of anti-aircraft artillery were a lingering counterpoint to British airship dreams of the 1920s.[23] French citizens during the interwar years also had reminders of wartime as Eckener flew his zeppelins over France to North and South America. One cartoon depicted the goateed captain arriving over Paris in his airship, allegedly twelve years late. A writer saw the peace zeppelin as a reverse of the war ship, its thirteen [*sic*] passengers easily replaceable by thirteen bombs, thus transforming the peaceful dove into a bird of prey.[24] One American has recorded his own childhood memory of the *Hindenburg* over New York City, feeling himself trapped in his closed play-yard, with the great ship swelling and roaring above him – an experience of total and overwhelming fear.[25] In our era, by comparison with our own memories of films showing screaming Stuka dive bombers, massive destructive air armadas, and the disasters of atomic strikes, the threat of a lumbering and vulnerable airship as a war weapon seems almost ridiculous. But before 1939, in the Western world at least, the rigid airship was a major example in popular memory of destruction from the skies. Eckener succeeded in overcoming that image with his peacetime zeppelins of travel and commerce, but in several lands there was still a persistent tinge of apprehension in response to the great silver skyships.

From these categories of benign and shadowed individual psychological responses to rigid airships we turn to the third subgroup manifestation, the role and behaviour of crowds. In fact, the individual viewer was most frequently not alone. Almost inevitably people were caught up in collectives of somewhat dispersed and heterogeneous individuals, all focusing their attention on the passing phenomenon overhead. Usually, the airship crowd was drawn to a particular place of arrival or exhibit of the airship. Pre-revolutionary France had witnessed the first outbreak of mass enthusiasm for airships, at that time, of course, free or tethered balloons. Contemporary accounts then indicated that tens of thousands attended balloon ascensions in various French cities, accompanied by fireworks and military music in a carnival atmosphere. Though an instance of superstitious peasants 'slaying' a downed balloon was reported, or of crowds becoming unruly when an advertised ascent failed, the crowds were usually friendly. Indeed, there was a unique element in the many upper-class men and women who pursued their enthusiasm for the educated and popular pursuit of Enlightenment science by attending an *experience aerostatique*.[26] Most of these crowd characteristics appeared again in the twentieth century.

Recent psychological studies of crowds and crowd behaviour offer little explanation for the behaviour of an airship crowd.[27] Such works concentrate on the non-airship, militant, inflamed, and activist crowd behaviour quite unlike the American multitudes that came to witness and gawk at the silver skyships. These were open spectator crowds, a heterogeneous collective drawn by a single stimulus. An observer described the crowd at Los Angeles' Mines Field on 26 August 1929:

> Several thousand had already gathered ... The throng was growing by the minute. Streams of automobiles were bringing still more thousands along the dusty narrow road leading to the airport. Batteries of searchlights, floodlights, movie arc and klieg lights, their

generators throbbing incessantly, blazed under a massive cloud of bluish-white fog billowing over the area where the *Graf Zeppelin* would touch down. Now the word came that the *Graf* was picking up unexpected tailwinds and was making better time. The report [by radio] caused thousands more motorists to head for the airport. The traffic control task force of 325 policemen, 60 sheriff's deputies, 400 national guardsmen, and a detachment of troops from Fort MacArthur, was fast being overwhelmed. Deputy Police Chief W. L. Spellman put in an emergency call for 100 additional officers ... Los Angeles had never seen such excitement.[28]

For all its surging size, the crowd was anonymous, unorganized, accidental, and leaderless. Theorist Elias Canetti has commented on such spontaneous and 'open' crowds, with their infinite varieties of growth, form, rhythm, and disintegration. Here was also the 'invisible crowd', initially a dispersed, unidentified but emotional band of enthusiasts, personally unknown and unrelated to each other, congregating willy-nilly in a 'feast crowd' atmosphere to experience the gigantic aerial visitor.[29] This was the great happening that was soon called 'zeppelin fever' in America. And this was the phenomenon that alerted politicians of all sorts in the Western world to consider manipulation of the technology that had such wondrous attractiveness.

In Germany, the crowds attracted to the zeppelins were even initially of a more formed nature. True, they came from hither and yon into the streets and onto the rooftops of Imperial Germany; but they moved not only to experience the fabulous *Luftschiff*. They also responded to the attraction of an unseen 'leader' – to the new folk hero that was Count Zeppelin. By 1914 this response became a predictable certainty for German crowds exulting in German technological achievement, German scientific *Kultur*, and Imperial German military power. Although Germans lost the subsequent world war, their sense of the zeppelin as a scientific and cultural national achievement remained firmly with them. During the interwar years, especially in the Nazi era, German zeppelin crowds were thus more readily manipulable, whereas the multitudes that greeted airships in Russia, Japan, America, northwest Africa, and South America remained innocently attracted in less political contexts.

Very possibly these overt and sometimes subtle responses of humankind to the airship could have faded to psychological habituation, had the impressive skyships continued developing, increasing, and flying for several decades longer. Some psychological familiariza-

Introduction: Technology and the Human Psyche   11

tion was already beginning at the Lakehurst and Sunnyvale naval air stations by the early 1930s, as viewers diminished to watch the *Akron* and *Macon* in their workaday practices. By the later summer of 1936 the *Hindenburg* arrivals and departures no longer made daily news in America or Germany. Yet, her American east coast appearances continued to arouse almost as much attention among the masses as before, even upon her last arrival on 6 May 1937. Possibly some of this interest derived from newer stimulation of negative political reactions or of some anticipation of disaster. The fact remains, however, that, a handful of Goodyear blimps apart, only one rigid airship was then flying in all the world and just one other was about to join it; these alone still resisted the forces of familiarization and psychological desensitization.

What were the dimensions of this rarity of rigid airship construction and movement in Western industrial society between 1919 and 1939? Leaving aside the memories of airships in Imperial Germany and of their operations in World War I, the international public during the interwar years was aware, at best, of just 18 rigid airships. Consider these in contrast to the visibility of several dozen significant ocean liners, many impressive railroad trains, hundreds of racing cars, and thousands of airplanes. Of these rigid airships, nine appeared in England. Five of these were belated copies of wartime zeppelins, whose R34 achieved brief international acclaim with its first round-trip airship crossing of the Atlantic in 1919. The rest made only British news of trial, error, and failure. Of the remaining four in Britain, Barnes Wallis's unique R80 (1920–1) was lost to postwar economies, R38 was a sensational disaster in 1921, while R100 and R101 were the ultimate hope for British airship achievement by 1929–30. Seven zeppelins came out of Germany, all of them postwar designs, except for naval L72 (Works No. LZ114), delivered to France as reparations in 1921 and renamed *Dixmude*. Two were lost: *Dixmude* in 1923 and *Hindenburg* in 1937. The others were eminently successful. Of the five American rigids, only two were native postwar originals. For the rest: ZR1 was a domestic copy of German naval L49; ZR2 was the destroyed British R38; and ZR3 was originally LZ126. ZRS4 and ZRS5 (with the 'S' suffix, meaning 'Scout', indicating the capability of these ships to carry scouting planes) were both of German-American design and construction lineage. To complete the roster of publicly perceived sky giants, there should be added three Italian semi-rigids: the *Roma* of 1921–2 (acquired by the US Army in an abortive bid to reassert its role in lighter-than-air flying); the N1 (*Norge*) of transpolar flight fame; and N4

(*Italia*) with its months-long saga of polar disaster. Of these 21 skyships built and flown over two decades, 13 attracted wider international public attention: three British, one French, two Italian, four German, and three American – and of these, eight were lost in accidents that were spectacularly publicized. In an era of otherwise burgeoning avia-tion development, this baker's dozen carried the entire thrust of airship success or failure, together with all the accompanying public reaction and political attention.

Consistent with this perceivable rarity of airships was the scarcity of airship design teams and builders. In contrast to the dozens of other comparable entities constructing other types of transportation, during the interwar years there were just a handful of airship designer-builder teams, together with their related subcontractors. In Germany it was Luftschiffbau Zeppelin. In Britain Vickers Ltd and the Royal Airship Works (Cardington) did the work. Goodyear-Zeppelin carried its hopes for America. On the margins another handful of designers and builders, such as Schütte and Nobile, overlapped from the war years and failed in the competition. By 1928 there were just four designer-builder enterprises as foci for rigid airship construction – the Detroit-built *Metalclad* (ZMC-2) was an experimental loner. These four alone had to carry all the business responsibilities and maintain the expec-tant visibility for the entire transatlantic airship enterprise.

The corporate concentration of the airship builders further marked the scarcity of their enterprise. During the interwar years, when the rigid airship became internationally prominent, usually just one city in an entire nation laid claim to birthing the luminous skyships. Massive hangars and extended shops identified the skylines of Friedrichshafen, Akron, and Cardington. Their respective communities escalated their civic identities into national significance as they esteemed themselves in the prestige of their technological achievement – and yearned for comparable business results as well. All three thrived psychologically on their undoubted attention-getting qualities: Friedrichshafen as Germany's *Zeppelinstadt*; Akron with its aspiration to become an international airship centre and to overcome the smoggy tarnish of its significant rubber industry; Cardington distant in the countryside, though nearby Bedford took some warmth from the proximity of the Royal Airship Works. Battleship builders and locomotive constructors never rose above the grime and racket of their workplaces. Airships, however, were among the first of the twentieth-century clean indus-tries. By their size, scarcity, and prestige – certainly in popular aware-ness – they seemed to lead the way out of the noise and stinks and soul-cramping ugliness of the machine age.[30] All of this perception has been lost by now in the burgeoning military-industrial activities of the space age since 1939. But in its time and place, the airship construction enterprise briefly held its bright promise as it also struggled to survive the successive failures of its products.[31]

Clean though the airship industry was, its business foundations were always insecure. These companies continually had to balance the prospective hazards of airship flying with the tremendous unit costs of skyship production and the excessive manpower required in their handling and operation. Rigid airships were incredibly expensive; only the larger warships, passenger liners, or entire streamline trains were more costly. Unlike the ships and trains, however, airships were still mostly in experimental stages of development. Thus decisions about each airship unit or programme generated financial apprehensions of great cost and risk. Where government agencies were airship purchasers, each stage of planning, financing, and construction elicited much formal political attention. No airship enterprise or nation escaped these circumstances. With the exception of its earlier wartime activities, Luftschiffbau Zeppelin wrestled with its development, always close to the brink of insolvency until 1935, when the Nazis politically hijacked the zeppelin while giving it financial lifeblood. England endured the ultimately disastrous financial-technological competition of R101 with R100, accompanied by various political innuendoes. In the United States the airship had a more secure billet as part of a diversified corporation. Within the US Navy, however, it was always financially embattled, competing with rapidly emerging carrier aviation and going through heavy bureaucratic weather into catastrophic operational storms as well. Only the promise and popular attractiveness of the airship seemed to justify its otherwise largely irretrievable costs.

The airship, of course, was only the single most visible example of much aircraft development and diversification between 1900 and 1940. Psychiatrists have noted the unique relationship that can develop between humankind and its machines. Here emerges a curious animism that endows its mobile craft with qualities of a living creature and even a personality of its own.[32] Though airship designers and builders did not establish the intimate psychological relationships characteristic of a single pilot with his airplane, they did develop their own kind of empathies with their immense constructions. Most designers and builders of great engineering constructions such as skyscrapers, suspension bridges, and large maritime vessels, have had their own pride of identification with their achievements. Airships, with their unusual size and three-dimensional mobility, exercised their own unique fascination. One expert described structural engineer Vincent C. Richmond, chief designer of R101, as 'obsessed' from the moment he first saw LZ120 *Bodensee* in Germany in autumn 1919.[33] An airplane pilot testified:

> When one went to an airship station [in England, 1919–21] and saw what airships could do, and what they did do, and what they had done, and what he hoped they could do, then one became confident that the present lapse [in airship flying] was purely temporary. He went up to Howden and was taken into R33, and he must say that it was simply like stepping into fairyland. It was the most beautiful engineering structure that he had ever seen.[34]

American engineer and businessman Harry Vissering had the same experience travelling with LZ120 *Bodensee* as Richmond had had. Indeed, airship voyaging had a collective fascination for the entire airship crew. Towards the end of the zeppelin era, after its crews had languished and chafed at the bit awaiting helium for LZ130 *Graf Zeppelin II*, the word came to fly again with hydrogen for the Luftwaffe. When they then leapt to the opportunity with gusto, it was not enthusiasm for war or Nazism, but simply sheer joy to be in the air again with a new version of the ship they already knew and understood so well. In all three nations this remarkable empathy of designers, fliers, and skyship communicated itself readily to airship passengers and many others close to airship operations, including the realms of public relations and political perceptions.

Curiously and banefully, these same engineering and flying enthusiasms sometimes became poisonous when expressed towards competitors of their immediate kind, of other lighter-than-air craft, or of airplanes. No doubt naval engineer Johann Schütte contributed crucially important improvements to airship design that were then melded with zeppelins in wartime German production, but all through the subsequent 1920s Schütte and Eckener, together with their designers, fought a fierce internecine battle for exclusive recognition. A different but equally hard-bitten competition featured the diversities in building R100 and R101 in England. Even in America echoes of the German fight touched the fledgling Goodyear-Zeppelin Corporation, which also cast anxious side-glances at the *Metalclad* airship building in Detroit. Competition between different types of lighter-than-air craft was almost venomous in Count Zeppelin's time, when the Old Aeronaut vied with Major von Parseval's non-rigids, battled quite personally with Major Hans Gross (semi-rigids), and disdained the efforts of the Prussian Airship Battalion in general. While the war years proved the relative superiority of the rigid airships, echoes of these earlier quarrels lingered on into the 1920s in the derogation of Italian semi-rigids by various zeppelin adherents. The most widely observed conflict occurred between airships and airplanes. It was an unequal struggle, as airplane technology relentlessly improved and overcame the skyships by 1939. Because the airships were so scarce and the captains of their large crews so well identified with their accomplishments – and failures – these aviation conflicts often took on very personal tones, all the more so, since their personae appeared so prominently in the public eye. Engineering rivalries, design competitions, and contests for product superiority were endemic in western industrial society. But it was in the scarce airships that these competitive aspects appeared as highly publicized personal attributes of success or were dramatized as personal aspects of technological or operational failure.

Compounding the strains of airship design and engineering competitiveness were certain forms of institutional and governmental bureaucratic behaviour. The attractiveness and scarcity of the airship evoked an exaggerated kind of loyalty and devotion on the part of its several builders and fliers. This phenomenon was initially evident at the Luftschiffbau Zeppelin. A comparable enthusiasm was not seen at the Schütte-Lanz works because the charismatic leadership was lacking, the firm was in business so briefly, and its products became notoriously unreliable. Yet even here Friedrichshafen designers were stubbornly reluctant to accept Schütte's design improvements, while Schütte's group persisted inflexibly too long with wood girder frames and then belatedly was stranded in a blind alley of tubular duralumin experiments. Comparable strains were even greater in Britain, where the initial informal contacts between the design teams for R100 and R101 later gave way to a defensive wall of silence between the two parties. Here the politicking of personalities contributed to the animosities between the two teams. American airship building that had profited from the accumulated and refined zeppelin experience was hardly troubled by these kinds of problem, and no strong competitor emerged to challenge Goodyear's monopoly. Indeed, civilian and naval engineers collaborated effectively at Akron and the crews of their products echoed this accord.

The various governmental agencies also played different roles in each of the three nations. The bureaucracy of Imperial German military and naval procurement expressed a customary hesitancy towards weapons innovation, then was passively hostile towards rigid airships until three years before war broke out. The civil service of the Weimar Republic found Eckener's zeppelins an annoyance at best and once tried in 1925–6 to impede their development. The Nazis adroitly replaced bureaucratic negativism with ideological conviction and cajoled many of the zeppeliners into thinking of Berlin as a saviour of their cause. In Britain the new postwar Air Ministry was established within the civil service, which endowed airship building and flying with all the accumulated experience and behaviour patterns of His Majesty's Ruling Servants.[35] This bureaucracy contributed to the problems of the interwar British airship programmes. In America the naval airship design corps worked with the Germans from the birth of ZR3 at Friedrichshafen in 1922 through to the completion of ZRS5 at Akron in 1933. Where US naval bureaucracy had more problematical influence on airships, it was most likely in the troublesome areas of the presence and role of contrasting carrier aviation. On balance, the informal political behaviour and personal politicking of institutional and governmental bureaucracies was relatively least damaging to German airship enterprise, disastrous for the British, and became irrelevant on the American scene – where, by its multiplicity of functions, carrier aviation soon overtook the airship in importance.

Foregoing, we have examined two basic aspects that uniquely identified the rigid airship in its interaction with humankind. The first of these was in the realm of the psychological experience which the impressive skyships evoked. The second was the scarcity factor, which reinforced human psychological perceptions and reflected the great cost of airships. These two basic aspects constantly played into a third one – the workaday politics of the modern industrial world. Such political interactions were, of course, not limited to the rigid airship; but the role they played there became uniquely prominent.

In common parlance both 'politics' and 'politician' have various derogatory connotations. Such use is not intended here. We will deal rather with politics as the arts and practicabilities of governance. Here we encounter the competing groups and interests seeking to influence that governance and also the forcefulness of individual personalities in those endeavours. Such behaviour is generic in all societies. In the manipulation of airship technology it became especially visible.

Let us examine several categories and subcategories of political manifestations. Most readily recognized is the formal conduct of 'open' politics. This category comprises the activities of executives and legislatures, of election campaigns and all related phenomena, all of which are readily open to the media of the time. Behind, or within, these formal activities are various kinds of 'closed' politics. Analyst C. P. Snow here identified three subcategories: (1) committee politics (allegedly 'non-political' pressure groups and causes); (2) hierarchical politics (chain-of-command organizations such as armed services, civil bureaucracies, and business systems); and (3) court politics (power exercised by one individual or group not readily amenable to 'open' politics).[36] These variations serve as a bridge to the second major category of informal politics of groups or individuals seeking protection or advantage in various kinds of small-scale but sometimes significant 'politicking'. Airship technology was of itself far too visible, too expensive, and too obvious to lend itself to very much surreptitious 'politicking,' yet even here there were a few notable examples of that behaviour.

Finally, in yet another kind of political categorization, the airship loomed as large by influence as it actually appeared in the skies. Reference here is to the four major strata in the modern state, as identified by theorist Robert A. Dahl. Largest and quite unorganized is the apolitical stratum, comprising possibly a majority of innocuous citizenry. Next, Dahl finds a significant minority of the whole in an active political stratum. At the core of Dahl's model are two very small political groups: the active power-seekers and the established power-holders.[37] The airship impacted almost equally upon all four strata. The apolitical and politically active strata reacted similarly to the airship, whether as individuals or in crowds. Here they were impressed, moved, and rendered politically malleable to the efforts of the two small minority groups. The power-seekers tried to hitch their political wagons to the luminous airship star. The power-holders focused some of their energy even more directly to manipulate the airship magic to preserve or enhance their dominant command. There were also a few examples of governance in business, as in state affairs, where airship imagery played a significant role.

Indeed, here the ring closes: from individual and crowd fascination, by way of airship scarcity, through the airship awareness of power-seekers, to the active development and thrust of airship propaganda in the ways of the power-holders. Thus the airship came to play a lead role in heroic political theatre. Like all theatre, it appealed more to emotion than to reason, though the reasoned understanding of airship limitations and fallibilities were clearly in the ascendant by the early 1930s. The airship political theatre played to several different themes. Prominent was the personification of an individual struggle, such as the trials and triumph of Count Zeppelin himself. Another theme saw the airship as symbolic of the superiority and dominance of a particular national group: here strongly the Germans, more faintly the British, strengthening the faltering bonds of Empire, quite parochially the American Navy bolstering an established battle configuration against another more significant emerging one. A third, probably unique, theme of airship theatre played in the Friedrichshafen and Akron business communities. It was in all these propaganda dimensions that the airship made its greatest impact. Thousands of very affluent Germans took brief rides in the pre-war zeppelins and a few thousand citizens worldwide were interwar predecessors of today's jet set. Even today many thousands still perceive the skyward advertising of Goodyear blimps. But it was in the effort to impress millions on four continents, between 1919 and 1939, that the rigid airship became, however briefly, the greatest psychologically impressive propaganda instrument of the twentieth century to that date.

Modern psychological and sociological data offer new possibilities of understanding historical events in terms of the experiences of the observing and participating human beings. This work will draw upon those kinds of evidence as the skyward rivalries of the era unfold. Twentieth-century aviation stands at the culmination of several millennia of technological development making its impact upon the human psyche. Within the recent and most attractive three-dimensional world of airborne wonders, the airship still holds a place of unique psychological importance. Unlike the airplane, which by 1920 was becoming an everyday social experience, the experiencing of a rigid airship was mostly an unusual event. Given this fact, together with the awareness of the large crowds that airships attracted until their final days, both power-seeking and power-holding politicians sought to manipulate that technology to ends not inherent in the essential purposes for building and flying the impressive skyships. Such political calculation was less random and spasmodic than workaday political behaviour, for in its attractiveness the rigid airship was also fairly predictable in its measured movement, in the scarcity of its presence, and the great expense of its construction and operation. Thus the political history that now follows exemplifies a highly unusual account of politics interacting with technology.

1
Imperial German Precedents, 1890–1918

The invention and development of the rigid airship in Germany, from its inception to the end of World War I, occurred in a context of unique circumstances which spanned a gamut of intensifying political repercussions. These derived from arguments about weapons development, various bureaucratic interpositions, a widening psychological impact of the airship on the German public, and initial commercial ventures. By the outbreak of World War I there had emerged a technological instrument of great potential military threat and of remarkable national propaganda. Herewith also developed different kinds of political manipulation about the new technology. Initially, these efforts played in the confines of closed politics, where negative committee and hierarchical actions vied with Count Zeppelin's advocacy of his airship by way of court politics. Open politics gradually came into play as the Aeronaut's technological efforts became increasingly successful and soon spectacularly visible. Their culmination could be seen in nationwide public enthusiasm and the unique donation of 1908 that confirmed the Count's rise to heroic proportions and established his independence in airship construction and flight. Between 1908 and 1914 airship successes and accidents were constantly in the public eye to influence further development of the technology. By sharp contrast, the succeeding war years would see largely negative military decisions about airships concealed by censorship, while legends of airship wonder continued to command the popular imagination. This wartime disparity between airship reality and myth lived on into the postwar decade with significant psychological persuasion.

The politics of Imperial German society, wherein the rigid airship first developed, derived from a curious combination of aristocratic conservatism with less conservative middle-class democrats brought together in 1871 by Prince Otto von Bismarck. His constitution gave an appearance of parliamentary government. In reality, however, the popularly elected Reichstag was checked in its power by the much more conservatively functioning Upper House (Bundesrat), wherein the reactionary state of Prussia was dominant. Obscuring this semi-autocratic regime was a bright haze of broad public enthusiasm for national unification and imperial German militaristic patriotism, and several generations of South German opposition to Prussian power and aggrandizement had been assuaged by special constitutional privileges for the kingdoms of Saxony, Bavaria, and Württemberg. Newly-unified Germany was thus a potentially unstable mixture of semi-feudalism with conservative democracy, wherein the Prussian tail wagged the German dog, as all the while Berlin reactionaries manoeuvred to assert further power in constitutional areas that were unclear or unresolved. In this society Count Ferdinand von Zeppelin of Württemberg developed his military career and was then rudely deprived of it in 1890 at the peak of his capabilities.[1]

What brought the Count to such a fateful circumstance that totally redirected his energies from a military career to the political and technological realization of a rigid airship? Born in 1838, he prepared for a career in the cavalry at the Württemberg Military Academy followed by engineering studies at Tübingen University. Then, following three years of foreign travel he returned to Stuttgart, being appointed in 1865 as Adjutant to the King of Württemberg.

Like most Germans of that era, the Count participated in the great debates and conflicts of the 1860s about German unification. In the intra-German conflict of 1866 he supported the south German cause against Prussia, which in victory nevertheless dealt generously with the south German states and quickly deflected intra-German animosities into an all-German national enthusiasm for war with France. When the Franco-Prussian war came in 1870–1, the Count saw wide and distinguished service and at its end his military future in the new Prusso-German armies seemed assured.

For the next two decades Zeppelin moved steadily upward in his military career. In 1885 the King appointed him military attaché to the Württemberg embassy in Berlin, two years later elevating him to ambassador and member of the powerful German Bundesrat. It was Zeppelin's last act at Stuttgart's embassy in Berlin that totally changed his life.

In 1890 the Count had perceived what he considered improper Prussian interference in Württemberg military matters and filed an official protest in Berlin. Kaiser Wilhelm II personally received this document just a few days after he had dismissed Bismarck and expressed anger at these Württemberg accusations and noted in the margins of the document his amazement that such old 'particularist' notions still prevailed at Stuttgart. Among some Prussians this incident rankled sufficiently to precipitate an unjust verdict of failure for Zeppelin's performance at the Imperial Military Manoeuvres (*Kaisermanöver*) of autumn 1890. In consequence the Count had no alternative but to resign his commission and thus to abandon the career to which he had been so devoted.[2]

The King of Württemberg perceived the situation for what it was and promptly appointed the Count as a general-in-retirement, but for Zeppelin himself it was an appalling psychological crisis. His diaries indicate how desperately he wrestled with his humiliation and the loss of his life's work.[3] He was psychologically a changed man. Henceforth his efforts would be directed in compensatory behaviour towards restoring his military honour in the service of his King and Emperor. In addition, he would strive to serve his people and their nation by devising a superior military weapon that would make Imperial Germany pre-eminent in the world. Thus the Zeppelin rigid airship was born out of a national political dispute and a personal psychological crisis.

The Count's latent interest in lighter-than-air transport originated in 1874, after he had heard an address by German Posts Minister Heinrich von Stephan on possible use of airships for the mails. Later, however, Zeppelin's peaceful airship thoughts took a military turn, when he perceived with alarm the exploits of French captains Renard and Krebs with their semi-rigid military airship *La France*. In 1887 the Count wrote to the King that Germany must counter the French aerial threat with larger and more effective military dirigibles. There Zeppelin's efforts rested until his humiliation in 1890.

At that time the world of aerial hopes was lively with the knowledge of several generations of dirigible-balloon projects, notably in France. The armies of the major powers, however, had also been systematically perfecting the military capabilities of tethered observation balloons. By 1884, the Prussian military had established its Airship Battalion (captive balloons), fostering an infant industry in fabric production, mobile gas generation machinery, and instrumentation – altogether even then dubbed *Kriegsaeronautik*. Thus, when Count Zeppelin began to press the German Army with his rigid airship project, the stage was set for serious technological competition between several different lighter-than-air vehicles *and* for a contest of political wills – in terms of projected expectations of military effectiveness, comparative cost advantages, and characteristic bureaucratic behaviour. These circumstances would enliven the German airship scene into the years of World War I.[4]

Before 1859 Count Zeppelin had completed only introductory studies in the scientific and practical aspects of engineering, but from spring 1891 onward he pursued his airship studies with tenacious persistence, following two complementary avenues toward ultimate success. The first was his military aristocratic network. The individuals he could no longer associate with professionally were still open to him by contacts of genteel sociability. Thus in June 1891 he wrote to Count Alfred von Schlieffen, new Chief of the Great General Staff, requesting that he be assigned a qualified expert from the Prussian Airship Battalion to evaluate his project and assist in its further theoretical development. Thereupon Major Rudolf von Tschudi arrived in Stuttgart where he encouraged the Count to continue with his studies.[5]

The second avenue that Zeppelin now used was his own wealth, to employ talented theorists and engineers to refine and certify his ideas. He established early contact with the Daimler motor works to research a more efficient engine and engaged the services of Theodor Kober, who brought Zeppelin's original insights into harmony with physical theory and practical engineering. The King made available the various physical research and testing facilities of the Württemberg state, which were augmented by advice from other scientists in Stuttgart. By the end of the century the first successful rigid airship would make its initial ascent at Friedrichshafen – an achievement brought about by three significant factors: the unique blend of the Count's tenaciousness and imaginative intellect; the military-social network available for his manipulation; and the fact of his personal fortune. Had Zeppelin not suffered his professional disaster, and thus not turned his unique circumstances towards working out his psychological frustration, the rigid airship might well not have been developed in time to give it even that one generation of competitive advantage over the more rapidly and less expensively evolving airplane.

Between 1893 and 1895, the Count had a series of exchanges with the Prussian military authorities that would set the negative tone for his further relationships with them until 1906. Armaments development in Imperial Germany did not have the massive government resources characteristic of more recent times in industrial nations. The Reich was constantly short of funds so that new weapons development was left to private enterprise. Only when such innovations were operational and privately tested were they acceptable to the Reich military for final evaluation and ultimate purchase. In such circumstances Zeppelin submitted his first airship project to the German Army on 14 September 1893.

The Count's appeal to Berlin was more than just an opportunistic canvass for some well-endowed sponsor. He wrote with deep feeling about his personal sacrifices for the Reich over the past three years, which had been meant to give his nation a superior military weapon. Though phrased in the bureaucratic jargon of the era, his request ended on a note of aristocratic presumptuousness by indicating that the King would simultaneously be informing the Kaiser of its significance. Nevertheless an irritated Kaiser did in fact agree to setting up a panel of experts to review the Count's proposals, although eventually they decided against them. Thus Berlin exercised its time-honoured policy on weapons procurement, while also protecting the interests of its Prussian Airship Battalion. Here also first came into play two aspects of closed politics: the committee politics of the Army bureaucracy and the court politics of Zeppelin himself.[6]

Three months after receiving his rejection, the Count showed that he would not be put off by this display of committee and hierarchical politics. He fired off a fervent ten-page protest to the Prussian Minister of War, showing his displeasure with the committee decision by answering members personally point for point and justifying one technological aspect after another, as well as uttering a thinly veiled threat to make his invention available to some other nation. He gave especial political emphasis to his revised project by naming the airship *Deutschland*. All that happened was that the Count's arguments were rejected for a second time and even a personal plea to the Kaiser was unsuccessful, the All-Highest wondering where the money might come from to back such a venture.[7] Obtaining neither a further hearing nor funds, Zeppelin wrote to the Prussian War Ministry yet again in August 1895, citing new technological authorities for the effectiveness of his invention and stressing both its military and peacetime potentialities. For the next decade thereafter relations between the Prusso-German Army and the Count barely passed polite formalities.

In the meanwhile, however, the Prussian Army had systematically developed its aerial arm, establishing the first balloonist training station near Berlin in 1894. In 1896 the experimental projects of Major August von Parseval and Captain Hans Bartsch von Sigsfeld bore fruit in development of the kite balloon, into which were now introduced telephoto field photography and initial experiments with airborne wireless telegraph. Funding for these developments was never easy, but by the time of the manoeuvres in 1900 there were eight Prussian mobile field balloon units (and one Bavarian) with the most up-to-date equipment. In addition, four major fortresses were similarly modernized, with others soon to follow. This steady progress of the Prussian Airship Battalion also saw developing cooperation with the Imperial German meteorological services, with their burgeoning needs for all types of information-gathering balloon technology. By the first decade of the twentieth century, Major Parseval and Captain Hans Gross stood also at the threshold of non- and semi-rigid dirigible projects, ready to emerge normally out of regular military bureaucratic and budgetary circumstances. Little wonder that these established aeronauts had small concern for Count Zeppelin's eccentric endeavours at Lake Constance as they engaged in this first instance of twentieth-century skyward rivalry.[8]

While the Count had carefully maintained his useful social and military connections – he rarely missed the Kaiser's annual New Year's reception for generals of all the German armies – in late 1895 he sought civilian resources for support, becoming a member of the prestigious Association of German Engineers (VDI). In the presence of the King he delivered a major address to the Württemberg section of that society in February 1896. Late that year the directors of the VDI in Berlin launched an appeal for recognition and support of the Zeppelin project. At this point, the industrialist and manufacturer in aluminium Carl Berg, heavily involved with David Schwarz's all-aluminium airship construction, had also contacted the Count for possible use of Berg's metal products. During 1897 scientific attention was diverted to the ultimately disastrous non-rigid of Karl Wölfert and the fateful crash of the Schwarz airship in which its designer was killed. Now Berg threw in his full support with Zeppelin and the two negotiated rights settlements with Schwarz's heirs. At last the way was open for a civilian venture to build and fly Zeppelin's ship.[9]

The events that followed were largely non-political. A Company for the Promotion of Airship Flight was established in Stuttgart in 1898, its shareholders predominantly from Württemberg and notably buttressed by Berg's large subscription and the direct involvement of his aluminium enterprise. Nevertheless, the Count still had to underwrite more than half of the company. He transferred his activities to Manzell, near Friedrichshafen, where the King had supplied lake-front property for construction facilities. Curious tourists appeared in the spring and summer of 1900 to observe from boats the great skeleton being assembled and covered at the shed afloat on the lake. The King also kept the Kaiser informed of progress at Manzell. Newspapers around Germany that normally could have reported the technological event at Lake Constance were instead distracted by other events. A huge fire in Hoboken, New Jersey, destroyed the American termini for German transatlantic liners. The Boxer society rose in China and murdered the German ambassador in Peking. The Kaiser stood centre-stage at Bremerhaven, exhorting a German expeditionary force en route to besieged Peking to ravage China as the Huns had once done Middle Europe. The first three ascents of Count Zeppelin's first airship, the LZ1, between July and October of 1900 were thus mostly unreported. While some aviation circles were excited, observant laymen like young Dr Hugo Eckener, writing for the *Frankfurter Zeitung*, expressed their considered misgivings. A final consolation remained for the Count however: early in 1901 his imperial overlord conferred upon him the second-highest Prussian decoration, thus attesting the Kaiser's characteristic sympathy for projects of technological gigantism.

Encouraging though this might be, it was paltry recompense for the decade of effort and treasure that Zeppelin had invested. With no apparent prospect of further military or political interest in his airship he liquidated the company. The momentary interest of aviation enthusiasts waned and Zeppelin was hard-pressed to convince even the VDI to give continuing attention to his further studies of rigid airships. Meanwhile French military non-rigids continued to make news, and Brazilian Alberto Santos-Dumont got worldwide headlines flying his non-rigid airship on a short prescribed course rounding the Eiffel Tower in Paris. Unlike Zeppelin, Santos-Dumont reaped a rich financial prize, stimulated French military aviation, and quickened dirigible thoughts at the Prussian Airship Battalion.

Gradually the Count returned to his own research and financial investment towards a second airship. Two years were needed to clear away the organizational, material, and financial wreckage of LZ1. Young engineer-designer Ludwig Dürr, who had been with the Count since 1899, worked with a small team on new studies and materials-testing of useful remnants of LZ1. In 1903 the Count sent a personal appeal to 6000 wealthy men in Germany; the proceeds hardly covered his printing and postage costs, while producing a crop of derisive and affronting commentaries. The Prussian General Staff added its own measure of insult by confidentially notifying the men of its officer corps not to become involved in Zeppelin's venture. A public appeal for funds sponsored in mid-1903 by magazine publisher August Scherl yielded just a pittance. The great German public had not yet awakened psychologically to its later zeppelin fervour. Indeed, quite the opposite was the case. As he worked away in his reduced offices at Manzell, where Dürr was designing and would soon construct a new, fixed hangar on the shore of Lake Constance, Zeppelin seldom encountered inquiring journalists. And he turned one away with a brusque quip: 'I am not a circus rider performing for the public; I am completing a serious task for the *Vaterland*'. Thus he acquired marginal notoriety as the 'fool-Count' at Lake Constance, though his indulgent fellow-Swabians were more tolerant of his efforts in referring to 'the aerial dreamer down at the Lake' – *der Luftikus am Bodensee*.[10]

Zeppelin's second effort to build and fly a rigid airship coincided with a significant quickening of non-rigid developments abroad and at home. During 1905 construction of LZ2 was under way, with substantial support for the Count's own continued heavy personal investment: Berg's aluminium, Daimler's engines, Riedinger's balloon-stuffs, south German lottery funds, and containers for hydrogen on loan from the Prussian Airship Battalion. Concurrently the Prussian Army was also financing Major Parseval's first non-rigid at the Riedinger works. Into these leisurely-paced endeavours came a thrust from the Chief of the German General Staff that soon sharpened the focus and energized the efforts of official German airship activities. Early in November, Count Schlieffen, master-planner of a knockout blow against France, alerted his colleagues to the potential threat of the Lebaudys' successful military semi-rigid already in operation with the French Army. It was a grim irony of fate that just a month later Captain Gross (delegated from Berlin to Manzell and no doubt clearly aware of Schlieffen's alert) witnessed the accident at the first ascent of LZ2. Thereupon he submitted a detailed analysis of potential airship usefulness, as scout, transporter, and weapon. Here, ever arrogantly committed to his own preference for non-rigids, Gross found Zeppelin's rigid unacceptable by reasons of its great initial cost, its inflexible stationing requirements, and its excessive need for manpower in handling. Given this evaluation by Captain Gross and pressure from Count Schlieffen, the Prussian War Ministry established a high-level Commission on Military Airship Construction, which met four times between 27 January and 24 February 1906. By grim coincidence, just as official military circles were at last giving serious attention to airships, Zeppelin's LZ2 was wrecked in mid-January on its only flight. The Count briefly considered abandoning his whole venture, offering the fruits of his entire enterprise for sale to the War Ministry. At its first session the new

Commission unanimously rejected that offer and instead authorized construction of a small semi-rigid on designs developed by Gross and his engineer, Nikolaus Basenach. Inherently biased against maverick Zeppelin since the conflicts of the early 1890s, the Army establishment preferred the advice of its tested Prussian Airship Battalion; but in the national interest it still kept an option open for possible rigid airship success. Sensing the competition from non-rigids and manoeuvring for time finally to prove his rigid airship, the financially strapped Count began at the age of 68 a third aggressive campaign for his enterprise. He supplemented a vigorous defence of his design and experience with a public manifesto written with the assistance of Dr Eckener: *The Truth About My Airship*. Twice thereupon the Commission met with Zeppelin and Dürr, but the military had already cast its die for a prompt German non-rigid response to the corresponding French aerial units.[11]

For the second half of 1906, non-rigid and rigid construction and trials moved apace. In June the first Parseval non-rigid made some unsuccessful trials that pointed the way towards improved successors and the Reichstag approved funds for construction of the first Gross-Basenach semi-rigid. Concurrently the Count and his staff worked to redesign and reconstruct LZ2 into LZ3. In mid-1906 the Kaiser established a significant new research, support and publicity organization: the Motor Airship Study Society, supported by a number of major German companies. By year's end the Count had been promised a 100 000 mark loan interest free, but far greater advantage accrued to Parseval, who sold his airship and patents to the government. In its five years of activity the Society also sponsored other aviation projects, notably a scientific research facility that employed Theodor von Karman at Germany's first aerodynamic wind tunnel at Göttingen University, and initial projects to build airplanes on the Wright Brothers design. Overshadowed by this visible and well-funded Imperial Society, Count Zeppelin worked away at Manzell. With another Württemberg lottery authorized by the King, the Aeronaut developed increasing popular support in that kingdom, no doubt nourished by continuing anti-Prussian sentiments. Increasingly the broader German press gave attention to the huge new aluminium skeleton at the Manzell lakeside. At long last Zeppelin's endeavours achieved success with several long flights in early October; Prussian civilian objection to an earlier proposed lottery gave way and the Count belatedly received the interest-free loan already noted. At year's end, as a third, improved Lebaudy semi-rigid appeared in France, all three airship types were set to compete for performance and military orders in Germany.[12]

Each individual constructor, convinced as to the superiority of his respective ships, sought political support. Parseval and Gross worked in a comfortable partnership bred from two decades of incremental technological development within the hierarchical security of the Prussian Airship Battalion even though Gross found Parseval's ship too small and unpredictable to meet the French semi-rigid challenge. Zeppelin, by contrast, laboured in self-sacrificing loneliness, rejected and often disdained by the military authorities. Still, he continued to circumvent the antagonistic military command, manipulating his protective social network to reinforce the support of the King and to reach for the favour of the Kaiser. In the closed political contest of that time the Army used its committee politics to keep the irksome Count at bay, fostering the non-rigid projects it developed within acceptable bureaucratic and financial limits. The court politics of the Count, of course, challenged the hierarchical stability of the military establishment and stiffened its resistance. Thus both non-rigid and rigid proponents worked sometimes alongside, more often against, each other in the closed politics of early airship developmental rivalry.

With the advent of 1907 the arena of airship drama widened appreciably. Zeppelin now had the advantage of an emerging favourable public image: the genial, stalwart, dignified loner still enduring after 15 years of unrequited endeavour. Following upon the brief successful trial flights of LZ3, the Count appealed to the German Minister of the Interior. Here he argued that LZ3 and its improved successors were most likely to challenge successfully the French military semi-rigids and lead Germany towards world supremacy.[13] The upshot was that Zeppelin's venture would be supported financially by the Empire for its cultural, technological, and military importance; it was also decided that the Count's invention should be considered for purchase by the Reich, once the rigid airship had completed a 24-hour flight over a prescribed course. Coincidentally dozens of German engineering professors made an appeal favouring the Aeronaut's airship as of great technological importance in fostering Germany's world scientific reputation.

Now German civilian and military offices began competing among themselves for power to guide airship developments. The military still sponsored the airships of Parseval and Gross-Basenach, and found parallels in American, British, Italian, and French non-rigid ventures. In May, however, the Ministry of the Interior contracted with Zeppelin for basic improvements on LZ3 and provided Reichstag support of a half-million mark subsidy, including construction of a new floating hangar. A new Gross-Basenach semi-rigid took to the air, was found wanting, and gave way to military funding for a larger and improved type. At the same time the Army placed a trial order with Siemens-Schukert for a very large non-rigid that made various flights during 1911–12, when the zeppelins were already well established. Correspondingly, the Prussian Airship Battalion was expanded and a new motor-airship division was placed alongside the continuing observation balloon activities. Meanwhile, in south Germany, with the new floating hangar under construction offshore at Manzell, German officials, journalists, and tourists came to gawk and wonder at the improved airship taking shape. In late September LZ3 made four spectacularly successful flights, up to eight hours each and up to distances of 200 kilometres. The open skies at Lake Constance stimulated the open politics of further support for the Zeppelin Enterprise. The Reichstag enthusiastically voted a further two-and-a-half-million mark subsidy to assist in the construction of LZ4 and to provide for purchase of both ships by the military. At year's end, however, Zeppelin had still not achieved the requisite 24-hour, 700-kilometre test flight, and the military would not purchase either ship until the test was completed.[14]

The year 1908 would be the great turning point for the fortunes of Count Zeppelin and the future of rigid airships. In the first six months, however, circumstances hardly favoured the aeronaut's cause. Parseval's second military non-rigid performed to military satisfaction. The rebuilt Gross-Basenach semi-rigid took off and later broke all endurance records with a 13-hour flight. The elements were no less vexing than the Count's competitors. A winter storm partly sank the new floating hangar, inflicting damage on LZ3 that took weeks to repair before work could begin on LZ4. Similarly agitated were the Count's negotiations with official and business circles. Prussian authorities regretted that they had not snapped up his despairing offer of early 1906. For his part, Zeppelin now held somewhat exaggerated views of the dimensions and rewards of airship enterprise. For months tripartite negotiations went on between the Count, several companies (Berg aluminium, Krupp steel, Daimler-Benz motors, Continental-Hannover rubber), and military and civilian authorities in Berlin. Here in embryo were the several ingredients of a putative aviation military-industrial complex – issues of patents, cost allocations, guarantees, subsidies, royalties, ownership, and profits. Fortunately for the Count, he had his own enterprise firmly in hand, could delay any outside pressures, and went right on building LZ4. The others in the negotiations reached impasse after impasse, and finally gave up the endeavour. By this time, Zeppelin was well known in business and other public circles, and LZ4 was ready to take to the skies.[15]

Now there opened a wholly new era for the role and perception of the airship in relation to politics. As long as Count Zeppelin's efforts had resulted only in a haphazard succession of fragile ascents, failures, and then short trial flights, these impressed mostly the local inhabitants and some tourists at Lake Constance. However, once the rigid airship was up and away, it struck a totally new dimension of human perception. Then occurred the various individual reactions, soon escalating into multiplying and self-intoxicating crowd behaviour. As the new awareness electrified the general public, it simultaneously touched the significant minorities of political activists: those who would try to manipulate the new technology in order to influence their prospects, and those in power who would belatedly espouse the aerial wonder in ways to invigorate their established political control. But foremost it would be Count Zeppelin himself who would achieve his own personal political objectives.

On 1 July 1908 the aeronaut took off with LZ4 on an epoch-making flight. In superb weather he flew over south Germany, central Switzerland, and the northwest tip of Austria for twelve uninterrupted hours and a distance of nearly four hundred kilometres. Over a multinational geographical scene, to the acclaim of an international press, the rigid airship entered upon the threshold of international politics. At one stroke the Count advanced the development of aviation from the lumbering local efforts of elongated non-rigid balloons and brief airplane trips of less than a hundred kilometres to the flight of a vehicle of international transport with two dozen passengers and crew aboard. This was the multinational event that triggered the ensuing national German zeppelin craze, the fact that German technology and daring had received an international cachet of recognition and astonished approval. Immediately thereafter the focus of German attention concentrated on the Count himself, a man hitherto disdained, denied, and impeded, to celebrate his seventieth birthday on 8 July. Telegrams, gifts, and myriad other attentions poured into Friedrichshafen, crowned with Württemberg's royal gift of its gold medal for achievement in art and science. It was a national celebration, fresh and invigorating as compared to the frequent stale repetitions of official imperial pomp and circumstance.

Amidst this prolonged enthusiasm the Count set out in early August in LZ4 to meet the requirements of the Prussian War Ministry for ultimate proof of the military reliability of his airship – that uninterrupted

24-hour flight over a prescribed course at least 700 kilometres long. Now Germans in the southwestern fifth of the Empire had their initial experience of a zeppelin. And it was indeed an experience, much more than just a view. Five hundred feet long and almost fifty feet high, the *Luftschiff* passed at twenty miles an hour, its two Daimler motors in a throaty roar, often less than a hundred feet above the ground. Ever greater grew the masses of sightseers as LZ4 moved northward from Basel via Freiburg, Baden-Baden, Speyer, Worms, and Darmstadt towards Wiesbaden. Hourly bulletins, newspaper extras, and electrifying word of mouth sent people rushing towards the expected route of the airship. By dozens and hundreds they moved, soon to become crowds of thousands. The wonder and amazement of individuals became the new commentators' observed idealism, where materialistic sensation was seen transfigured into spiritual enthusiasm. Individuals' sense of pleasure and wish-fulfilment became in newsmen's jargon a realization of the 'dream of millennia', the achievement of human flight. Stuttgart's major news organ, the *Schwäbischer Merkur* rhapsodized:

> The streets filled up, people clambered onto rooftops. And one waits, patiently waits for another hour! And then after the long silence, the crowd cries out. Above the hilltops, just to the right of the Bismarck Tower, a silver, glimmering, wondrous entity appears. At first it seems to stand still, but then pushes itself slowly but steadily against the fresh morning breeze. One feels its power; we are overcome by a nervous trembling as we follow the flight of the ship in the air. As only with the greatest artistic experiences, we feel ourselves uplifted. Some people rejoice, others weep.[16]

Thus were incongruity and bewilderment also registered, though most typical was the surging crowd at Oppenheim that broke out in joyous singing of 'Deutschland, Deutschland über alles!' Walls of people formed from the streams of individuals that came on foot, by wagon and car, and in trolleys, jubilant crowds in a carnival mood. Thus occurred the transformation of passive individual onlookers into active participants in a great national patriotic drama. Technology and nationalism intertwined for greater nationalist dreams and modernist visions. If machines were the measure of men in the new modern era, then airships (and later, airplanes) became a new measure of nations.[17]

Still, it was not to be initially the success that Count Zeppelin sought – indeed, quite the opposite. Stubborn motor trouble made him turn southeastward from Mainz to Stuttgart, where the Daimler works could eliminate the problems. Arrived there, and awaiting the engine experts, a sudden afternoon rain squall tore the airship from its moorings and generated the spark that caused an instant hydrogen explosion. In a few minutes the culmination of the Aeronaut's life work was reduced to ruin. Horror swept the gathered thousands assembled to admire LZ4 just pausing in its record-breaking flight. Here was the first in a succession of flaming calamities that would bedevil all airships until the consummate disaster of the *Hindenburg* in 1937. The German press raised its zeppelin excitement to a crescendo of national melodrama.

And now, almost miraculously, occurred a nationwide secular epiphany that is the very stuff of vivid social history. With its impression of success instantly transformed into catastrophe, and its awareness of the Count's lonely work of nearly two decades turned to ashes, the German public released an avalanche of public compassion and financial consolation. Telephone calls, telegrams, and letters poured into Friedrichshafen from all corners of Germany. Many are the stories of pennies taken from children's money boxes, of marks squeezed from housewives' kitchen budgets, and of a thousand other small, heartfelt contributions from the common man. More financially significant, however, were large gifts from the Imperial purse, from princely and other aristocratic donors, from German industry and business, and from systematic collection campaigns sponsored by a host of newspapers. Further tens of thousands of marks came from the Count's immediate suppliers and subcontractors: the Daimler motor works, the Riedinger balloon factory, Carl Berg's aluminium business, and others. Mannheim manufacturer Karl Lanz, who would later join with engineer Johann Schütte to become Count Zeppelin's energetic competitor in rigid airship design and production, contributed 50 000 marks. The final tally of all this financial generosity came to over six million marks, worth twenty times that in today's purchasing power. What a contrast to 1903, when the Count's 6000 requests for funding produced barely 8000 marks! It was an event hitherto unequalled in German experience. As Theodor Heuss averred half a century later, it was an occurrence of fundamental political significance: by such massive participation in this public fund-raising, the people sensed a consummation of national unity never experienced before in Germany to such an extent.[18] Accordingly, both the Count and his prominent successor, Dr Hugo Eckener, considered themselves ethically obligated to the German people for proper management of that donation and fostered the zeppelin as a unique national technological treasure.[19] Like the phoenix of classical mythology, a new technological wonder would arise from the ashes.

As airship technology conveyed the passions of human endeavour into the open skies, there to be seen and interpreted by everyone, so did it produce an open political manifestation. The ashes of the wreck at Echterdingen had not yet cooled when Chancellor von Bülow telegraphed his sympathy to Count Zeppelin and promised further support for airship efforts – with copy to the Foreign Office press bureau. Perfunctory imperial condolence and praise arrived the next day, simultaneously broadcast by the Wolff newsagency. Then, the old closed committee politics reasserted themselves. Visibly impressed by the rapidly accumulating monies in popular support for the Count, and understanding that this was indeed an unparalleled manifestation of the German nation – all without imperial planning and sponsorship – the Kaiser tried to impose imperial administration on those funds. He sent the Minister of the Interior, Bethmann Hollweg, to request the transfer of the fund to Berlin for management there by a traditional national board of trustees. Zeppelin deftly dodged these machinations by establishing a foundation under German law, with a board of regional aristocrats and businessmen, himself at the head, and legally seated at Friedrichshafen. Thus was born the *Zeppelin Stiftung*, which would have momentous importance for the development of industry at Friedrichshafen and whose influence persists there to this day.[20]

As the Count manoeuvred to secure his national gift in the Zeppelin Foundation, an event occurred that immediately dramatized the new importance of open national politics. A major consequence of the secular epiphany of August 1908 was the frequently expressed conviction that new insights and ideals had been awakened in the German nation. This new awareness contrasted dramatically with hitherto stale political attitudes, mundane habits, and imperial banalities. Open and latent anti-Prussian sentiments found expression in the presence of the zeppelin, and not just in Württemberg. Many Social Democrats found the new airship an acceptable expression of all-German working-class accomplishment. Other Germans could cheer the industrial workers' contribution to the greater technological glory of the *Vaterland*. New excitement in the skies for everyone overshadowed tasteless and hollow conservative *Stammtisch* patriotism.[21]

Into this environment of fresh self-awareness came a vivid reversal of roles for the Kaiser and the Aeronaut. In late October 1908 Wilhelm II raised much public displeasure by his maladroit handling of a widely publicized interview with the London *Daily Telegraph*. Indignation appeared on all sides in Germany, questioning the behaviour of the emperor, the dubious role of the chancellor, and the conduct of German foreign policy generally. In political *extremis*, the Kaiser detoured from his annual autumn hunting trip in south Germany to visit Count Zeppelin. On 10 November, the very day the Reichstag began its formal inquiry into his diplomatic indiscretion, the All Highest came with great ceremonious publicity to be with the Aeronaut at his Manzell works. Here the Kaiser arrived at the heart of the anti-Prussian 'particularism' that he abhorred: summer residence of the Württemberg King, home of Count Zeppelin, and retreat of Hermann von Mittnacht, retired Württemberg minister-president. Laden with gifts the Kaiser came: a confirmed military purchase for LZ3, Prussia's highest decoration for the Count, and a ringing accolade that Zeppelin was the greatest German of the twentieth century. The Emperor's effort to divert attention from his political distress in Berlin, and to ride the new wave of national idealism, was only partially successful. For the Count, however, the visit was of momentous significance. With this imperial demonstration he was fully embraced again by the establishment that had cast him out two decades before. Here the first of his two political objectives was achieved. His honour was fully restored. Henceforth his person would grace the highest echelons of imperial observers at every subsequent peacetime *Kaisermanöver*.[22] It still remained for him, however, to achieve his second political objective: to make his aerial weapon fully acceptable to German military and naval authorities. That effort would fully tax the Count's political energies for the next six years.

It was his unique financial windfall combined, however, with his own entrepreneurial experience, that in late 1908 produced the world's first military aircraft industry, the *Luftschiffbau Zeppelin* in Friedrichshafen. Various production subsidiaries soon developed in motors, ballonets, gas production, metals testing, wind-tunnel experimentation, airship hangar production (in Berlin) and, by 1915, the specialized gear and drive-train production of the Zahnradfabrik. Although military airship building would become an industrial dead end within the next decade, this nascent industry stimulated sophisticated technological innovations that benefited all aviation of the era. The combination of public adulation for the Count and his dramatically restored service prestige gave his new company an extraordinary version of the military cachet requisite for big business in Imperial Germany. Henceforth the messages from Friedrichshafen would have more political clout than business appeal in Berlin.[23] Complaints were heard that here was unfair competition. But only one significant rigid airship competitor appeared, the Schütte-Lanz works of Mannheim, founded in late 1909. At the outbreak of war, these two impressively visible construction centres overshadowed a dozen emerging small airplane producers, also privately financed and hungry for scarce military orders. Major German industries would not risk investing in a field of such dubious prospects of profit.[24]

Airships of the era 1908–14 are generally remembered only for the trials and pleas of the Count to make his dirigible militarily acceptable. Actually, the political scene was enlivened by the continued Prussian military preference for small non-rigids (seen as preferable support for the planned *Schlieffen* advance into France) and by the emergence of the Schütte-Lanz rigid competition. Parseval and Gross-Basenach, however, were in technological decline, losing their initial advantages of low cost, easy handling and rapid deployment as they became more expensive with constant changes towards ever-larger dimensions and more powerful motors.

Just as the non-rigid opponents of the Old Aeronaut were wrestling with these problems in Berlin, the new *rigid* competitor appeared in the person of Johann Schütte, who adopted basic marine engineering principles to produce streamlined hulls, single-unit rudders and elevators at the stern of the ship, and engines in pods outside the hull with direct-drive propellers. Such evident features of the later well-remembered 'zeppelin' were still lacking even in the last ships launched, just before the war, from Friedrichshafen. Schütte made three further improvements not evident to outside lay observers: a fully extended internal keel, internal vertical shafts to conduct and discharge valved hydrogen securely upwards out of the ship, and improved internal wire bracing. He had informed the Ministry of the Interior, which in turn had notified the Count, about these innovations barely a month after the LZ4 disaster. Since the Old Aeronaut declined to find these improvements useful, Schütte resolved to build his own airships.

Schütte soon won the hearts of civilian and military bureaucrats alike. By early 1909 he had stimulated the interest of the Kaiser, the War Ministry, and the Inspector of the Prussian Airship Battalion. They still favoured the non-rigids but found the young engineer a welcome negotiating diversion from the insistent folk hero down at the Lake. In spring 1909 Schütte joined with Karl Lanz, a manufacturer of agricultural machinery and forest products, to form the *Luftschiffbau Schütte-Lanz* at Mannheim, which used laminated plywood for girders, Daimler engines, Riedinger ballonets, and Siemens electrical equipment. In November 1911, SL1 finally took to the skies. Inevitably, major further changes were necessary, but for Schütte a military contract was quickly forthcoming for his next ship. With SL2, in early 1914, Count Zeppelin could see a dirigible superior to his own in basic ways, and a keen competitor. Incredibly, however, just a year into the war the SL airship developed fatal hull flaws – the unstable laminated plywood girders from Lanz's basic forest products enterprise – that were never overcome. But many of Schütte's improvements lived on in subsequent SL designs that marked the first skyward rivalry of two domestic rigid airship builders and persisted in the wartime forced marriage with the zeppelin technology.[25]

As Schütte was just getting under way in late 1908, the production of new zeppelins and business reorganization were order of the day at Manzell. Notable was the arrival of a modern business manager for the new Zeppelin Company. Alfred Colsman, son-in-law of aluminium supplier Berg, had been aware of the Count's work since 1899. He thus came to Friedrichshafen thoroughly experienced in up-to-date business practice – a twentieth-century bourgeois executive to help realize the technological dreams of the nineteenth-century aristocrat. The Count considered Colsman below the salt, but readily sought his advice and seldom failed to act upon it. Thus Colsman gave the new company its essential structure and guided its development into great wartime prosperity and beyond into painful postwar reorganization.[26]

The curious social relationship of the Count with his business manager was soon put to practical test in an environment of public acclaim for the Aeronaut but of faltering official interest in his product. In early 1909, rebuilt LZ3 went to the Army, new LZ5 soon followed, and LZ6 was begun (the last ship built at Manzell) on expectation of further military orders. But none came. Meanwhile great publicity attended several zeppelin events. In late August of 1909, the Count at long last arrived in Berlin with LZ6 to visit the Kaiser and thrill the citizens of the capital. Two weeks later a special train carried several hundred Reichstag members to the Lake for zeppelin flights that Gustav Stresemann (later Weimar foreign minister) blessed as an event unifying the German people of all parties and all confessions in a spiritual concord. A bit later it was all capped by a splendid visit of Austrian Emperor Franz Joseph to the Count at Friedrichshafen. Now a great new construction hangar stood ready for work at the new Riedlepark airfield – and stood empty for months on end. Concurrently, all through the summer of 1909, varieties of aircraft had exhibited and performed their feasibilies at the great Frankfurt International

Aviation Fair. LZ6 carried by far the most passengers aloft for short rides and long views. That autumn, with still no further orders in sight from Berlin, Colsman got the enthusiastic support of Frankfurt and other city officials for a proposal to establish airship stations with services at a network of major German urban centres and supplying them with passenger zeppelins. Taking this project to the Count, he found the aristocrat indignantly opposed. Zeppelin was not about to have his great technological gift to German military prowess debased by civilian commercialization. As Colsman later recalled:

> He saw his conception profaned if airships were used to earn money through such a company. That enterprise thus remained for him, the feudal aristocrat and old soldier, a tradesman's venture ... In a patrician context such as his, a merchant was just not socially acceptable.[27]

But, reluctantly, the Count finally gave way and in November 1909, the German Air Transport Company (DELAG) was established at Frankfurt, half of its capital subscribed by various air-minded German city governments. Forthwith the Zeppelin Company began building airships for its commercial subsidiary, countering the absence of military orders for the next two years.[28]

Formation of the DELAG had two further consequences for Germany's airship development, and for its political impact at home and abroad over the next generation. First of these results was Colsman's recruiting of Dr Hugo Eckener as public relations tactician for the passenger service. As of 1892 a trained behavioural scientist, he never developed that expertise professionally but later used it frequently in practical application around the world. For most of the 1890s, Eckener had been a journalist in his native Flensburg. By 1900 he was down at Friedrichshafen writing on labour economics, and it was here that he reported Zeppelin's ascents for the *Frankfurter Zeitung* in 1900 and 1906, finally himself becoming an advocate of airship possibilities. Eventually, after a spell in the north, Colsman enticed him back again to the Lake. Henceforth his name and career were indissolubly bound up, first with the Count's venture, then with Germany's intercontinental enterprise until its end in 1940.[29]

The second consequence was its association in mid-1910 with Albert Ballin of the Hamburg America Line (HAPAG), which took over ticket sales for the new company. Now upper-class Germans flocked to book their airship voyages. With DELAG aerial guidebooks in hand, with

HAPAG caviar and champagne at their side, thousands went aloft in the commercial airships that increased in number and multiplied in flights between 1910 and 1914. Most Germans, who could not afford trips costing more than a month's average wage, cheered the spectacle from below. '*Zeppelin kommt!*' became a nationwide chorus of anticipation and excitement. Here came into play the psychological phenomenon of individual and mass wish-fulfilment, which for most Germans expressed itself in admiring and acquiring a host of zeppelin mementoes.[30] Manufacturers by the hundreds pasted zeppelin logos and images of the Count on their mundane goods. The hero figure appeared in miniature busts and statuettes, dolls and nutcrackers, and other mass-produced kitsch. Altogether those phenomena were evidence of a self-replicating and expanding social propaganda that was remarkably immune to a succession of four major accidents in 1910 to Army and DELAG ships. No lobbyists, PR-agencies, or political spin doctors – who would appear during the interwar years – were needed to foster the zeppelin craze. That informal heroic political theatre was generic to Germans of the pre-war decade and would be renewed in the 1920s and 1930s.[31]

As the first wave of national enthusiasm rose, the zeppelin became a focal point for new studies in aviation in international affairs. In 1910 the Count arranged an expedition to Spitzbergen to initiate studies of arctic exploration by airship, contributing the article on meteorology in a book subsequently published.

For all these peacetime diversions, however, the Count continued to advocate the military potentialities of the zeppelin – against a barrier of negatives. The German Army, still eyeing the improving French military semi-rigids, went on testing all three types of airship. At the *Kaisermanöver* of later 1909, the zeppelins performed poorly and shortly afterwards there were accidents to ZII for which no replacement was ordered. The three DELAG accidents that occurred between April and September 1910 caused grave operational soul-searching at the Lake. They also caused the General Staff to begin serious consideration of airplanes for military use, for the non-rigids were not performing well, either. The German Army stood irresolute at an aviation crossroads.[32]

Neither the Count's determination nor much of public enthusiasm was affected by these very visible airship crashes, fortunately without fatalities – no doubt the phoenix phenomenon again at work. With only one delayed army order to replace ZII finally in hand, the Count reactivated his social-political network. In August 1911 he addressed another fervent plea to the Kaiser on 'Contemporary and soon-to-be-realized Performance of Z-ships and their Utilization in War'. Passionately and selectively the Count praised the achievements of his ships in the past and for the future.

If this appeal marked the nadir of Zeppelin's fortunes with the German Army, it was also the opening gun in an aggressive political campaign by the *Luftschiffbau* to press the government for more military orders. Hereupon followed an invitation for Colsman to address prominent civilian and military leaders in Berlin, where he continued the Count's adroit intermixture of zeppelin fact and fancy. From the alert public relations bureau of the DELAG Dr Hugo Eckener supplied the German press with a stream of stories and pictures to continue nurturing zeppelin enthusiasm. Fortunately he could build on the records of the new DELAG LZ10 *Schwaben* and LZ11 *Viktoria Luise*, which together would make over 700 flights by mid-1914, conveying nearly 18 000 passengers and crew. These ships were stationed and rotated through a growing network of airports and hangars, notably at Potsdam. Meanwhile, down at the Lake, the Company established a new division to increase effectiveness of armament and wireless telegraphy for its intended military airships. Concurrently, as army orders still faltered, a stream of correspondence from Friedrichshafen hit Berlin, relaying inquiries of foreign purchasers for zeppelins. Accompanying these papers were various intimations about the need for homeland orders, failing which the Company would be forced to seek export markets. The German military was moved by these political pressures toward further acceptance of military airships, beginning with subsidies for DELAG ships as units in military reserve. At a crucial meeting of Berlin officials with the Count and Colsman, the die was cast on 26 August 1912: Berlin ordered a third zeppelin for the Army (in addition to replacements for ZI and ZII) and two for the German Navy, with subsidies for the DELAG increased (thus facilitating its acquisition of LZ17 *Sachsen*). It was a remarkable *tour de force* for the wily Old Aeronaut and his wily business manager, but it would not have succeeded without the continuing all-German zeppelin craze.[33]

More than airships, indeed, the popular enthusiasm had also begun embracing aviation in general. Clubs and associations (some of them linked in national networks) held sessions, attended aviation meets, and spawned a growth industry in books and magazines.[34] Widespread was a patriotic commotion rooted in visions of three-dimensional war. Beginning in 1907, Rudolf Martin, a civilian government councillor with a facile pen, fanned popular military airship enthusiasm with a series of articles and books. Thus developed *Luftmilitarismus* – militarism of the air in a world already redolent with gunpowder. Martin's first book, *Berlin–Bagdad. The German World Empire in the Airship Age (1910–1931)*, about German rigids achieving military-political supremacy sold several editions. In February 1909, the Count addressed the exclusive Military Society of Berlin with details of airships conquering terrestrial space, deep into enemy territory, wreaking havoc on installations and troops. Concurrently Martin's latest novel, *War in the Air*, excited his readers with details of the aerial bombardment of Paris, while the fantasies of other writers saw England similarly enveloped in destruction. In its most exaggerated form this new *Luftmilitarismus* was viewed as superseding the effectiveness of all existing fortresses, armies, and navies.[35]

In this air-militaristic context the rapidly developing technology of the rigid airship had its next international repercussions. British culture had little inclination for technological megalomania (unless it was for their planned superliners *Titanic* and *Gigantic*), but it did have a thousand-year-old fear of invasion. Thus air-militarism first came to general British attention in H. G. Wells's novel of 1907, *The War in the Air*. Here the master chronicler of Martian invasion detailed a global military conflict launched by Germany with fleets of zeppelins. Soon thereafter appeared an English version of Rudolf Martin's realistic military airship fantasies. In May 1909 British newspapers sensationalized a phantom airship scare, and two months later Louis Bleriot made the first flight across the Channel in a spidery airplane. Now H. G. Wells railed against a Britain, slack, dull, and defenceless against 'foreign-invented, foreigner-built, and foreigner-steered' aerial machines. In the following year a German vision of the world a hundred years ahead included an essay by an Englishman on the devastation of the British Navy at Lowestoft by German airships. Between 1909 and 1914 British sensationalist journalism produced an increasing flow of military aviation fantasies, most of which featured many zeppelins in a Germanic threat.[36] Actually, 1907–12 saw the delivery of only four warlike zeppelins, three to the Army and a first to the Navy.

During 1912–14 official German air-militarism finally hit its stride. Crucial was the decision of the German General Staff on 27 September 1912 to abandon flying with all non-rigid airships. Henceforth the focus was on rigids alone, with plans to acquire twenty of them by late 1915. Simultaneously Berlin also emphasized an all-out commitment to develop airplanes, which had been featured since summer in the imperially sponsored *Nationalflugspende* that staged a host of aviation meets throughout Germany and garnered over seven million marks for the Imperial Treasury to foster airplane research and purchases. Still, the major focus was on airships. DELAG flights were demonstrating their increased reliability and winning thousands of influential adherents who travelled skyward as pampered guests. The German military also overestimated the effectiveness of Italian airship bombing and scouting forays in Libya and Asia Minor during the Italo-Turkish war of 1911–12. Important, further, was an impact from revisions of the Schlieffen Plan for German victory in the next war. As the contemplated thrust into France was weakened by strengthening its eastern counterpart, so were expanded the areas requiring continental troop-support of all kinds. New estimates indicated the need for very heavy bombs to smash the Belgian fortresses likely to impede the German thrust westward. And with the more numerous airships came the need for more airport facilities along the western and eastern fronts – which the Zeppelin Company's hangar construction subsidiary busily supplied. As of 1914, the Zeppelin Company was Germany's (and the world's) largest military aviation firm. However, more than a dozen private aviation enterprises were graduating from their bicycle-workshop stage to require networks of parts subcontractors to meet their growing military orders. When war broke out, Germany had the best-developed aviation military-industrial complex in the world.[37]

Now the German Navy finally entered the scene. Admiral Tirpitz, the arch-innovator of German–English naval rivalry, sought an additional advantage beyond the enervating ship-for-ship construction race. Colsman steadily wooed the Admiral, and naval crews joined their military comrades as frequent fliers on DELAG ships. When (naval airship L1) made its final test run, it covered over 900 miles, often at heights up to 6000 feet, in 31 hours of uninterrupted flight, and with a bomb-load potential of half a ton. Shortly thereafter Tirpitz began a programme for ten zeppelins within five years and built a central naval airship base at Nordholz, west of Hamburg. Thus emerged the naval airship service, whose hostile use of its zeppelins would soon have a psychological impact in major Allied nations that would leave lingering political odium against rigid airships well into the postwar years.[38]

Outstanding among the political positives of the time was a significant social-political development in the *Zeppelinstadt* itself. The Count slowly became aware after 1909 that his rapidly growing enterprise was stimulating unscrupulous land speculation, rent-gouging, and price manipulation in basic life necessities for his workmen, and he met the challenge head-on. On the occasion of celebrating his seventy-fifth birthday in 1913, he established the *Zeppelin Wohlfahrt*. This was a community-oriented enterprise to provide housing (sales and rental), food and household essentials, medical services and recreational facilities for his burgeoning workforce. The venture fostered the company during its massive wartime armaments boom, helped the entire city in the postwar depression, and became a model for sociopolitical innovation in other German cities – again carried by the magic of Zeppelin's name.[39]

The airship negatives that occurred during 1913 were the worst yet. In April military airship ZIV caused an international incident when, fogbound, it made a forced landing in Lunéville, France. Already the German military had made a provocative gesture in stationing ZI and its two successors at Metz from 1909 onward. Sane heads prevailed on both sides in face of the press sensations about this first 'aerial invasion' of one sovereign nation by another. Meanwhile, delays in releasing the ship permitted a thorough technical reconnaissance that promptly benefited French rebuilding of its single Spiess rigid and was passed on to Britain to shape construction of its rigids early in the war.[40] In the following autumn two naval zeppelins exploded and burned with almost total loss of life, the first great disasters of the airship era. At the funeral for the crew of L18 (naval LZ2) the public witnessed an unseemly row between Admiral Tirpitz and Count Zeppelin about the alleged deficiencies of his airships. Henceforth the Navy would press for incorporation of various Schütte innovations in the LZ ships it ordered. Maximilian Harden, publisher of the dignified *Zukunft*, seized upon the disasters as symbolic of German megalomaniac destructiveness. His command of the negative evidence was impressive, but the majority of Germans shuddered briefly, and then praised the phoenix rising again from the ashes.[41]

By now the airship had become both popularly and officially the symbol of German national and racial superiority. The government was using it in formal ritualistic political theatre. American ambassador James W. Gerard described the pomp and ceremony of the annual *Schrippenfest*, held at the new palace in Potsdam in May 1914. It was replete with their Imperial Majesties and their families, a host of highly decorated aristocrats and officers, open-air divine services, row upon row of ceremonial soldiery, a great military band, and choir boys from the Berlin cathedral. 'The occasion was very impressive,' wrote Gerard, 'and not less so because of a great zeppelin which hovered over our heads during the whole of the service'.[42]

However, much more than political theatre was at work in Germany by then. An extraordinary half-billion mark supplementary military expenditures bill was passed in the Reichstag in 1913 to meet alleged dangers from the new French three-year service plan. Monies for aviation soared from seven million annually to fifty-two million. More than a dozen fully equipped or planned zeppelin bases appeared around the rim of the Reich to serve the twenty planned airships. New directives made the Navy responsible for a line from Britain, over the North Sea, and eastward into the Gulf of Finland, while the Army commanded all continental airspace, east and west, from France to Russia. Winged aircraft multiplied and developed to supplement the great rigid airships. Germany became the leading air power of the world.[43]

By this time British official circles were seriously debating their possible responses to the German airship threat. In early 1913 a veritable panic broke out in England over alleged sightings of a zeppelin on Britain's east coast, supposedly on a secret round trip from Germany. Churchill felt that Britain needed a fleet of airships to counter the German threat, a view not accepted by the Committee on Imperial Defence and the Asquith Government. Nothing effective was done. British attaché reports from Berlin stressed the continued public attraction of DELAG ships, also serving in reserve military status by training crews for the Army and Navy.[44] In September a DELAG ship (LZ13 *Hansa*) visited Copenhagen and flew in demonstration over units of the British Fleet then visiting Denmark. Just before that, Colonel Erich Ludendorff, long an airship advocate in official circles and later to attain supreme military and political power in 1916–18, telegraphed the Count on his seventy-fifth birthday: 'With firm confidence in the accomplishments of the Zeppelin airships in the war that at long last is coming, I send your excellency in deep admiration my most respectful best wishes.'[45]

At year's end one of the Count's admirers wrote to him about visiting London 'with its immense wealth in buildings, goods, and banks that twenty zeppelins could in one day devastate with incredible losses in property values and war materiel'.[46] The Count's company expert in military armament reported on a long discussion with the Aeronaut on 29 July 1914, wherein Zeppelin insisted that Britain must participate in a European war at the very outset, even be provoked by Germany to ensure its involvement, lest it remain aloof to snatch the spoils of victory from the exhausted participants.[47] Thus questions of the technological perfection of Germany's aerial superweapon produced a political impasse in Britain while advancing prospects of the German grasp for world power.

The role and development of rigid airships in wartime service can readily be summarized in the context of four questions. How effective were they as military weapons? What importance did they continue to hold in popular imagination? Were they subject to any wartime political manipulation? And finally, how well did they develop technologically during the great conflict?

The great pre-war expectations of *Luftmilitarismus* were soon clouded by frustration and ultimately doomed. Of a dozen ships ready for action in early August 1914, half were destroyed by year's end, either by military action or accidents. Winged aircraft also took severe losses, but the airplane rapidly adjusted to new conditions of combat. Pressured by civilian authorities who were still mesmerized by the illusions of airship gigantism, the military High Command in early 1915 reluctantly ordered two dozen newer, larger, and presumably more effective airships. Always hampered by weather and operational hazards, the zeppelins could not keep pace with the far less expensive, more easily constructed, and more versatile airplanes. By late 1916 the Army had had enough and turned its few surviving ships over to the Navy. There, six Navy scouts had been ready by late 1914, but the Navy itself undertook only limited fleet actions requiring much reconnaissance. Perforce the airships began bombing British seaports in 1915 and by midsummer initiated their notorious raids on other British cities. Although the first attacks on London achieved some destruction, loss of life, and panic, the ensuing raids increasingly stimulated a powerful positive psychological advantage for Britain, especially as burning zeppelins were seen falling into English suburbs. Despite later erroneous impressions that zeppelins had played a decisive scouting role in the Battle of Jutland in late May of 1916, airships never attained the significance as crucial naval auxiliaries that the Kaiser, Tirpitz and others had anticipated. At the end of the war the balance sheet of all wartime airship participation was appalling. Of more than a hundred zeppelins and SL ships in service 37 were shot down, 40 were lost in accidents, and the rest were scrapped during the conflict or sabotaged by their crews on 23 June 1919, when the German Navy held captive by the British at Scapa Flow was scuttled by its officers. It was a dismal failure for the *Luftmilitarismus* so arrogantly displayed in the pre-war decade.[48]

As regards the widespread popular image of pre-war airships in Germany, as soon as the guns began to speak, the great airships disappeared from public view, out to the land and sea frontiers. The public was left only with the facile pens and pictures of the journalists. Here came lurid descriptions of airships attacking Belgian fortresses – replete with images of bursting bombs, dying soldiers, and panic-stricken civilians. All this reached a crescendo from mid-1915 onward with airship raids on London, and imagined scenes of panic, and destruction at popular tourist sites there. Far more exciting were the reports of returning U-boat commanders and individual airplane pilots, who could convey all the detail of destruction and glories of residual chivalry still dear to the public at home. So the airship giants vanished into the murk of censorship and obscurities of high flight, the sufferings of their often battered crews unreported. The one remarkable zeppelin accomplishment of the war – the long-distance Africa flight of L59 in late 1917 – remained a military secret until revealed after the war. Meanwhile the exciting and sportive U-boat commanders and airplane fighter aces became the legendarily propagandized – and quite unanticipated – new military heroes of the German nation.[49]

If the politically manipulable airship image had thus disappeared from public awareness by 1918, it had still exerted some influence in German internal politics in 1914–16. Count Zeppelin himself was the aviation star at the outbreak of hostilities, begging the Kaiser to let him command the first raid on London, as – so he averred – the German people expected of him. Only by mid-1915 was his image overshadowed by the now emerging 'wooden titan' von Hindenburg. As the war lengthened into the grim stalemate in the trenches, civilian impatience generated behind-the-scenes agitation for unrestricted use of the aerial superweapon. Radical conservatives, even to the right of the Kaiser, were still enthralled by the promises of pre-war *Luftmilitarismus* and mostly ignorant of the actual limitations of the zeppelin in combat. Now they used their demands for unrestricted zeppelin warfare as a political bludgeon against the relatively moderate civilian government that was allegedly impeding use of the wondrous military airship and that had certainly constrained public discussion of wild annexationist war aims. The Count continued to address 'private' military and civilian audiences and in one such speech to many members of the Prussian State Assembly he put the old Zeppelin political magic to work in a direct attack on his former technological advocate, Chancellor Bethmann Hollweg, for allegedly hobbling German victory by failing to send dozens of massed zeppelins in raids on England.[50] This was the kind of political venom that shortly was switched to a more likely weapon – unrestricted submarine warfare – which did indeed topple the Chancellor in early 1917. By then the Count had already sensed the limitations of his invention and had refocused his energies to build huge four-engined winged bombers that wrought more destruction on Britain in 1917–18 than his airships ever did.[51] He did not live to see this last success. When he died in March 1917, he was still in many minds the greatest German of the twentieth century – a man who had praised the arrival of the de facto Hindenburg-Ludendorff military dictatorship in August 1916, which was intended to breathe new vigour into the allegedly faltering civilian government. In that struggle the zeppelin had played, if only briefly, its final political role in Imperial Germany.

Despite their surprising wartime operational failures, the zeppelins steadily improved technologically during the conflict. Down at the Lake, naval construction experts superseded the influence of the now mostly absent Count. Colsman oversaw the prodigious growth of wartime production, with additional new factories at Potsdam and Staaken, both near Berlin. Personnel grew to over seven thousand, including the Dornier airplane works and further subsidiary airplane production. The airships tripled in size, doubled their speed, and soared to heights over 20 000 feet. By 1916 the ships emerged from their construction hangars at a rate of one a month. Thus was produced naval L59 of the Africa-trip record: an uninterrupted voyage of nearly 4000 miles, en route for 95 hours, and with a load of 22 crew and 15 tons of war materiel – realizing the earliest dreams of Count Zeppelin for an aerial military transport and foreshadowing postwar achievements in transoceanic commercial flight.[52] Dr Eckener had left Friedrichshafen early in the war to command the naval airship instruction school at the new Fuhlsbüttel base. From here he sent evaluations of the ongoing operational limitations and successes, wisdom that was used to improve airship building. Crucial to all these developments was the government's forcing the Zeppelin Company and Schütte-Lanz to share each other's designs. Both parties agreed to postpone settlement of their respective claims for patent royalties and profits until victory was won – which then led to long litigation in the postwar years of defeat and recession. From this technological shotgun wedding was born the 'Zeppelin' that became so well-known worldwide during the interwar years. Strangely, while Zeppelin thrived in the rush of orders, Schütte went – after his first important design innovations – from one practical construction failure to another during the war years, culminating in the Navy's refusal to accept any more of his wood-girder ships after 1916. Still, in the wartime armaments boom Schütte profited handsomely from his dual airship and subsidiary airplane production. Colsman and his firm also became wealthy and further technologically expert in their business. Indeed, as of 1915, the company could reimburse the Count for all his financial outlays since 1891. Eckener's wealth was garnered in the priceless wartime operational experience that he would use to great advantage in the postwar years. Thus technological knowledge of the zeppelin steadily improved while its military operational effectiveness just as steadily declined. It was a paradoxical outcome for all the pre-war aspirations of the valiant Old Aeronaut and the preposterous visions of *Luftmilitarismus*.

The invention and first development of the rigid airship in Imperial Germany set in motion a complex of hitherto unperceived behavioural responses to the new technological phenomenon. These novel psychological attitudes, and the initial political responses thereto, would later be repeated in perceptions and policy manoeuvres in a worldwide arena. What in sum were these Imperial German precedents for the airship era between the wars?

First of all was the wide spectrum of public psychological reaction in experiencing those great skyships in majestic motion above all humankind. Herewith, the zeppelin became a German and international sensation – with immediate latent international political significance. The awakening of wonder, excitement, wish-fulfilment and other positive responses were almost universal in Imperial Germany. Subordinate to these crowd-gathering enticements were feelings of uncanniness and apprehension that surfaced only momentarily on occasions of airship wrecks or the two fatal disasters of 1913 – events that in Germany were uniquely subject to the phoenix phenomenon, a powerful and curious confidence in technological rebirth. Conversely, in neighbouring nations that had pre-war felt militarily threatened by armed airships, the war turned these fears into initial outright panic that was later only partially assuaged by Allied aerial victories over the zeppelins. In Germany, however, that wartime failure of the superweapon was never popularly perceived. Enthusiasm for the zeppelin just slowly subsided into the German psyche, dormant there until its postwar reawakening in a renewed image of German pride and peacetime power.

German airship design, engineering and business organization also set significant precedents for postwar developments in Britain and the United States. Essentially, airship building was a monopolistic enterprise, yet despite its unique free-enterprise beginnings, Count Zeppelin's company soon became quite dependent on government business. As of 1911, the company was already busily politicking at various official levels to stimulate Berlin's orders for its enormously expensive and still experimental aircraft. Count Zeppelin was the individual who developed the most spectacular career from his intimate airship association. Subsequently others like Colsman, Eckener and Schütte also began developing national identities in their respective spheres of airship endeavours. Design and production engineers like Dürr at Friedrichshafen, or Schütte's several capable and creative associates, remained publicly undescribed and unpictured – their works were armaments secrets. These characteristics of business procedure and certain luminous individual careers would replicate elsewhere in the postwar era.

The broader politics relating to airships in Imperial Germany were at first fought within the closed arenas of committee, hierarchical, and court struggles. When private discussions among a few industrial leaders in 1906–7 failed to establish an airship industry, the Reichstag funded the new Manzell hangar and airship orders in open debate. In mid-1908, the airship instantaneously achieved wide public attention that brought the whole matter of airship funding and use fully into open politics. Men and women from all walks of life – that large political stratum comprising a majority of innocuous citizenry – awakened together in great emotional crowds to cheer the Count and experience his aerial machine. These were the circumstances that Theodor Heuss later identified as *the* compelling political event of modern Imperial Germany, for they created a new dimension of national awareness to supplant the stale political inheritance from the later nineteenth century.

Now the very small and active political minority – the power-holders and the power-seekers – moved both closely and openly to exploit the possibilities of new technological gambits in their political games. The Prussian Military, holding to its non-rigid preferences, moved only very reluctantly and unconvinced toward the rigid airship. The Kaiser, however, caught in momentary political *extremis* by the *Daily Telegraph* affair, made his sudden and dramatic open visit to the Count at Manzell – in the process thrusting an unwanted rigid airship on the German Army. Thus was broken the anti-Zeppelin clique, as the Kaiser defected to join the cheering masses.

Politics in Imperial Germany were pursued, however vigorously, within well-defined limits of staid conduct. Great issues were fought between inflexible and bureaucratically controlled political parties that strongly emphasized ideological principles and major economic interests in their strategies for political gain. Individual politicians were firmly subject to party discipline. In peacetime Count Zeppelin did not exploit party affiliation for himself. His work was for the German nation. He held himself 'above politics' and the enthusiastic millions gave him no specific party-political identification. Indeed, before 1914 the socialists maintained their support for his contributions to German science and culture, though voicing their anti-war ideology in condemning airship weaponry – a stance that wore thin in the mounting pre-war enthusiasm for *Luftmilitarismus*. Even in the great internal political shift of the 1912 elections, when the Social Democrats swept to an impressive one-third of Reichstag seats, no one used the Count or his airship in political propaganda. The postwar era, in Germany as elsewhere, would be rather different.

The second wartime year did produce an exception to that peacetime political conduct. The Count increasingly agitated for the unrestricted zeppelin warfare that pre-war visions of *Luftmilitarismus* had found so compelling. Increasingly the Pan-German, Prussian, and military opponents of civilian Chancellor Bethmann Hollweg used his alleged neglect of the aerial superweapon as a cudgel to drive him from office. The image of the All-Highest Emperor rapidly receded from public awareness as he abandoned his frequent pre-war posturing and gave the limelight to his generals. Indeed, the Kaiser came under oblique criticism for restraining the powerful battleship fleet and initially forbidding zeppelin raids on his relatives in London. The new power-seeking clique combined power-holding Prussian reactionaries with other conservative losers in the 1912 elections. Together they whipped up wartime emotions about lagging military successes to combat pre-war democratic and socialist gains, founding a broad new *Vaterland* party, which the aged Count himself joined. When it became clear by early 1916 that the military zeppelin could not be made effective, they continued their efforts and simply switched to another wonder weapon. That campaign for unrestricted submarine warfare achieved its purpose in early 1917, with other, quite unanticipated political consequences. By now the Kaiser, and Count Zeppelin, were quite overshadowed by the new publicly acclaimed personalities of Hindenburg, Ludendorff, and various aviation and U-boat heroes. The death of the Old Aeronaut early in 1917 coincided with the fade-out of his once-vaunted aerial superweapon.

The wartime zeppelin precedents reverberated twofold into the wider world. The initial terroristic impact of bombing airships was soon overlaid – but not concealed – by the evidence of their destruction high in the skies. Henceforth no nation would consider the airship as a reliable weapon in combat, though the United States would develop a unique airship scouting function for its Navy in geographic circumstances totally different from the restricted dimensions of Europe. Zeppelin construction and operating experience of wartime would, however, play the determining role in commercial rigid airships of the interwar period and also pass over into their American naval scouting counterparts. And a new generation of masses, in Germany and elsewhere, would respond again to the great emotional wonder of airships, with their renewed political manipulation by other power-holders and power-seekers, in a renewed outburst of skyward commercial airship rivalry.

2
Zeppelins in International Politics, 1919–21

Six years elapsed between the final costly zeppelin raid on London in 1918 and the triumphant transatlantic zeppelin flight of 1924. The victorious Allies moved promptly to eliminate German military airships and to prevent Germany from gaining any commercial benefit from their undeniable technical expertise and wartime operational experience. Britain and America sought to command German airship advantages for their own use. London soon abandoned rigid airships in naval use and sought to develop them for Empire-wide commerce. Washington alone developed naval airships as scouts for its battle fleet. Paris and Rome hovered briefly at the edge of airship development, receiving allocated zeppelins and losing them in operational accidents. While German power languished in defeat, the Zeppelin Company privately activated commercial airship building and operation. This venture was fraught with Allied interdiction, but finally it culminated in the construction of a zeppelin for the American Navy, a project that became a masterstroke of technical and international political acclaim – an opening chord in renewed international skyward airship rivalry.

With the Armistice most of the German Navy arrived at British bases for internment. The battle fleet went to Scapa Flow, the submarines to Harwich, where the surrender was imperially overseen by British rigid No.23 in a final symbolic gesture of victory over the zeppelin fleets that had so stimulated British apprehensions during the previous decade. The remaining zeppelins were grounded in Germany to await their fate. The military stipulations of the ensuing Versailles conference were clear and immediate. According to clauses 198–201, Germany would have no airships in the future, its construction and maintenance facilities to be destroyed. An aeronautical Inter-Allied Commission of Control had sovereign power to supervise the elimination of German aviation. These clauses were part of an Allied political thrust to cripple all German military power. They were also meant to prevent Germans from developing postwar commercial airship projects and to transfer all German airship technological expertise to the Allies for likely postwar improvement of their own commercial aviation. The postwar Allied search for German zeppelin secrets and personnel foreshadowed the much more intensive victors' scramble for German nuclear and space technology in 1945. For an interim year, however, while the Treaty was in negotiation, much German non-military and commercial activity began anew in an uncertain limbo.[1]

From 1917 onward, several German firms had already begun planning for peacetime air service and adapting military aircraft for passenger use, the Zeppelin Company among them. When the war ceased in 1918, the German government was immobilized by defeat and revolution, but private enterprise promptly sought postwar development. Down at the Lake, Colsman had wisely secured some of his company's prodigious wartime profits in inflation-resistant material assets. He also successfully rode out revolutionary labour unrest, reducing the wartime thousands to a few hundred trusted local workers. Momentarily he kept airplane developments at the Dornier subsidiary and at the Berlin-Staaken works, where several four-engine R-giants were in completion. The Allies still permitted such construction, hoping to acquire the latest and best for their own use. At Friedrichshafen, Colsman focused on converting the aerial warship building complex into peacetime consumer goods production. Eckener, however, returning from his naval airship training command, had a very different concept in mind for postwar development of the Zeppelin Company. Now he would dedicate the resources of Count Zeppelin's great venture to grasp Germany's aviation future with commercial airships, for domestic and international flight. Initially these divergent paths did not preclude collaboration between the two executives to beat zeppelin swords into ploughshares, but within three years their project and personality differences brought the two men to a latent hostility sometimes only bridgeable in consultation by interoffice memoranda.[2]

As of late 1918, wartime reminders were everywhere about them. Secure in its hangar, almost complete, stood the latest naval zeppelin, L72, while a delegation from the Inter-Allied Control Commission under Brigadier E. A. D. Masterman, Britain's premier airshipman, had already made its first appraising visit to Friedrichshafen. Other Allied airshipmen soon appeared as well: Dr Jerome C. Hunsaker of the US Navy, Commander Jean du Plessis de Grenédan of France, and

Umberto Nobile of Italy. Among the returned German airship veterans was young Ernst A. Lehmann, pre-war captain of the DELAG *Sachsen* and new head of the construction division at Luftschiffbau Zeppelin. He urged an immediate postwar political mission for L72: a surprise transatlantic flight to New York 'in order to reestablish Germany's prestige in the world'.[3] Both Colsman and Eckener were intrigued by the proposal but found it psychologically foolhardy. For the time being, Lehmann prevailed with support of Baron von Gemmingen, head of the Zeppelin Foundation, who would soon release new guidelines for the postwar mission of the Foundation. Here he fixed a revised image of Count Zeppelin which would dominate German awareness well towards the end of the twentieth century. He argued that the war had had the unfortunate effect of distorting the Old Aeronaut's primary objectives. These had been to use the generous German national gift of 1908 to further the scientific understanding and operation of airship flight and to devise the technological means to perfect the rigid dirigible. The demands of the war had interrupted pursuit of the Count's ultimate objective – to achieve transatlantic flight as a cultural blessing and to bring nations more closely together. It was a bitter irony that naval Britain was avidly recognizing Zeppelin's military achievements while Germans had lost their faith in the airship by reason of its wartime failure. Now the Zeppelin Foundation would take up the stiff competition with England – a nation seeking to utilize all the Count's work to extend its mastery of the seas into the air. By achieving his peacetime objectives the good name of Count Zeppelin would be restored in the world.[4] The L72 flight was vetoed in Berlin, probably as Lehmann later averred, by the influence of Masterman, who was no doubt aware of British plans to send R34 across the Atlantic for the same prestigious purpose. It was the first round in the postwar Anglo-German political contest for airship supremacy.[5]

Concurrently with the L72 discussions, and while Colsman began his diversification of the Zeppelin Company, Dr Hugo Eckener embarked on his new career as a postwar peacetime airship builder and flier. Born at the Baltic seaport of Flensburg in 1868, he had early developed a sailor's experienced empathy with the meteorological moods of the sea. He took his doctoral degree in 1892 in behavioural psychology with Professor Wilhelm Wundt at Leipzig. Considered the world's most prominent psychologist at the time, Wundt rooted his studies in fundamentals of human perception by feeling or by vision. Eckener was probably impressed by that aspect of Wundt's studies and theories that focused on folk psychology, which constituted a psychic bridge from individual impressions to the broader community – a folk soul that developed from commonality of experience.[6] How readily the pre-war German passion for airships would seem to confirm those observations! Eckener later always understood that his behaviour in context of the airship and its German folk-resonance would be crucial to the success of his enterprise. His bearing in that relationship was disdained as shallow posturing by his opponents in the camp of designer-competitor Schütte, though praised as genial leadership by his friends and admirers. But those characteristics would only develop later in Eckener's career. Between 1892 and 1909 he had no firmly developed occupation, vacillating between jobs as cultural news commentator in Flensburg (1892–9) and Hamburg (1907–9) and with private studies in political economy at Friedrichshafen. When Colsman hired him as publicity director for the DELAG in 1909, Eckener's quick and perceptive intelligence, together with his experience in sailing, soon led him to qualify as a licensed airship captain and become an expert layman-engineer in all aspects of airship construction and operation. Here he was in constant touch with Count Zeppelin, for whom he developed the deep admiration and respect that marked the rest of his life. His vast wartime experience as commander and flyer at the naval airship school bound him to airships for life and deepened his conviction that he must carry on the work of the Old Aeronaut and confirm Zeppelin's obligation to the German people for their devotion of 1908 and thereafter.[7]

Venturing a new commercial airship business in defeated Germany in 1919 did not seem as hopeless then as it does in retrospect. The Allies would not close Dornier or Berlin-Staaken for another year. The quiet hangars at Lake Constance held a full range of surplus airship parts. Chief engineer Dürr still presided over a nucleus of experienced design and construction crews. The reactivated DELAG ordered two small airships and on 20 August, LZ120 *Bodensee*, with twice the lift and speed of DELAG's last pre-war ship, began its scheduled flights. With German rail transport bedevilled by strikes and breakdowns, and with revolution in Bavaria, the new airline catered to travellers and businessmen coming north from Switzerland. Almost every trip was booked solid up to the private DELAG airfield at Berlin-Staaken. Several Allied men with future airship significance enjoyed zeppelin flight when commercial airplanes were few and puny: Colonel William M. Hensley (soon to seek a zeppelin for the US Army); Lieutenant Colonel V. C. Richmond (ultimate designer of the British R101); and Harry Vissering (later godfather of Goodyear Zeppelin). All were stimulated in

55

Departure of the *Bodensee* from Munich, bound for Berlin, 1919

ambition for their services and nations. The German people, however, staggering under news of the crippling terms of the Versailles Treaty, had no care for the plucky private airship revival. Even at Friedrichshafen the plump little zeppelins appeared as a sad come-down from the last sleek wartime height-climbers three times their size. But the Allies had immediate apprehensions. After a hundred successful flights, with 3000 passengers and tons of mail, the DELAG was shut down in early December.[8] Here, allegedly, was a new threat of air militarism in commercial disguise, no doubt built and operated by top wartime airshipmen. Such success by the recent 'baby-killing' Huns was simply not acceptable to Britain or France. It was high time to identify the real victors of the war.[9]

The German government had hardly noticed the DELAG revival. Quite contrary to the pre-war era, when Count Zeppelin, engineer Schütte, and their airship production held attention centre-stage, the immediate postwar era found zeppelin builders and fliers under Allied pressure for elimination, and shunned in Berlin. Compared to other disarmament terms of the Versailles Treaty, zeppelins were just a tiny fraction of the vast disarmament required – but they still held their high international awareness. So Berlin had its vexing airship tasks: coping with the political fallout of the seven zeppelins scuttled by their crews in June 1919; processing a long-delayed delivery of seven other airworthy ships to the Allies; and long arguments about dismantling all the airship stations and construction works remaining as of November 1918. Relations with Berlin were further strained by Schütte's five-year law suit (1919–24) to force payment by the Weimar Treasury of unpaid debts incurred by its imperial predecessor. It also sought satisfaction from the Zeppelin Company for its infraction of Schütte patent-rights and failure to pay requisite royalties for use of his technical innovations – altogether hardly the stuff for airship enthusiasm anywhere. For their parts, Eckener and Colsman maintained passable relations with personalities in various Berlin agencies, but they required little of them except clearances from the new Transport Ministry for the DELAG flights. For the rest, Luftschiffbau Zeppelin financed itself, operated from its own private landing fields in Berlin and Friedrichshafen, and got little resonance from either the government or a public that was burdened psychologically and economically by the punitive measures of the victors. Later, with the construction of LZ127, the Foreign Ministry, the German Cabinet, and several other ministries would become actively involved with Eckener's very aggressive activities to re-establish the zeppelin as a symbol of German technological and cultural prowess – but in dismal 1919 that was at least five years in the future.

Just as the DELAG was getting under way that summer, Colsman and Eckener made an alternative bid to rescue zeppelin technology for German advantage and to improve their company's finances. Contacting the American military attaché at The Hague, they offered to sell L72 (still seen as company private property), together with zeppelin patents and expertise, to any American group interested. Promptly the War Department sent Colonel Hensley to Germany, where he entered vigorously into negotiations with the Zeppelin Company and was frequently under way with the DELAG *Bodensee* during the second half of 1919. Reporting that the men at Friedrichshafen would rather destroy L72 than see her go to Britain or France, he got their enthusiastic instruction in technical and operational details, including their assurance that she could be readied for a flight to America in two weeks, provided the Americans could supply the necessary fuel. When L72 was then allocated to France by the Allies in late September, Colsman and Eckener proposed building an ultra-modern new zeppelin for the American Army. For the next two months activities hummed down at the Lake, updating existing plans for a transoceanic zeppelin and conducting simulated transatlantic crossings. In late November Colsman signed a definitive contract with Hensley for the new zeppelin, about a third greater in size and capabilities than the lost L72. When the War Department then abruptly cancelled the order because America was still technically at war with Germany, Hensley stayed on briefly in Friedrichshafen, as Colsman and his co-workers continued refining their designs, periodically raising their price to adjust for inflation, and still instructing the American in zeppelin technology and operations. By May 1920, Colsman finally lost patience with the venture and set out for America on his own. During the summer of 1920 the last echoes of the project were perceived in the urgent billing of the Zeppelin Company to the War Department for four and a half million marks to cover work to date – all denied in Washington.[10]

Meanwhile, they continued sharpening their wits at Friedrichshafen with simulated transoceanic zeppelin flying. It was an obvious fact in 1919 that only an airship, fully loaded, could reliably cross the Atlantic, as British R34 had proved in July. It seemed that the future of intercontinental aviation must rest with the airship. By contrast with the technologically more mature airship, the airplane was still in its infancy. Its major improvements in engines and propellers, construction materials, wing configuration, and a host of other refinements were yet to be achieved. Yet, already short commercial airline spans were developing, where zeppelins like the *Bodensee* would soon be outclassed by the improving airplane advantages of cost, speed, adaptability to weather, and ease of handling. It was still anticipated, however, that only the airship could master the transoceanic distances. These were the perspectives that compelled attention at Friedrichshafen. While Colsman wrestled with adjusting to postwar business, the airshipmen pursued four major tasks. Generally they were all preoccupied with various aspects of airship development: new facets of construction, propulsion, and handling; systematic study of Atlantic meteorology, with imaginary flights attuned to actual weather conditions; and anticipation of commercial schedules, passenger handling, and goods transport.[11] Second, was an immediate flurry of activity by engineers Paul Jaray and Karl Arnstein to design LZ125 for the abortive American Army order. Third, were several days of intensive negotiations by Eckener at Stockholm in October 1919, to complete plans for the international service of LZ121 *Nordstern*, a prologue to his later activities: journalistic celebration of his airship career, popular excitement for airship travel, and planning for all aspects of the operation. Finally, initial negotiations were under way with commercial interests in Spain to establish a zeppelin service between Seville and Buenos Aires. The game was afoot for international and transoceanic airship service and these Germans were not about to be left behind in the competition.[12]

The Treaty of Versailles came into effect on 10 January 1920. All interim German aircraft conversion and construction ceased. Dornier looked to establish new factories in Switzerland and Italy. At Friedrichshafen the stock of surplus duralumin served for a new line of kitchen and industrial containers, nostalgically marketed as Elzett [LZ] ware. Colsman attempted to open discussion with the British airshipmen about prospects for developing German–European collaboration to foster inter-European and transoceanic commercial airship service. Meteorologically speaking, he argued, several areas of the continent offered more favourable prospects for transoceanic departures than the gale-prone British Isles. Financially, single nations could not afford to start costs that logically should be shared among several cooperating countries. It was not worth converting used wartime airships for peacetime commerce; new ships were needed based on up-to-date technology and the best of operational experience. Finally, he concluded, it was senseless to demolish all German airship facilities, some of which could be converted to peacetime European use. Obviously, Colsman sought to maintain his company and its prospects. Equally, Masterman hoped to surmount the financial difficulties at home, to abolish the hated German weapon, and to eliminate German airship competition. He made no response to Colsman's plea.[13]

Meanwhile, Allied airship personnel, notably Commander Ralph D. Weyerbacher (designer and builder of America's ZR1, now under construction) and visitors from Goodyear continued to arrive at the Lake factory. Like Dornier, the zeppelin works still tried to seek its fortune abroad. That summer, when Colsman led a Zeppelin Company trio to America, they were respectfully received in New York, at naval air stations, and at Akron and Detroit. But Colsman tried to drive too hard a bargain and returned empty-handed.[14] Concurrently Schütte was also exploring in America. Like Colsman's, his enterprises were exposed to possible Allied sanctions or confiscation, and, like Eckener's, his tiny remnant design staff was also producing projects for a transatlantic airship.[15] All this futurism, however, was blighted by Allied claims on the few surviving wartime ships. In the second half of 1920 the image of Count Zeppelin reappeared ghostlike on the German scene, as the popular press reported various zeppelin captains on their final flights, delivering two airships each to France, Britain, and Italy. L72 was not destroyed by her builders, as they had earlier vowed, but arrived in France with her interior liberally bestrewn with insulting and pornographic greetings in French to her new owners.[16] In mid-1921 the final blow fell: the Allies' demand for financial compensation from Germany and delivery of the two new DELAG ships in amends for the seven naval zeppelins destroyed in the scuttling of June 1919. Meanwhile all surviving airship stores and hangars were being obliterated. Schütte was wiped out. Friedrichshafen alone survived in limbo; August 1921 was the nadir of Germany's postwar airship era.

Despite all the alarms about German zeppelins in England between 1908 and 1914, these valuable years for British aviation development were mostly frittered away in disputes and delays. In contrast to the forthright German programmes for developing rigids from 1912 onward, assisted by self-motivating private interests and integrated design and production teams, Britain had not yet left the starting line in that aspect of the armaments race. When war broke out, few decision-makers had even seen a zeppelin, though Admiral Jellicoe (later the British naval commander at Jutland in 1916) had flown in a DELAG ship in 1911. Those pre-war years were spent in service disputes, disagreements among scientists and engineers, incredible decision delays, and military–civilian political conflicts – all compounded by echoes in their respective lower staffs. At the beginning of the war Britain had just half a dozen faltering non-rigids, though airplanes had made better progress. All this pre-war bureaucratic behaviour would bedevil airship design, procurement, and operation through the rest of Britain's airship era.[17]

While the war years saw a hundred non-rigids achieving varied results as submarine searchers and off-coast scouts, there existed neither consistent government policies nor forthright procurement of rigids. Just as naval policies were in frequent ad hoc revision, so it was with airships. Four major constructors worked, beset with frequent delays and changes over three distinct design cycles. Most Britons, in their haste to confront German zeppelin scouting and urban bombardment, believed that those airships, with all their size and stealthy menace, must be met with comparable opposing British weapons. London had no option but to imitate the few examples of zeppelin technology that fortuitously fell into its hands; thus the final British ships were always three or four years behind the zeppelin state of the art current at that time. Plans derived from the fog-bound landing of ZIV at Lunéville in 1913 did not materialize with variations in the 23-class British rigids until autumn 1917. The next two series, based on zeppelins downed in England, were equally belated. Training for airshipmen, sometimes transferred from non-rigids, only began at Masterman's Howden flight base in mid-1916, three to six years behind comparable German crews. Concurrently there was a prodigious task to establish and staff three major rigid airship stations. That progress did not conceal continuing differences about airships within the Royal Navy and the even greater conflicts between the Admiralty and the Ministry of Munitions, with its comprehensive wartime scope and power. As a result of exaggerated perceptions about the alleged effectiveness of zeppelins scouting for the German Fleet at Jutland in 1916, with its serious loss of British warships, some Britons finally began to develop basic operational doctrine for airships in service with the fleet – notably Masterman's studies of later 1917. Concurrently also began the first instance of intra-service rivalry between advocates of the airship and supporters of the nascent aircraft carrier, highlighted in July 1918, as planes from the flight deck of HMS *Furious* dealt aviation's first on-shore carrier strike against the zeppelin station at Tondern. When No. 23 made its victory flight over German ships surrendering at Harwich in late 1918, British airships were still not yet an operational force. Despite great service and civilian efforts, barely five airships were flying at the end of the war – all technically outdated, too late to serve in the conflict, and their crews still learning their skills.

Most of the characteristics of the flawed wartime development would persist into the postwar era: first, imitation and adaptation of German accomplishment; second, intra-service rivalries, especially now extended to inter-service friction with the new Air Ministry (since April 1918) and the Royal Air Force (RAF); and third, frequent disagreement between service and civilian offices – all accentuated by the myriad problems of demobilization and firm requirements for postwar budget economies.[18]

Notable during the postwar decade was the evident lack of spontaneous and positive airship resonance in the British public. Pre-war British apprehensions about zeppelins escalated during the first two years of conflict into fear and repugnance towards the 'Hun babykillers'. Dowager Queen Alexandra wrote in July 1915:

> We have been living through some gruesome moments here – just a fortnight ago we had those beastly Zepps over us. We were all sitting in Victoria's room when we were suddenly startled by an awful noise! and lo and behold, there was the awful monster over our heads.[19]

Then, quite unlike the Germans, many British people actually witnessed the destruction of several zeppelins and were saturated with propaganda about their flaming extinction, and it was not hard for them to add to their initial negative image of airships a delighted celebration at zeppelin destruction. Consequently the characteristic structure of psychic response to airships was basically impaired. The British public saw very little of their own rigid airships in the last year of the war and had therefore no positive picture of London's airship progress on which to build a new peacetime appreciation for commercial airship prospects. Even when wartime anti-zeppelin emotions faded, there remained a fundamental popular scepticism about the airship per se. This was the problem that Lord Thomson would later confront with his propaganda for the Imperial Airship Scheme. However, that was not the focus of problems in 1919–20. Here rather was the phenomenon of nearly a dozen British airships contractually multiplying at their builders, or actually emerging from their hangars, like products from some technological Sorcerer's Apprentice. Wrestling with this now unwanted abundance of airships brought the whole panoply of political interest and gamesmanship into play.[20]

It was evident that the great and usually apolitical majority had been thoroughly and negatively inoculated against positive airship enthusiasm by British wartime experiences. Only two small groups responded positively to airships. First was the tiny nucleus of experienced designers, engineers, and fliers who had been emotionally seized by the practice and promise of airship technology. Second was a larger group of men in transport, commerce, and government who were open to reasonable persuasion that the airship was a key to postwar imperial enterprise and prestige. Together these two groups constituted a loosely functioning airship lobby. Both sought to deprive Germany of her dirigibles, with the aims of combatting a military zeppelin resurgence, and eliminating German competition in future transoceanic commerce. Those in power wrestled to close down wartime airship activity as expeditiously as possible, thus to end its very visible drain on the public purse. Still, they had to keep a weather eye on the promise of postwar commercial airship success that could bring international political prestige to London and the Empire.[21]

Every facet of decision-making in the postwar decade felt the impact of one or several government entities:

First, from wartime experience, the Admiralty, which was still paying for the British airship programmes and would continue flying the airships until that function was turned over to the Air Ministry in October 1919.

Second, the Air Ministry, established in April 1918 soon to oversee all commercial aviation and thus to become involved with the fate of the remaining naval airships and with planning for transoceanic airship projects.

Third, the Cabinet, together with its subordinate Air Council.

Fourth, Parliament, notably the Lower House.

Fifth, the Treasury, England's most formidable hierarchy of civil servants.

Finally, the ministries of Commerce, Transport, and the Post Office.

This was an impressive list of ever-ready participants in British airship decision-making.[22]

Outside the government was a spectrum of private interests and individuals promoting their projects for postwar commercial airship development. For the first half of 1919 the Admiralty and the Air Ministry fenced adroitly to escape from costs of airship procurement. The former anticipated receiving a few of the newest zeppelins as war booty and had already planned a totally new R38. A few of the older ships they kept for training, the rest they cancelled or tried to dump on the Air Ministry. The Royal Navy itself felt happily rid of the gas craft, vesting its future in the aircraft carrier and protecting those carrier-borne planes from Air Ministry grasp. Sir Hugh Trenchard, founder of the RAF, agreed only to assume control of airship personnel, while leaving airship costs with the Admiralty. Air Minister Winston Churchill was chairman (1919–21) of the new Air Council where now, ever-negative about airships, he moved, reversed, compromised, and moved again to appease all interests, from airship proponents to the stern budgeteers of the Treasury. It was a tiring game of airship musical chairs.[23]

Matters became urgent in February 1919, when the Cunard Line and two airship builders proposed a commercial service to New York and pressed for a skyship demonstration flight. Soon afterwards, an American aviation group invited the new British R34 to fly to America. Before such a flight could be undertaken, an American naval flying boat made an eastward crossing in stages, soon followed by Alcock and Brown's non-stop flight in a Vickers Vimy biplane. The airshipmen now chafed at the bit to show positively what they could do.[24]

Both the new R33 and R34 (German design vintage 1916) took to the skies in mid-March of 1919. Preparations for the transatlantic flight of the R34 culminated in a 56-hour flight of 2000 miles eastward into the Baltic and along north Germany, where, in a curiously misconceived effort at psychological manipulation, some Britons thought thereby to press the Germans into signing the Treaty of Versailles. While the Germans then signed for other reasons, the airshipmen had a thorough workout for their coming venture.[25]

On 2 July 1919, R34 was finally set to take off for America. The Admiralty had relinquished all but some lingering scouting interest in airships, with a latent claim for future wartime requisition. The Air Ministry had finally accepted overall responsibility for civilian airships to which the Air Council and the Cabinet had made miserly short-range expense contributions, while the Post Office had considered some future mail subsidies for aircraft. American aviation circles paid for stationing R34 at Mineola, Long Island. The US Navy and Army compromised in their contention for political visibility: Lieutenant Commander Zachary Lansdowne (later captain of the ill-fated ZR1 *Shenandoah*) flew as a westward observer; Colonel William Hensley flew eastward to temporary stationing in Britain, whence he soon departed to negotiate the secret contract in Germany to build LZ125. The R34 proved that 30 men and 25 tons of fuel and supplies could successfully make the transatlantic crossing. Wrote the *New York Times*:

> The R34 is the pioneer of the air fleets of commerce and pleasure, which in a very few years will make the flight from the New World to the Old, a brief, luxurious, and comparatively tame enterprise. The [Navy] airplane flights of 1919 were gallant adventures; the voyage of R34 is the real beginning of the new age.[26]

This record defined the undeniable advantage of airships in long-range commerce for the next fifteen years and set the stage for the commercial skyward rivalries of the next two decades.

The homeward flight was faster and more routine, but the political welcome there was notable by its absence. Whereas thousands of Americans had streamed to Mineola to view the ship, and officers and crew had been socially lionized in New York for several days, the British official and public responses were negligible. It was ironically symbolic that a British service band at the arrival station spiritedly playing 'See the Conquering Hero Comes!' was suddenly doused with a water ballast discharge. News publicity, in contrast to New York, was perfunctory and the Treasury gave no funds to capitalize commercially on the crossing. The American Naval Secretary had approved awarding Navy Crosses to the entire flight complement of R34 in recognition of their feat. But when the British government, which had recommended knighthoods for airmen Alcock and Brown, failed to give any recognition to the men of R34, the American Navy deferred. As seen by Americans, the flight had real Anglo-American significance, but the British appeared unmoved, distracted as they were by the problems of demobilization and still affected by the continuing negative wartime image of airships.[27]

These adverse effects spurred on the British airship activities. Soon R33 made a 30-hour flight over southern England, trailing banners exhorting Britons to buy victory bonds, while a small brass band played full blast on a gun platform atop the ship. Huge crowds were out in London as the skyship criss-crossed the city, but they were more likely attending events commemorating the proclamation of peace than drawn to admire the airship. More directly, the airshipmen were now pressing to improve their skills in an ageing veteran of Class 23, with wooden R32, and with the relatively more modern R33 and R34. Altogether, nearly two thousand hours were accumulated in flight. Elsewhere there were experiments with airplane hook-ons to serve either as military scouts or to facilitate commercial on- and off-loading that could obviate expensive landings. But the lobbyists still had to contend with the swell of political negativism. They were haunted by Labour election posters in later 1919 that featured airships as instruments of the capitalist armaments industry. Nor was their cause buoyed when R36, converted from a war craft to peacetime use with an underslung elongated passenger car, failed to live up to its publicized capability of flying to Suez. The ship nearly crashed on her maiden flight in April 1921 with a complement of high-ranking Air Ministry officials aboard and two months later, another 'publicity' flight with almost 50 Members of Parliament failed to secure any positive political recognition. What the airship lobby thus failed to achieve politically at home, the technological shortcomings of its skyships prevented it from recouping abroad with another international success like the flight of R34.[28]

Between late 1918 and mid-1921 the Admiralty and the Air Ministry had done various Empire-wide studies on sites and likely opportunities to develop commercial ventures for all types of aircraft, including airships. Just after the war Masterman had distributed his optimistic 'Notes on Airships for Commercial Purposes', which anticipated using the best zeppelins thought soon to be available. In September 1919 both R32 and R33 made demonstration flights over Amsterdam with scanty, improvised passenger accommodation to greet the first postwar international aviation exhibition. Soon thereafter the Cunard and P&O shipping lines offered their tentative plans, all based on expected government subsidies. On and on went the dreams, with projects to overfly French battlefields, open service to Rome or Scandinavia, reach Egypt and ultimately India. Chief Engineer H. B. Pratt of the Vickers armaments firm authored the best contemporary book on commercial airships. His projects were twice the size of the most recent zeppelins and visualized luxurious accommodation for a hundred passengers. This was a design concept that would influence British commercial airship thinking for the next decade. Despite Pratt's undeniable engineering expertise, his calculations on airship lift, profitability, and required government subsidies were far too optimistic when reality fully intruded in 1929–30.

A more immediate reality was the Cabinet decision of late July 1920, which decreed that all airships should be sold or given to commercial interests, or barring that, to be scrapped. With no takers found, demolition of the older ships proceeded. The Admiralty, however, was still financially responsible for two new ships finally emerging from their construction hangars. R36 was a great disappointment, but R38, almost complete, had happily been sold to the Americans to be their ZR2. There were prospects that a successful R38 might well lead to further American orders for British airships, thus establishing Britain as a premier builder and exporter of airships. Still, neither the Admiralty nor the Air Ministry could any longer contend with the accumulating bad airship news: the publicized mishaps to British airshipmen; the long-delayed arrival of the two best zeppelins, now deteriorated almost beyond repair. Added to these was the heavy burden of airship financial history, cumulatively almost two hundred million dollars since 1911 – enough to build a dozen record-breaking liners like the *Mauretania*. Faced with such perceptions, the government finally closed down all its airship activities on 31 May 1921, leaving only R38 to be completed and delivered to the Americans. Three other recently built British airships remained to be sold to private interests or scrapped. England could at that time no longer endure the stressful process of learning to fly the temperamental skyships, nor could she afford to fund their continuing prodigious expense.[29]

Both the rather frustrated British airship lobby and the enthusiastic Americans looked forward to completing and testing R38. First conceived by the Admiralty in mid-1918, then taken over by the Air Ministry a year later, design of this largest airship ever built was especially subject to dilemmas, political rivalries, and strong emotional attitudes on both sides of the Atlantic. The R38 was essentially derived from the 1917 German L49, a height-climber intended for specialized, high-altitude, thin-air bombing missions. Yet she was being reborn as a workhorse scout for low altitudes in dense air. Could the design have been redone for safe high speeds at low altitudes? Author Higham's considered commentary stated:

> In the first place, the contract with the American Navy had already been entered into and changes may have required a species of international agreement. Secondly, there was the generally hostile attitude to airships which existed both within and without the Air Ministry and the Admiralty. This in its turn made design-change a matter of face, an admission that earlier work had not been properly done. Though an Air Ministry airship staff came into being, the design team was in fact seconded from the Royal Corps of Naval Constructors and was, therefore, still composed of the same men. Thus no outsiders with competent experience appeared to be available. Only Vickers really had a design team of its own with long

experience. But could these civilians be asked to scrutinize the work of a government department? And, last but not least, there was the press of economy.[30]

Already another factor was becoming evident that would bedevil British airship activities for the rest of the decade – the emergence of technological defensiveness in the Admiralty-Air Ministry design team. These men had been at work since 1915, with much theoretical design experience in adapting German specifications and little corrective from operational experience, becoming psychologically isolated, technologically speaking, from airship flying. Furthermore, as of 1918, they seemed to suffer the disdain of the RAF-minded majority in the Air Ministry, with its burgeoning enthusiasm for airplanes. Here also they bore the stresses of long delays in practical realization of their designs and then the rude rejection of their accomplishments by hurried postwar demobilization and Treasury resistance to further funding. The result was a developing in-group defensiveness, expressing itself in some illusion about the technological superiority of their craft and a perceived higher quality of their engineering speciality, the nobility of the cathedral-like construct of rigid airships. Thus began to emerge subtle pressures for defensive group uniformity and stereotypical resistance to other designers in similar or different aviation projects.[31]

As interim design and building tests were being made on R38 during 1920–1, some structural features were changed or strengthened. Despite some urging for even further changes or rebuilding, most Britons were agreed on closing the British airship chapter and delivering R38 to the Americans as quickly as possible. The Americans, in turn, were overly anxious to acquire the prestigious ship (as it was seen at home) and to gain the political profit of a well-advertised successful Atlantic crossing before the heavier weather of autumn set in. On 23 August 1921, Britain's greatest airship undertook her final trials over Hull (to the east of Howden), already displaying her new American designation of ZR2. Most of her American crew were aboard, but the British were still in command. At a crucial point in these trials the British commander ordered sharp turns at high speed and low altitude. Tragically, the British designers had failed to anticipate the heavy aerodynamic stresses of such manoeuvres. The airship simply crumpled in the air, broke apart, and burst into flames. The cream of British airshipmen (with General Maitland, Head of Training at Howden, Flight Lieutenant Pritchard, the officer in charge of the trials, and chief designer C. I. R. Campbell) perished, as did all but one of the neophyte

American crew. It was an appalling climax to a decade of British airship muddling through.[32] Thereafter defensiveness among these British designers only strengthened.

Evaluating that decade, various analysts drew their respective conclusions. Most idealistic were three American engineering contemporaries of the men lost over Hull. They paid tribute to the innovations and daring of the British designers, averring that life was always dangerous and sometimes fatal out on the frontiers of aviation science. They did not then know of the political limitations of British airshipmen who failed to respond to the invitation of Colsman to share German airship knowledge with them in return for German participation in postwar aviation.[33] Two commentators later described the completion of R38 in an atmosphere charged with antipathy to airships, or of British engineering inexperience propelled by overconfidence in circumstances severely limited by the stringencies of peacetime political economics.[34] A third opined succinctly: 'The British airship program was more remarkable politically than technically or operationally.'[35] It was a momentary victory of the short-range politics of the public purse over the longer-range politics of commercial airship enterprise then still within a range of conceivable feasibility.

It was in a tethered artillery-spotting balloon that Count Zeppelin had made his first ascent during his American tour of 1863, and after that war ex-army balloonists found jobs at county-fair ascents and sporting events. By 1904, American air enthusiasm was evident at the St. Louis World's Fair, where half a dozen elongated balloons were gathered to sway at their moorings and make tethered ascents, and one actually completed a single flight. Meanwhile, the Wrights were into the air and nationwide backyard shops were building primitive airplanes. Such domestic ventures found international emphasis with Walter Wellman, who in 1906–7 planned a semi-rigid airship expedition for polar exploration. Establishing a base and hangar at Spitzbergen, he flew his airship *America* for several hours there, only to strand on a nearby glacier.[36] Soon after, the news of Count Zeppelin's successful flights reached America, finding enthusiastic reception especially among that eighth of its population of first and second generation Germanic descent. This German-American element would remain a constant positive factor in national enthusiasm for airships over the next 30 years. In 1910, Wellman set off with a rebuilt airship and a crew of five to cross the Atlantic. After three days of failure and drift they were rescued northwest of Bermuda. Most important here was the echo of this flight in the financial support and wide publicity of American journalism.[37] Concurrently, both Britain and Germany were hearing echoes of airships as harbingers of future destructive wars, but Americans saw these as distant in geography and time. Of greater immediate interest, along with more airplanes, was the attempt in 1912 of Melvin Vaniman (Wellman's aeronautical engineer) to cross the Atlantic in the first airship built by the Goodyear Tire and Rubber Company.[38] Named the *Akron*, this non-rigid made several test flights before blowing up with the loss of its crew soon after departure eastward from New Jersey. Still, already before World War I, the American public had its first excitement of airship anticipation, not for war (as in Europe) but for polar exploration and ocean commerce.[39]

By 1913, at least one leader in the US Navy was already alert to the potential importance of airships for naval scouting. Admiral David W. Taylor accentuated his life-long advocacy of naval aviation by sending young naval constructor, MIT Professor Jerome C. Hunsaker, to study airship developments abroad, notably in Germany. His subsequent report on European airships opened a distinguished career with American naval airships and with Goodyear-Zeppelin at Akron from 1930 to 1938. Even before America entered the war, a few younger naval officers pioneered shipboard aircraft take-offs (1910–11), as well as float-plane (1913), and small non-rigid (1916 onward) operations. During the war naval airshipmen were sent to England for advanced training by their British counterparts. Concurrently, and possibly as a result of fallible wisdom derived from the Jutland battle in 1916, naval planners determined to acquire a rigid airship of their own. A far-sighted agreement among high-ranking service colleagues to avoid interservice friction produced a Joint Army-Navy Airship Board, where Army members soon deferred to their naval colleagues because of the great technological complications and cost of building a rigid airship. By the spring 1919, the Navy General Board, firmly supported by Admiral William S. Sims (the maverick naval technological innovator of the early twentieth century) and up-and-coming Captain Ernest J. King (early advocate of carrier-borne aviation, and naval chief during World War II), decided that America must build and develop large scouting airships. America's need for long-range scouts was predicated on her world strategic position between the Atlantic and Pacific oceans and her unique possession of the world's only supply of non-flammable helium. Since the Navy was then woefully short of cruisers for scouting with the Battle Fleet, airships were seen as a crucial component in overcoming that deficiency. In addition, they had three times the speed of the fastest vessel afloat and could carry many times the load of existing winged aircraft. These would be the justifications for the enormously expensive and fragile experimental airship during a postwar decade of public anti-war sentiments, neo-isolationism, and constant demands for greatly reduced federal budgets.[40]

The Navy's major problem, however, was less with a neo-isolationist and thrifty public than with the Army Air Service. Since 1916 almost all Army pilots had been training and flying with winged aircraft, anticipating wartime service in Europe. Future naval airshipmen began training with float-planes at Pensacola, then with non-rigid instruction in England. Other naval aviators were flying planes and learning about English experimentation with their first aircraft carriers. Already the questions were being posed: what would be the most useful craft for American naval operation, the carrier with its planes or the scouting airship? And what would be left for the float-plane or the flying-boat to do? The results of Army and Navy war aviation experiences were thus quite different. Army pilots had an immediate, well-developed, and unified sense of their aviation, with easily defined tasks for observers, fighters, and bombers. The airmen of the Navy, by contrast, faced a greater variety of tasks and potential technological alternatives: on-ship, off-ship; on-shore, off-shore; heavier-than-air, and lighter-than-air (three types). Consequently the Navy's wartime aviation experience was diffused, only partly developed in each of the differing operational and technological areas, and inherently disunited. Inevitably, the Navy airmen developed deep emotional loyalties to whichever specialized technological vehicle they had trained with and anticipated using in a service career. Thus the stage was set for an American Army-Navy political confrontation over the future of all American service aviation and for continuing intraservice naval conflicts about the proper development of naval air power.[41]

The centre of the approaching political storm was Brigadier General William Mitchell (1879–1936), commander of the Army's Flying Corps in France. Early in 1919 he returned to America from a brilliant aviation career, already reputed as a flamboyant and experienced political operator within the Army bureaucracy. While abroad, he had worked closely with British General Hugh Trenchard and saw Britain's development of an independent RAF as a model for future American service aviation. Soon at odds with his own service superiors for his razzle-dazzle public appearances, he still had their support in speaking for Army aviation generally and in his criticism of the Navy for its alleged outdated weapon technology. The American Navy had been the politi-

cal darling of the American public since the Spanish-American war and
Theodore Roosevelt's international posturing with the Great White
Fleet between 1905 and 1909. During World War I, however, that same
Navy was quite overshadowed in its successful anti-submarine warfare
by American soldiers and airmen in France. Soon the Navy would bear
the brunt of Mitchell's political campaign with his sensational experimental bombings of outdated warships in 1920–1 to demonstrate naval
vulnerability to aviation – in this case, specifically to Army bombers.[42]

Already in 1919, Mitchell was apparently involved with Army efforts
to acquire a zeppelin from Germany. Though Americans were by then
quite aware of the well-publicized airship raids on London and in 1917
had seen movies depicting futuristic pictures of their Capitol and New
York under zeppelin attack, they were still, in 1919, more open to positive service or commercial airship expectation than the British. In
droves they had visited R34 during her brief American visit, while
newspapers and newly devised newsreels carried the exciting message
from coast to coast. Into that psychological climate came the Colsman-
Eckener offer to the Army to do business in America. Various Army
eager-beavers, possibly uninformed about the Joint Army-Navy Airship
Board, rushed their internal negotiations entirely by cable, while
Colonel Hensley aggressively pursued his part of the venture in
Germany. The initial spur to action – fear that the Germans would
destroy L72 if ordered to fly her to France – was then followed by a
vision of the finest airship ever, built to serve Army needs. Three arguments were persuasive: the unique opportunity to acquire zeppelin
technology and experience; the notion of getting it all at a fire-sale
price; and the chance to acquire a great propaganda vehicle for the
Army – including an initial project for a spectacular delivery flight to
America eastward via Russia, the Philippines, and Hawaii. Further
dreams saw the Army Air Service sponsoring commercial airship service
or flying the mails non-stop across the continent in 30 hours. Airship
historian Richard K. Smith later wrote:

> As it turned out, Hensley was being watched by Anglo-French intel-
> ligence services. They turned over their findings to the US State
> Department. The legalists [there] shot down the Hensley Zeppelin
> by pointing out that America was still technically at war with
> Germany and that his contract with the Zeppelin Company violated
> the Trading with the Enemy Act. It was a crazy episode; *opera bouffe*
> cum Zeppelin! But it illustrated how far Billy Mitchell's 'empire of
> airpower' was prepared to go to obtain a zeppelin in 1919.[43]

Curiously, although Masterman had heard of Hensley's negotiations and reportedly had vowed to get his scalp, the American Navy remained quite unresponsive to the Army venture. A boast by General Mitchell before the Senate Military Affairs Committee on 7 October 1919, that the Army had almost bought the largest airship in the world at a knock-down price, caused no tremor among the admirals. Not until half a year later did the Secretary of the Navy indignantly inquire of his Army opposite number what that 'not understandable' military action meant. The question was by then moot, for the Navy had gained the exclusive right to acquire and operate rigid airships.[44]

In contrast to that curious lapse of late-1919, the airship was now moving towards the heart of naval strategic thinking. Three factors converged to influence this new trend and interacted with the newly emerging prospects for naval aviation. First was the continuation of the 'cult of the battleship', derived from several centuries of British experience with ships of the line, invigorated in 1906 with construction of the *Dreadnought*, and a focus of envisaged sea battles in all navies until 7 December 1941. The German and British Fleets had fought at Jutland in the context of this conception. While the Germans did the greater damage to their foe and escaped by a daring fleet about-face and night manoeuvre, England retained strategic control of the North Sea and maintained the crippling blockade of its enemy. Despite this element of climactic interruption in the battle, the lessons derived from Jutland fortified naval leadership worldwide in its conviction that the capital ship was the ultimate and crucial instrument of naval power, whose significance dominated all other craft and armament. Here ruled the 'battleship admirals', members of the so-called 'Gun-Club', who coordinated all naval elements and craft towards the great culminating fleet action of opposing lines of capital ships to decide the outcome of a war. Jutland was seen as just an incomplete example of this preconceived confrontation of sea power. As of 1919, both submarines and aerial weapons were meant to assume subsidiary roles to the long rifles of the Dreadnoughts. British evaluation of Jutland also yielded the short-lived misconception that zeppelin scouting before or during the battle had given the Germans an advantage in escaping the jaws of the British Lion. This erroneous conclusion fostered a brief British belief that a climactic battle action must include the participation of scouting naval airships – a view that then found acceptance in some American naval circles.[45]

A second major factor that strongly influenced postwar American naval thinking was the anticipation of a conflict with the Japanese

Navy in the western Pacific. Naval staffs worldwide had long since developed strategic planning for confrontation with their most likely future opponents. These, for America before the war, became plan BLACK against the Germans (in a curious Caribbean war) and plan ORANGE against the Japanese. Planning for ORANGE developed from 1897 in several variations, all aimed to regain the Philippines (presumed lost early to Japan) and then to defeat the Japanese near their home islands. After 1918, ORANGE conjured with the prospect of rapid movement by the Atlantic Fleet through the Canal for defence of the Panama–Hawaii–Alaska strategic triangle and subsequent offensive westward. During the 1920s ORANGE was refined in many studies at the Newport Naval War College and elsewhere. Attitudes polarized between 'thrusters' and 'cautionaries'. 'Thrusters' prevailed between 1916 and 1922, strengthened by their powerful 'Gun-Club' advocates with concepts of a climactic Pacific super-Jutland. The 'cautionaries' strengthened from 1919 onward, with realities of postwar military cutbacks and the impact of the Washington Naval Conference (1922) on naval strategy: notably the loss of island bases west of Hawaii, while Japan held all the Marshall and Mariana Islands under a League of Nations mandate. Between 1925 and 1929 the 'thrusters' were again briefly dominant in their activity which a later critic dubbed 'ridiculous as strategy but excellent as fantasy'.[46] After 1929 the 'cautionaries' again strengthened, now with initial concepts for the island-hopping that became the basic strategy of the naval war in 1942–5. Crucial, however, until late 1941 in all variations of ORANGE planning was the anticipation still lingering of the great battle line of Dreadnoughts sailing towards a super-Jutland climax in the western Pacific.[47]

The third, and ultimately decisive, factor in postwar American naval thinking was the impact of emerging naval aviation on the political culture of the 'Gun-Club' and on war plan ORANGE. By 1919 naval aviation had produced small but inexperienced cadres in different types of naval aircraft. There was also awareness of Britain's venture with its first aircraft carriers. Now the competition sharpened: how could aircraft of whatever kind best improve the Navy's fighting capabilities? Earlier the focus had been on scouting ships, represented since the later nineteenth century by fast, thinly armoured and lightly armed light cruisers. Now aircraft promised to expand vastly the effectiveness of naval scouting by supplying aerial ships of greater speed and broader range than hitherto conceived. In May 1919, the Navy flying-boat NC4 made the first aerial crossing of the Atlantic, albeit with intermediate landings. Meanwhile the Jutland zeppelin myth stimulated the design of an American-built rigid and fostered the purchase of British R38. Concurrently plans were also drawn to convert a new naval collier into an aircraft carrier with 32 planes. All these craft were intended initially for the specific task of scouting for the Battle Fleet, quite under control of the 'Gun-Club' admirals – a limitation soon resisted by carrier airmen once they had mastered their art of flying at sea. Technological improvement wrought other great changes in naval aviation. Each battleship continued to hold a pair of float planes for artillery spotting and close reconnaissance. Naval flying boats increased their range in single scouting sorties and gave promise of wider use in naval communications; still, they were mostly limited to their assigned scouting function until 1941. Similarly, rigid airships never deviated from their intended reconnaissance purpose. Indeed, by the early 1930s, *Akron* and *Macon* were built as mother ships to launch, capture, and relaunch half a dozen planes in a day to survey a hundred thousand square miles of ocean between dawn and sunset. But it was the aircraft carrier that would upset the proverbial apple cart, goad the 'Gun-Club' admirals into frustration, and set off rivalry with the airships for funds and function. By 1929 airmen from the carriers had developed diversified specialities, with fighters, dive bombers, and torpedo planes to challenge the battleship monopoly to deliver destructive blows against enemy fleet units. Once the 'Gun-Club' admirals were successfully challenged by the carriers in their exclusive fighting purpose, who would still have need of scouting rigid airships? These questions bedevilled intra-Navy relationships for the entire interwar era, though the airships fell victim to other circumstances six years before the Pearl Harbor crippling of the Dreadnought fleet.[48]

The creative and guiding force for all naval aviation was Admiral William A. Moffett. His death in the *Akron* crash of 1933 distorted an awareness of him as being primarily committed to rigid airships for naval aviation. In fact, together with Admiral David W. Taylor, he constantly pressed for development of all types of naval aviation, notably carrier development. From 1920 onward, when he came ashore from his command of the new USS *Mississippi*, his influence was felt in every naval aviation sector: long-term aircraft and engine procurement, development of technological aviation research, search for more effective carrier aviation, and maintenance of special flight pay for naval aviators. His early and crowning achievement was establishing and developing the naval Bureau of Aeronautics (BuAer). Increasingly BuAer would contest with the 'Gun-Club' and from here Admiral Moffett as Chief pursued a vigorous campaign, including political manipulation of all naval aviation technology, to foster nationwide interest and support for the Navy. Float and patrol planes performed for the public at shore bases; carriers were frequently open to public visits at ports along their prescribed routes – and film crews were always ready to add aviation sequences to the stereotypical images of great battleships plunging through heavy seas. But Moffett's propaganda star would be the rigid airship, magnetically attractive in its awesome magnificence and capable of appearing on schedule or impromptu at almost any place in the nation, at any time.[49]

The political campaigns that Moffett waged to procure and maintain all naval aviation encountered a different set of circumstances from those present in either Germany or England. The American Navy, which had no rigid airships as of 1919, faced different political hurdles from those abroad. First, was a powerful American executive – the Presidency which, although deferential to congressional powers, still played a key role in policy initiatives and in access to the media. Marked was also its role in naming special committees to examine publicly specific problems, such as the Morrow Board of 1925 after the crash of ZR1. Second was the House of Representatives, with its unique function of controlling expenses of the armed forces. Its activities were not hampered by the intrusion of the Treasury or the Bureau of the Budget (unlike the comparable situation in the British House of Commons). Crucial were the long-established congressional committees for armed services, appropriations, interior (for helium), and commerce. From these derived the hearings and powers of investigation – a veritable Pandora's Box for potential political problems and manipulation. Third was the Senate, equal in significance to the House and fourth was the Navy itself where its top personnel were in close contact with Members of Congress.

Finally, much more so than in Germany or England, into all these complicated relationships came the intrusions of business and regional lobbyists who pressed to influence decisions in favour of their respective clients and interests.[50]

Characteristic of the political roller-coaster ride in seeking funding was the experience of naval aviation appropriations for budgetary 1920. Though barely 5 per cent of the total, naval aviation had a budgetary battle to fight within the service as well as a technological one. The process began with the Navy's mid-1918 budget of $225 million being reduced at war's end to $85 million, and then cut again to $46 million in early 1919. The civilian Secretary of the Navy lopped off another $10 million. The House Naval Appropriations Committee pared the sum to $25 million, although the House voted only $15 million. The Secretary of the Navy appealed to the requisite Senate committee, which raised the sum again to $36 million. That rescue subsequently fell to $25 million in the joint-committee resolution. The appropriation passed Congress in its final form on 11 July 1919, no doubt assisted by the widely publicized presence of R34 at Long Island, where it arrived just five days before. Of the full $25 million for all naval aviation, $3 million was reserved for the new construction hangar at Lakehurst, $2.5 million for the purchase of R38 from England, and $1.5 million to begin building ZR1. Thus almost a third of that hard-won budget went on an aviation technology buoyed by the myth of zeppelins at Jutland which was at that time unavailable, untried, and untested in American experience. Passage of that budget within the Navy and in Congress was an early tribute to Moffett's focus on technological innovation and his political perspicacity. Rapidly he had learned his way among military and civilian bureaucrats in Washington and successfully practised the nuances of influential politicking with congressmen and lobbyists. And no doubt he fully stressed the remarkable and fortuitous feat of the R34's crossing to emphasize the great scouting potentialities for American naval airships.[51]

With funds in hand, the Navy purchased R38 in late 1919 and within six months had sent a contingent of officers and ratings to Howden in England for airship flight training by the British. General Maitland took command of the activities there, hoping against hope that the American connection would rescue the floundering British airship programme. In their training the Americans had full use of over-aged R32, access to technical exploration of the recently arrived but deteriorating war-booty zeppelins, and occasional flights with R33 and R80. These neophytes soon developed firm professional ties with their British instructors, while the news press in New York and London gave details of building and training. A single American construction engineer worked on the building of the R38 at HM Royal Airship Works at Cardington as an observer-learner with designer Campbell and his staff and in steady contact with Hunsaker and others in America. Thus they hovered around as the ship neared completion: uneasy about its outdated specifications, avoiding involvement with intra-British tensions, conscious of their own tight budgets – and yearning together with the Howden trainees to demonstrate their own proficiency by flying the world's biggest skyship across the Atlantic. When R38, already designated as ZR2, crashed at Hull on 23 August

1921, sixteen Americans perished together with several of the best British airshipmen.[52]

With the congressional appropriation of 1919 that had bought R38, Moffett had also received funding to begin building ZR1, seen as the first step in creating an American airship industry. But before materials and component parts could begin flowing towards the new Lakehurst construction hangar, many months were spent in basic technical conceptualization and design refinements for America's own naval scouting airship. Here MIT engineer Charles P. Burgess and naval constructor Starr Truscott joined Hunsaker in beginning to derive ZR1 from the German specifications for L49. Moving at a deliberate pace, they updated and revised their plans in light of their uneasy learning from the British and from specifications of L72, which the French sent them in later 1920. Occasional trips to Friedrichshafen rendered few insights from the evasive Germans, but did result in hiring Anton Heinen, pre-war DELAG and wartime zeppelin commander, who came to America as consultant and flight instructor with the Navy from 1920 to 1923. So deliberate was the American design pace that barely a fifth of the funds for ZR1 were used before the appropriation ran out. Now Moffett's political acumen again came into play, as he manoeuvred to get further funds specifically for the airship from a newly arrived Republican Congress that looked askance at 11 million dollars already given for two airships and two airship stations. But by 16 August 1921 – just eight days before the R38 crash – new funds were in hand. Subsequently the American team would fundamentally reconsider the entire ZR1 design, with assistance from a special outside technical panel of engineering and scientific experts, while politicians and armchair airshipmen flayed the Navy for wasting money on faulty technology seen as better developed by an independent American department of service aviation.[53]

In 1921, General Mitchell furiously pursued his campaign to separate aviation from the Navy, plans that were opposed with effective resolution by Moffett. When the new Republican Congress became deadlocked over Mitchell's endeavour, President Harding intervened in mid-April by proposing to centralize all naval air policy in a new Bureau of Aeronautics. Congress struggled briefly with the issue, then confirmed presidential and naval wishes. It was a signal victory for Moffett's political astuteness that came just in time to ward off the impact of Mitchell's spectacular bombing of old German warships off the Virginia Capes and the loss of R38 (ZR2). Moffett became an Admiral and first Chief of the new agency, a post he held until his death in 1933. Thus was confirmed a Joint Board decision of 1920 that the Navy alone would control and operate all rigid airships. The Army was left an option to use non-rigids; confirmed in its responsibility for all operations from land bases, it was restricted to off-shore flights of less than a hundred miles. Now the Navy was firmly set for its exclusive development of rigid airships and aviation dominance of sea warfare for the next generation.[54]

If Navy airshipmen found the Germans at Friedrichshafen wary of their inquiries in 1921, that was not the experience of civilians like Harry Vissering and Goodyear executives or in parallel contacts of Johann Schütte with American aviation circles and young Franklin D. Roosevelt, Assistant Secretary of the Navy in the Wilson era. Vissering, the successful owner of a railway equipment business in Chicago, had fallen in love with zeppelins during a DELAG flight in 1919 and was often down at the Lake thereafter. As this American waxed enthusiastic about potential airship markets in his country, Eckener gave him a flood of technical, operational, and pictorial information about the zeppelin past and its prospects for the future. Captain Lehmann stayed several months with him at his Kenilworth estate, where earlier Warren G. Harding had also been a guest during the Chicago Republican convention in the summer of 1920. With Lehmann's assistance Vissering wrote a laudatory book of zeppelin advocacy, while steadily prodding the Goodyear executives to bring their airship interests into alignment with the Germans so that both could realize their common technical and business objectives.[55]

In early 1921, Roosevelt encountered Johann Schütte, who had also been in America the year before, trying to salvage his enterprise by technical and business arrangements with the Americans. Spending a day with Army aviators, including General Mitchell, and the succeeding day with naval airshipmen and top Navy brass, he opined that both groups were appallingly ignorant. Similar was his reaction at meetings in Akron with the Goodyear executives, where he pointedly stated that he had not come over to give aeronautical instruction but to do business. His capable American representative, Frederick S. Hardesty, set up the contact with Roosevelt that eventuated in establishment of the American Investigation Corporation (AIC). The initial prospectus of this financial venture tried to lure investors by extravagant praise of German and British airships, proposing building aerial giants for two hundred passengers (based on distortions of Schütte concepts), and foreseeing routes from New York to Chicago and on to California, together with transatlantic trips in two and a half days – all to yield annual profits of 20 per cent on the investment. Roosevelt pursued the enterprise with great enthusiasm, took instruction in aviation law, and was set to become an aviation business tycoon. Just days before he was stricken with polio he wrote to a friend:

> I was horrified to get a cable from London the other day saying my mother had flown [by plane] from London to Paris. Wait until my dirigibles are running, and then you will be able to take a form of transportation that is absolutely safe.[56]

'His' dirigibles were, of course, to be derived from the patents and accumulated experience of Johann Schütte.

These American businessmen stood excitedly on the threshold of America's romance with rigid airships, almost innocently fostering German efforts to thwart the destructive purposes of their French and British adversaries and barely daunted by the flaming destruction of R38 and its 16 American crew.[57]

In retrospect, the three years from mid-1918 to mid-1921 saw quite opposite experiences in the fortunes of the three major nations involved with rigid airships. German success plunged from the culminating technological accomplishment of their latest height-climber into total airship loss and business despair. German public attention veered from its vivid recollection of Count Zeppelin's pre-war propaganda successes into the maelstrom of defeat, revolution and postwar dejection. In Britain, airship participation changed from belated, budget-breaking production success and transatlantic flight accomplishment to intermittent flight failures, culminating in the spectacular crash of R38 – all played out against public attitudes still negative on rigid airships in any version. In America there emerged the vision of naval airship scouts sweeping the wide Pacific ocean. Here the glamour of technology triumphed over momentary dismay with the loss of R38 (ZR2) and lived on in the expectation of better airships to come.

Nevertheless, mid-August of 1921 marked the first of eight palpable airship disasters that would signal an increasingly negative punctuation to sixteen further years of energetic skyship development until the *Hindenburg* exploded in 1937. Public attention in Europe and the Americas would alternate between psychological attractiveness and the awful immediate realities of each accident. To be sure, each successive disaster soon found its corrective in scientific explanations, technological improvement, and partially renewed belief. But in time the sands of confidence in airship advantage over winged aircraft for transoceanic flight ran out, as it also encountered ever more rapidly progressing airplane technology. For the moment, however, prompt evaluation of the R38 failure opened the way for revised airship design in Britain and saw an American naval initiative to exploit German technological prowess and experience to replace the destroyed ZR2. That thrust, in turn, would give the Germans a complete reversal in their airship fortunes toward renewed success and reborn public enthusiasm. It was all a remarkable turn of events.

3
Zeppelin Reborn in America, 1922–24

On 5 May 1921 the Allies sent Germany a harsh ultimatum, demanding immediate delivery of the two postwar DELAG dirigibles and forthright demolition of the remaining airship construction works. Schütte's factories were already in the hands of wreckers, and now the final bell seemed to toll for the Zeppelin Company. Facing this threat, and recalling his work for the Hensley project (with those bills still unpaid), Colsman wrote in mid-June to the American military observer in Berlin, offering to build an improved LZ125 for less than a million dollars. The initial American response would in time lead to building LZ126 (later ZR3) and her notable transatlantic flight of October 1924. In the interim, however, there was almost a year's delay until negotiations among the Allies and with the Germans were completed. So it was still a dismal time in Friedrichshafen. Early that summer Eckener flew LZ120 *Bodensee* to Italy, where she would function until 1928 as the *Esperia*. LZ121 *Nordstern* soon followed in delivery to the French Navy, where she remained deteriorating in the distant shadow of L72, now named *Dixmude*, focus of a brief and ill-starred naval scouting career. With the zeppelin hangars empty, Colsman focused on the further transformation of his industrial conglomerate to consumer goods. Eckener held his attention on dirigibles, as he nursed the lagging and interminable negotiations with Madrid for airship service to South America – a political vision of Imperial Spain revived with zeppelin galleons to carry the business wealth of the new world. Vissering was now the Zeppelin Company's official representative to corporate America, prodding the new managers of a reorganized Goodyear Company towards prospects for airships and sponsoring Lehmann's intermittent American visits. All around, the German airshipmen were treading water, hoping for some favourable German, Spanish, American, or even French developments.[1] Early in 1922, the Allies cleared American purchase of the new German zeppelin. Eckener honed his skills in manoeuvring with officials in Berlin. As he often did later, he cut bureaucratic corners sharply to achieve his goals, leaving angry and frustrated civil servants in his wake. Now he dealt directly with Foreign Minister Walther Rathenau, bypassing the Weimar Treasury, which had to finance his project. Despite its displeasure with Eckener's behaviour, the Treasury could not escape its obligation to process Reichstag funding of the zeppelin construction. It had its momentary political revenge in 1924, however, when Eckener could not get insurance for his projected transatlantic delivery flight and the ministry delayed payment on the project, Eckener having to win the Treasury over by pledging the assets of the entire Zeppelin conglomerate for the venture. This decision he reached in bypassing his business manager Colsman, an act precipitating a top-level company struggle that became the turning point in their duel for direction of the entire industrial enterprise.[2]

Official Berlin in the early 1920s considered zeppelins at best a frustrating minor irritant, with disarmament pressures from the Allies and Schütte's interminable lawsuit against the Treasury to collect unpaid wartime debts. The new Army (Reichswehr) and the equally curtailed postwar Navy had more pressing concerns than zeppelins. Each transformed its personnel into an ultra-conservative force: the Reichswehr secretly developing forbidden weaponry in the Soviet Union, the Navy focusing on new technology to outwit Versailles limitations on the few ships it could build. Both services looked with favour on a new aviation enthusiasm that began sweeping Germany in 1921 and gave support to civilians engaged therein: a phenomenal development in the theory and practice of glider flying and burgeoning propaganda in its advocacy. This enthusiasm attracted the many surviving wartime airplane pilots and spread rapidly to much of German youth. Glider associations mushroomed in various enterprises, cities, and regions – Germany's only legitimate opportunity to participate in worldwide aviation enthusiasm. Here developed new dimensions for understanding aeronautics and meteorology. Here were exciting opportunities to pit youthful prowess against the forces of nature, flouting danger and death itself. Great publicity attended this growing sport, usually identified with national defiance of the Versailles aviation restrictions on Germany. It was a replay psychologically of the pre-war zeppelin fever, men – and now also women – taking to the air in expression of a national conviction. Ballooning, not colourfully glamorized or propane-powered as it is today, survived in staid ascents. Schütte presided on one occasion at the launch of Germany's largest balloon ever, christened *West Preussen* in defiance of Polish possession of a former German province. A zeppelin in the offing, glider-flying, and balloon ascents all combined to give German aviation a muted political message.[3]

Even before the final contract with the Americans had been fully negotiated and signed, it became evident that the Germans would raise serious difficulties for the US Navy in constructing LZ126 (later ZR3). Learning from their unfortunate experience in dealing with the British in the construction of R38, the Americans now sent a small team of airship designers and builders to Friedrichshafen under Lieutenant Commander Garland Fulton, which pressed for full participation and interim evaluation in every phase of the work. Since the Allies had stipulated that America receive a *civilian* airship from its recent wartime producer, objections and resistance developed among German personnel in nearly every sector of the company, complaining that they were being forced by their enemies to give up unique and valuable commercial trade secrets. When resistance failed, evasiveness and lack of good faith emerged to bedevil the situation. Only Eckener's and Fulton's diplomatic skills assuaged the recurring disputes, no doubt helped by the ultimate German realization that failure to build for the Americans would result in prompt Allied demolition of the company. Within this strained combination of circumstances gradually emerged the visible results of Dr Karl Arnstein's design and construction talents, assets which the company had hitherto skilfully hidden away in the recesses of the business.[4]

Meanwhile, Eckener had continued to keep several other irons in the fire. In October 1922 Fulton wrote to Hunsaker from Friedrichshafen:

Vissering is here and is buying champagne for all the Zepps. The 'Z' crowd think he is a whiz, and he does do an excellent job in keeping them informed as to what goes on in America. Young (Goodyear) is with Vissering. Goodyear is V's candidate as an American partner for Z. They have been having long sessions with Z, and the result, if any, will come out later, I suppose ... There are rumours of an early and happy conclusion of the Z-Spanish negotiations. Lots of Spanish money. Three sheds to be started at once. A 160 000 (!) cubic meter ship to be started very soon, and so forth ... They have had the Spaniards here for nearly a month ... With

Vissering, Young, Boothby [British], and the Spaniards here, the Zepp have been going around in circles and getting very little work done [on LZ126]. It looks like much prosperity to them – through very rosy glasses, of course.[5]

Indeed, despite the presence of Vissering and Goodyear on the premises at the Lake, Eckener was most enthusiastic about the commercial project of a Spanish entrepreneur using zeppelins and German airship expertise in service between Seville and Buenos Aires. The first in a succession of contracts was already signed in early 1921. In the autumn of that year Eckener had travelled to Argentina for an extended study tour of facilities and oceanic meteorology. Then the negotiations just dragged on. Spanish General Rivera signed a revised contract for German supply and services in late 1923. Now profitable mail subsidies were in the offing and King Alfonso XIII was due to become a major stockholder. But final plans for capitalization and opening of business would not be achieved until 1927, then only to dwindle away.[6]

Fulton's mention of Boothby indicated a wartime British naval airshipman with some notions of postwar commercial development. More capable and serious was a project of Commander Dennistoun Burney (1888–1968), wealthy wartime inventor of the paravane, who planned to develop a network of imperial airship routes. For his ambitious interim proposal of an Anglo-German airship organization, Eckener proposed a very large airship to carry 150 passengers and 11 tons of mail and freight at 80 miles an hour. In May 1923, Burney and his airship expert Barnes Wallis (1887–1979), designer of Vickers R80, sojourned in Friedrichshafen to view LZ126 in construction and further develop their own planning with the Germans.[7] These efforts came to naught in the face of British delay and political conflicts at home, while Eckener's negotiations through Vissering finally eventuated by late 1923 in the creation of the Goodyear-Zeppelin Company. About that time the heavily-involved and much hoped-for Spanish project stalled for lack of Iberian funding.[8] But Eckener had at last achieved a firm technological partnership with the American Navy and a viable zeppelin future with Goodyear in America. What would happen in Germany still remained to be seen after the epochal flight of LZ126 (later ZR3) across the Atlantic in October 1924.

In England, just before the crash of R38, anticipations of an Empire-wide airship network still held official attention. Leisurely liner service to Australia at that time took about six weeks, whereas a fast airship

was expected to cover the distance in ten days. The Imperial
Conference of July 1921 heard a proposal by the London Agent-
General of Tasmania for an Imperial Air Company to be funded by the
four dominions, major colonies like India, and public subscription –
with the British government supplying R36, R37 (construction almost
complete), and a successor to R38, plus sizeable mail subsidies and
deficit guarantees for the first decade. The project foundered after
several meetings of a subsidiary Imperial Air conference that were
blighted by the loss of R38, by revitalized public negativism, and by
the improbable chances for financial success. Commander Burney,
however, now came on the scene, with excellent naval contacts and a
well-established position at Vickers Ltd (which had manufactured and
installed the anti-mine paravanes on wartime British shipping), with
proximity to Vickers airship designers Pratt and Wallis, and with strong
interest from British-based Shell International Petroleum Company. In
early 1922 Burney conceived a project to fund, build, and operate an
Imperial airship service. Here he planned to incorporate the remaining
ships and facilities of the Air Ministry, to build as many as four new
enlarged airships (initially by the Germans, later by Vickers), and to
anticipate substantial government subsidies for a privately held and
profit-making enterprise. This forward-looking proposal launched three
years of contention with hydra-headed postwar British politics, in
which he participated vigorously as the elected Conservative parliamentary member for Uxbridge.

As compared with Eckener's or Moffett's relatively uncomplicated
circumstances of airship conceptualization and achievement, the
British scene presented a formidable array of competing positions and
interests. In 1922, moderate David Lloyd George's coalition government was encountering heavy political weather. Facing revitalized conservatism and energized socialism, he steered a course providing
continued social benefits and proper (but not excessive) defence
budgets – a policy that found little favour for the very expensive airships. Many Conservatives favoured the Burney scheme with its imperial vision and favourable business provisions. Concurrently they also
advocated successfully the founding of Imperial Airways, a govern-
ment-subsidized private company given a monopoly of airplane services abroad. Labour, of course, denounced such government fostering
of capitalist aviation. Parliament reflected these divisions and concerns, with somewhat broader opposition to various programmes
requiring government subsidies. The deliberations of the Cabinet were
plagued by a proliferation of conflicting advice from powerful subcom-

mittees: the subsidiary Air Conference of the 1921 Imperial Conference and its own subcommittees on Imperial Defence, Imperial Shipping, and the Air Council. The Admiralty strongly favoured the Burney project and sought to regain control of airships while at the same time getting the government out of all airship development and future Empire-wide ground organization. The Air Ministry was rudely thrust on the defensive. On the one hand, it contended with Navy and Army efforts to reverse the RAF decision of 1918; on the other, it feared losing control of its airships and air stations like Cardington to the intrusion of as yet unclearly defined extra-governmental enterprise. Invariably the Treasury blew very cold on proposals for such huge isolated expenditures. And finally, the surviving airshipmen themselves, a diminished and embattled elite at Cardington, vigorously opposed the threatened invasion of their construction and operations turf by the 'civilian outsiders' from Vickers. By mid-1923, after the unproductive Burney-Wallis visit to Friedrichshafen, a new Conservative government had come to power and the airship negotiations impasse was partly overcome by indirect guidance from the throne. The way was cleared to establish the new Burney operation, the Airship Guarantee Company, though the Air Ministry still refused to give up its remaining ships and the stations at Cardington and Howden. Into this still unresolved dilemma came two further events: the loss of the French airship *Dixmude* (ex-L72) with all hands on 21 December 1923, and the Conservatives' fall from power in early 1924 to make way for Britain's first-ever Labour government.[9]

The *Dixmude* was the ill-fated lone star of postwar French airship aviation. Her captain, Jean du Plessis de Grenédan, was one of that tiny minority of younger postwar French military officers who – like Charles de Gaulle – saw beyond the limited horizons of wartime experience towards greater weapons mobility in the future. In 1916, he was posted to naval non-rigid service which awakened his theoretical and operational enthusiasm for airships in fleet operations. Made commander of an Astra Torres non-rigid in September 1917, his reputation for scientific knowledge thrust him into the centre of French studies of downed German L49 just a month later. Thenceforth he produced a series of theoretical, technical and operational studies of rigid airships in naval service, together with several further studies on projected commercial rigid airship operations in the French Empire. When the Germans delivered their Army LZ113 to the French military and L72 to the French Navy in later 1920, du Plessis flew the naval airship to Cuers (near Toulon) and began systematic training for French naval rigid airship operations. While the French Army left its German booty to rot in its hangar, du Plessis constantly pressed a reluctant naval bureaucracy between 1920 and 1923 to refit and update *Dixmude* for Mediterranean scouting and northwest African aerial reconnaissance. Just one of few Frenchmen with enthusiasm for rigid airships, du Plessis cited German technological zeppelin successes and warned that France must not fall behind Britain and America in the race for global airship development, notably within the French colonial empire from Africa to the Far East. His firm determination to achieve experience and the perceived propaganda benefits of airship flying finally moved the French Navy to put *Dixmude* into minimal operational order. During the autumn of 1923 du Plessis pressed on with long scouting flights around the western Mediterranean, into North Africa and the Sahara interior, and planned a further bold thrust to the French West African naval base at Dakar. Always conscious of the need to arouse public enthusiasm for an airship mission in her colonial empire, he completed his scouting flights with extended cruises over French home territory. On one such extension that brought him up to northwestern France, he broke the world long-distance record of R34 and may have begun to weaken his nation's aversion to *le zeppelin*. His final pre-Dakar test flight was breaking both German and British records for men and cargo aboard airships, when the craft exploded aloft on the night of 21 December 1923, with no survivors. It was the second internationally reverberating airship disaster.[10]

Varied were the characteristic responses in nations with airship awareness. French public opinion mourned its wasted dead and reinvigorated its rejection of airships, while official policy condemned its two remaining zeppelins to terminal rot. German airshipmen had politely treated du Plessis like a leper when he came to Friedrichshafen in 1920 to accept assignment of L72, the only Frenchman to fly with her German delivery crew to France. Indeed, they refused to give him anything but the most minimal instruction or flight training, though Eckener did point out that L72 was built as an especially fragile height-climber. Now Germans were indignant at yet another instance of inexperienced foreigners mishandling a height-climber in low-level flight. The German press expressed malicious satisfaction at the enemy's failure to profit from its illgotten war booty. For the rest, the men at Friedrichshafen reconfirmed their design and construction principles and continued building LZ126. The American airshipmen there, in Washington, and at Lakehurst (where ZR1 *Shenandoah* was in her fourth month of test flying) were not deterred in their efforts. They thought and built and flew for the future – and they carried American public opinion along with them. As several engineers expressed it in a memorial lecture for designers of R38, held some weeks before the *Dixmude* loss:

> We, who follow them, must proceed in all humility and with full appreciation of the lessons which their splendid sacrifice has made available ... The design of a rigid airship is the boldest and most exacting engineering adventure that man has ever attempted. [They] realized the known and the unknown elements of the problem and dimly glimpsed the unknowable.[11]

The political impact of knowing that both R38 and *Dixmude* were wrecked by structural and operational failure was not lost on the new British Labour government. It now proceeded cautiously to negotiate its own revised Imperial Airship Scheme. Initially, Labour had simply to learn practical ways to achieve its policies. In that process the party realized that, with its slim majority and some of its own internal division, it had to rely on the votes of the Liberals to produce majorities. However, since the Liberals represented some elements of free economic enterprise, Labour had to make some uncomfortable compromises with its socialist principles in order to pass its legislation. Finally, Labour sought out experienced and talented men who were not of working-class origin to bridge the sizeable social behaviour gap between the majority of individuals in the British governmental establishment and the small group of often idealistic and sometimes confrontational working-class advocates.

   Enter thus Brigadier General Christopher Birdwood Thomson. Born in India of an Army family, he was schooled in England and developed a successful career in the Royal Engineers. Between 1912 and 1917 he served in the Balkans and the Middle East on diplomatic and military assignments. His negative experiences as an adviser at the Paris Peace Conference in 1919 confirmed his culminating dismay with current British politics and precipitated his resignation from the Army. He espoused socialism and stood in three losing Labour campaigns in the next four years. Still, his enthusiasm, talents as a speaker, and evident ability to move between the two social worlds of his recent past and the Labour present, prompted the new Prime Minister Ramsay MacDonald to secure Thomson's elevation to the peerage and appoint him Secretary of State for Air where he at once celebrated his new-found enthusiasm for airships by taking the title Lord Thomson of Cardington.[12]

After two years of delay from the early Burney proposals of spring 1922, a revised Labour airship programme was opened to full-scale debate in both Houses of Parliament in mid-May 1924. Rejecting the original Burney project as an unacceptable business monopoly like Imperial Airways, Labour still confirmed its commitment to plan for fast communication within the far-flung Empire. To achieve this goal, MacDonald proposed a comprehensive programme of research and development at Cardington, together with construction of an airship twice the size of R38 and of an intermediate base in Egypt on the England–India route. Canada and India were each expected to provide fully-functioning airship terminals, with the expectation of comparable facilities later in South Africa and Australia. Concurrently, the Burney enterprise would be offered a contract to build a similar second ship for commercial service, with government option for final purchase, once the airship had passed requisite testing. The government's financial exposure was projected as amounting to £5 500 000 over the next fifteen years, with six million immediately at hand. In the Lords, Thomson argued for the proposal on commercial, naval, and military grounds. In the Commons, MacDonald emphasized the professional, cautious, and safe advance of the Cardington team, while offering the Burney proponents the challenging opportunity to build a single airship by private enterprise. Since so much argumentation had gone on in the previous three years, discussion in Parliament moved with little excitement. Fundamentally, there was agreement on the need to strengthen the ties of Empire after the disruptions of the war. This need was especially important in the case of India, where the National Congress had derived great vitality from repressions of the wartime Defence of India Act and the postwar emergence of Mahatma Gandhi as a leader in agitation for Indian independence. As for airships to strengthen Empire ties, British public antipathy to the airship had – unlike the case in France – died down somewhat, especially in light of the promise of the new programme to discard allegedly unsafe zeppelin construction principles and to replace them with technology derived from new empirical British engineering research. Here Thomson and Burney were enthusiasts in a tepid crowd. Cardington, the airship lobby, and the Navy all found their interests served. Socialists warmed to the idea of the people, through their government, building and operating attractive symbols in a new era of social behaviour. Business interests chafed at the comedown from a broad programme to just a single ship but willingly accepted the implied challenge. The Treasury, with veteran airship opponent Winston Churchill at its head, remained curiously tolerant of this Imperial Airship Scheme with its small coterie of technically innocent conservative and socialist proponents, the ill-starred experience of its surviving government design team, and the next dollop of funding required for its fulfilment. In retrospect the words of author Higham bear consideration:

> Ground had already been lost by 1922 when the first Burney proposals were made. Politics gave up more. The Labour scheme with its experimental nature and fine scientific approach ultimately ruined it. Such conclusion is not based on any consideration of private versus nationalized business enterprise, but solely on the fundamental criteria that no technical weapon, device, or programme is going to prosper from constant changes in policy.[13]

So at least the policy was set, but the next six years would still see further political interference in carrying out the details, notably in the building of R101, the government ship, and in developing unfortunate rivalries between the two design and construction teams.

Turning now to American developments between mid-1921 and later 1924, we should first take note of two post-war events which uniquely affected the development of American airships. The first was the emergence of inert helium as a physically and financially viable alternative to flammable hydrogen. The second was the continuing naval armaments competition that led to the Washington Conference decisions of 1922, with their impact on American naval construction and strategic thinking.

Helium, first isolated in a British laboratory in tiny amounts at great expense in 1895, still cost $2500 per cubic foot. Soon , however, discovery of its presence under Texas oilfields resulted in major production. Severe naval budget cuts after 1918 stifled these initial efforts, but with the explosion of the hydrogen-inflated R38 and mishaps to several navy blimps, helium was open to serious consideration. In late 1921 the first naval helium non-rigid cruised over Washington, yet the inert gas still cost about fifty times more than hydrogen. The die was then cast, when in early 1922 the huge new semi-rigid *Roma*, recently acquired by General Mitchell from Italy (with much fanfare and mobilization of Italian–American enthusiasm), dived out of control and collided with high-tension cables, exploding with a loss of 34 army aviators. Thereafter, cost what it might, helium would be required for all American airships. The Department of the Interior, in cooperation with the Navy, got massive federal support to expand its facilities and the cost of helium soon dropped to barely six times that of hydrogen.

Thenceforth helium became the propaganda byword for successful naval airship operation. Given America's unique possession of almost all the world's supply of natural helium, the Navy and Congress pressed for prohibition of its export as crucial to national defence. Although a few military non-rigids would still fly in Italy, France, and Russia, this prohibition would primarily affect the development of commercial airships in Britain and Germany, making helium unavailable to lift either of the two British aerial giants in 1929–30 or the *Hindenburg* in 1936–37.[14]

The pre-war naval armaments race in Europe had already drawn justification from the studies of American Admiral Mahan about the influence of sea power in history – and the crucial role of battle fleets in climactic confrontation – just as the United States was emerging as a great power. With World War I under way, and already before the Battle of Jutland in 1916, the American Navy and the Congress planned a vigorous programme emphasizing capital-ship construction to attain parity with England by 1923. At war's end a lingering American naval antagonism to Britain took strength from Anglo-American disputes over Wilson's promise to attain freedom of the seas and from revelations that England had given Japan support for her claim to German island colonies in the Pacific. With American rejection of the Treaty of Versailles, the American Navy pressed for completion of the Big Navy Program of 1916, now primarily focused on Japan, which was also avidly enlarging its own fleet. In all three nations, however, a public groundswell for disarmament and economy brought the political leadership into conflict with its respective naval builders. By mid-1921 Anglo-American discussions produced an invitation from President Harding to the major naval and Far Eastern powers to confer in Washington about territorial disputes and to seek sensible limitation of their naval armaments. The resulting Washington Treaty of 6 February 1922 produced a bouquet of agreements on political and territorial issues in the western Pacific. Agonizing for the 'Gun-Club' admirals were limitations on the capital ships of the three major Pacific powers, which cost America eight partly completed super-battleships and six projected battle cruisers. The notorious 5–5–3 ratio for future naval construction that seemed to assure Anglo-American predominance was impaired by questionable Japanese assurances that they would not arm their mandated former German Pacific islands, for which America pledged to develop no new bases west of Hawaii, leaving her with a semi-developed naval presence in the Philippines and Guam. How would the American Navy overcome this weakness?[15]

Given the new treaty restrictions, which also curtailed construction of the light cruisers upon which the Navy had heretofore relied for fleet scouting, both 'cautionary' and 'thrusting' proponents of war-plan ORANGE welcomed new technological solutions to the restric-tive dilemmas. Here the newly-arriving prospects of naval aviation appeared as a godsend, either as planes from carriers or as airships. Actually, concepts of both types of flight preceded the Washington Conference decisions. During 1921 the Navy converted a new collier to become America's experimental carrier: the *Langley* (with its initial 15 scout planes) joined the fleet in March 1922. The airship ZR1 had been conceptualized in 1919, though its construction would not begin at the new Lakehurst hangar until late April 1922. As already noted, scouting airship ZR2 would have joined the Navy by autumn 1921, had she not exploded in Britain. And the later ZR3 was just in the pre-liminaries of acquisition from Germany about two months before ZR2 was destroyed. These beginnings could now be developed to enhance the Navy's planning for action in the western Pacific. Forthwith, the Navy in 1922 also rebuilt two merchantmen as seaplane tenders and decided to convert two of the battle cruisers under construction to become the later fabled carriers *Lexington* and *Saratoga*. These were all still experimental ventures, directly focused on scouting, eyes for the great Battle Fleet. Full evaluation of their effectiveness would be delayed for more than a decade. The two great carriers would not join the fleet until 1929. Of the airships, ZR1 would founder in 1925 after two years of service and ZR3 could not directly join the fleet because of its 'civilian' status. But the later *Los Angeles* did yeoman work in technological experimentation, crew training and long-distance flying. The lessons of these years in both airships accrued to benefit the new aerial giants of the early 1930s, the *Akron* and the *Macon*. By then both the carriers and the airships would be viewed from quite different naval perspectives – the carriers because of their remarkable independent effectiveness, the airships because of their operational frailty.

Back in the summer of 1922, however, American airship prospects appeared luminously bright. Naval ZR1 was finally taking shape at Lakehurst with much publicity, and the German–American contract to build ZR3 had just been signed at Berlin. Still, it was another civilian airship enterprise that momentarily seized the limelight – an American projection of Johann Schütte's postwar ambitions for commercial airship development that had already enlisted the enthusiasm of F. D. Roosevelt and his fellow investors.

As of early 1922 the Roosevelt-Hardesty-propelled AIC was attracting an impressive group of American capitalists and by June AIC had signed contracts with Schütte for the German to build several huge airships of his design and to manage their commercial operation. Forthwith the American public received widespread publicity about the proposed airships and their expected service. *Current History* glowed with enthusiasm about 'The Advent of the American Air Liner', saying:

The intention is to make the first route a practical demonstration between New York and Chicago, which by air is only 750 miles. The travelling public will need, and should have, proof of reliability and safety before undertaking overseas voyages in airships. All details of improved construction and operation will be assured on this short run before attempting the cross-continent and transatlantic routes … The first airship will have a capacity of 4,000,000 cubic feet of helium and should cover the distance between New York and Chicago in ten hours' average time. About 100 passengers will be transported at night in berths similar to those on steamships. In addition to passengers, an airship of that size will be able to carry thirty tons of mail, express, or other cargo. The method of mooring to a tower and means of supplying gas, fuel and water to a moored airship are interesting; so are the details of the engineering planning data; but those subjects cannot be discussed in brief space and are more appropriate for a technical article … The airship has passed from the experimental to the reliable commercial stage … Coastlines or mountain ranges no longer are barriers requiring a change in transport methods. St. Louis and Denver are as likely as any seacoast cities to have direct airship communication with Europe, South America and Asia.[16]

Soon, however, investment enthusiasm for AIC began to fade and disaster dogged Schütte's footsteps at home. He was unable to save his factories in Germany and no alternative construction sites seemed likely in Britain or America – certainly not the Goodyear Company that Vissering was carefully nudging towards agreement with Friedrichshafen. Yet, its public relations desk still ground out its alleged good news. In early 1923 Schütte and AIC launched a paper airship operating company called General Air Service, indicating that two giant helium airships were in the offing. Editorially the *New York Times* praised the event: 'Capital is available, and American promoters have never lacked courage.'[17] Soon the widely read *Literary Digest* enthused:

'Coming: Overnight Airships, New York to Chicago!'[18] In fact, the AIC syndicate was disintegrating. Soon it defaulted on its payments to Schütte and sank slowly into a morass of lawsuits forcing Roosevelt futilely to seek some lifelines from Vissering in Akron. It was just three years from boom to bust for the first German-American venture in commercial airships.[19] Just one aspect echoed into the future. *In extremis* AIC tried to link up with Ford aviation in Detroit and made abortive agreements with the future Metalclad Airship Company which later built an experimental metal-hull airship for the Navy, designed by Ralph Upson and built by Carl B. Fritsche, who would still have ties with Roosevelt in the White House in the mid-1930s. Even at that distance the earlier association fostered FDR's animus against zeppelin products, whether from Friedrichshafen or Akron.[20]

Unlike the activities of AIC and Schütte, the more realistic prospects of Goodyear's fusion with the Zeppelin Company matured unobtrusively while the construction of ZR3 was under way in Friedrichshafen. Differently from Colsman, who in 1920 sought to use Goodyear as a marketeer for zeppelins built in Germany, the ubiquitous Vissering represented Eckener in seeking a business association with the Akron airship builder. Goodyear's Paul W. Litchfield had since the end of the war enthusiastically sought to make his firm America's sole builder of rigid airships, for which he had the support of Admiral Moffett and naval airshipmen. In the summer of 1922 negotiations began seriously between the two firms. Late in the year it became evident in Akron that their non-rigid airship division would soon be out of business if no rigid activity could be found as an alternative. Further delays ensued as Goodyear tried to get a Navy contract to build a small rigid; but Washington delayed awaiting delivery of ZR3 from Germany. Finally, in September 1923, agreement was reached to establish the Goodyear-Zeppelin Corporation. Eckener, still faced with Allied demolition of his enterprise when ZR3 had flown to America, now pledged all his patents, plans, and accumulated building and operational experience to Akron. In return the Zeppelin Company got one-third ownership of the new Goodyear-Zeppelin Corporation and participation in its various future ventures. Immediate evidence of this new association was Eckener's reluctant promise to send engineer-designer Karl Arnstein permanently to Akron, together with a dozen top construction specialists. Arnstein and his 'twelve disciples' arrived in Akron just two months after ZR3 was delivered at Lakehurst. Thus was established for the next 15 years Goodyear's German-American commitment to rigid airships for American defence and commerce.[21]

Broad American enthusiasm for all aviation was, of course, the rising tide in the 1920s that carried the optimism for airships as well.[22] Here Admiral Moffett continued pressing for systematic procurement of naval planes, urging-on the fledgling pilots learning their skills with the new experimental carrier *Langley*, and seeking for naval fliers equality of status and opportunity seamen. But most prominent and concentrated was Moffett's focus on the completion and first flights of ZR1 in September 1923 – for Army Air Force General Mitchell was rampant again. Ever since the naval 'Gun-Club' had lost its envisioned and cherished super-battleships by decisions of the Washington Conference in early 1922, Mitchell and the Army brass had been increasingly pressing the Navy to release another two over-age battleships for further unwelcome bombing tests. Early in September 1923 the new exercises finally occurred off Cape Hatteras in the presence of 300 Washington dignitaries of all political stripes and dozens of news and cameramen. Both ships were dramatically destroyed in the spectacle, leaving the Navy with only its laboured excuses of 1921.[23] Fortunately for the Navy, Moffett and ZR1 were ready with drama of their own. Coincident with the Hatteras demonstration, the BuAer Admiral thrust the new airship into the public limelight, providing full radio, film, and news coverage for her maiden flight on the day after the battleships were sunk by Mitchell's Army bombers. The new *Shenandoah* (an Indian name allegedly meaning 'Daughter of the Stars') criss-crossed the mid-Atlantic states in demonstration over New York, Philadelphia and Washington – an inspiring image of noble sovereignty over the smoke of Mitchell's bomb clouds. Early in October ZR1 flew to the National Air Races at St. Louis, with return overflights at Chicago, Toledo, and Cleveland. All these 'hand-waving' excursions had their requisite radio broadcasters, film crews, and newsmen aboard and on land en route. Moffett's political manipulation of his airship technology at this crucial time strengthened BuAer's standing with the 'Gun-Club' and benefited the entire Navy that still felt its setback in public esteem as a result of its unspectacular role in the recent World War.

Indeed, this publicity role of ZR1 distinguished her brief career with the Navy. Only 13 of the 59 flights recorded in her logbook were directly related to her avowed purpose of service with the fleet. There was immediate enthusiasm to revive earlier American romanticism in a flight to the North Pole. Naval airshipmen plotted routes northwestward to Alaska and then across the Pole to Spitzbergen. Planners for fleet movement surveyed accommodation at both remote points and engineers considered possible structural improvements in the airship itself. However, some political and operational voices were raised by this accelerated pace in early 1924. In mid-January, a sudden storm tore the ship from her mast, but happily a skeleton crew aboard brought her back to safety. As polar plans went on hold pending the necessary repairs, more doubts were raised about the trip in naval circles and in Congress, with the result that President Coolidge cancelled the flight altogether. It was clear, however, that the serene naval airship aloft was as great a naval propaganda asset in the age-old competition with the Army as the image of great grey battleships plunging through heavy seas.[24]

In the background of all these developments – of big-gun naval concessions and General Mitchell's attacks, of private enterprise efforts to establish airships in America, and of completing and flying ZR1 nationwide – a third naval airship was being conceived and built in Germany. It had its origins in June 1921, when ZR1 was still in design and ZR2 was test-flying in Britain. At that moment, just after the Allies had given their stern ultimatum that shortly sent all remaining zeppelins to their respective Allied recipients, Colsman offered to the US military observer in Berlin that he should build and deliver an improved LZ125 for America. It was to be a bargain at $800 000, *provided* the Americans would save the Zeppelin Works from impending postwar Allied demolition. Although the service designation of the projected airship was initially unclear, Berlin was pressed to finance it in compensation for two wartime craft earlier allocated to America but undelivered. However, unexpectedly difficult negotiations developed with America's wartime allies in London, Paris, and Rome.[25]

Vigorous opposition of these Allies stemmed from their emerging skyward rivalry as of July 1921. Britain had great hopes of becoming Europe's premier airship builder and could not tolerate renewed German zeppelin activity. France wanted no survival of zeppelins in any form whatsoever. Italy had earlier sold her doomed semi-rigid *Roma* to General Mitchell and still hoped for a larger American market. Successfully the Allies pressed America to reduce the size of the ship by a third and wrung from Washington a commitment that it would not be a military vehicle and serve only commercial purposes. A month later these American concessions were battered by the further Allied demand that America should be content with two 'commercial' airships of a million cubic feet each, since anything larger would be considered 'military'. This message reached Washington two days after the R38 disaster. Now the American Navy was bereft of the single operable airship it so desired, but eventually London gave way to the earlier American compromise for a single larger ship, although all parties also agreed that completion of this craft, the ZR3, must be followed by the complete destruction of Zeppelin Company facilities and dispersal of its personnel. So it was all that America desired but just a terminal postponement for the Germans.[26]

Thereafter followed two years of vigorous participation of American personnel in the design and construction of ZR3 at Friedrichshafen, which was marred by two irritating conflicts. First was the resentment of the German builders that they were living on borrowed time for their technological expertise and careers as they shaped their last airship for delivery to a recent enemy. Yet, the Americans were determined not to repeat their role as distant observers of the R38 construction in England, and at Friedrichshafen they pressed for full access to all aspects of design, research, and construction – a process that the Germans considered outright theft of their trade secrets, since they still dreamt of an airship future beyond the ZR3. Fulton wrote Hunsaker in mid-1922:

> The Z. Co. has received us very cordially, but not with open arms. They want to work along on the airship design without any consultation and then propose to submit it fairly thoroughly worked out … Their attitude results from nervousness about [our] 'inspection' … You have received a letter about letting Z. sell data to Japan. I believe the Zepps are in good faith about it, but like to keep my guard up. Their suggestion about supplying fake data indicates an unhealthy state of mind and one must guard against it for ourselves – but that's why our Inspection Office is here.[27]

Experienced Dr Ludwig Dürr, who had designed every zeppelin since 1900, was a focus of technological resistance to the Americans but fortunately Fulton's diplomacy was reciprocated by Eckener's more sophisticated evaluation of circumstances and prospects.[28] Into these developments Vissering played his facilitating role that resulted in the birth of the Goodyear-Zeppelin Corporation, which would build naval airships in the future that, in turn, would be seen as prototypes for American commercial ships.

The second irritant in American naval activity at Friedrichshafen was General Mitchell's episodic pressure to wrest the new German airship from the Navy for Army use. It had, after all, been the Berlin military attaché to whom Colsman had sent his offer, and perhaps still hoped to recoup bills left unpaid from the 1919–20 negotiations for the LZ125. At the inter-Allied negotiations of later 1921 both Army and Navy representatives together pressed the American case for the airship. The Army's representative, Major Harold Geiger, was intermittently at Friedrichshafen half a year before Lieutenant Commander Garland Fulton arrived there for the Navy. Each service group suspiciously watched the other while publicly maintaining a united posture towards the Germans. When General Mitchell made a vigorous personal lunge in March 1923, the naval chiefs and their Friedrichshafen personnel were forced on to the defensive, lest the still unreconciled Allies consider the ship indeed a military one and renew their efforts to crush the venture. Fulton expressed it thus in a personal letter to Hunsaker:

> I do not believe that we should make any compromises with our A[rmy] friends in regard to final disposition of ZR3 ... I feel it is a Navy job and if we take a strong stand the A[rmy] hasn't a leg to stand on. We must take a strong stand or they will knife us in the back.[29]

A year later, ZR3 was almost ready to fly, and it was now, after a nine-month tour from the Philippines to India that Mitchell focused on writing his 300-page tour de force on the prospects of a great Pacific war, in which he believed Japan would open with sneak attacks on Hawaii and Manila. Ultimately that war should be won with unified American air power, securely under the influence of the Army. His study reached the desks of Army chiefs just as ZR3 was crossing the Atlantic toward assured naval possession, but Mitchell would be heard again a year later when ZR1 crashed dramatically in Ohio – far from action with the fleet.[30]

The completion and flight of ZR3 was a joint German-American emotional experience. While both nations had the satisfaction of overcoming Anglo-French resistance to building the airship in Germany and delivering it to American ownership, each had its own unique perception of the experience. For the Germans it was a deep bitter-sweet awareness of their technological competence encased in their political impotence. For their part, the Americans had the easy thrills of seeing the sensational transatlantic delivery of *their* airship and then knowing that their nation was the only one in the world to possess and fly two sky giants considered as keys to their Pacific defence and as harbingers of promising commercial future.

Wariness was the cue to Eckener's stance in all aspects of building and delivering ZR3. Although the ship would be lost to the Germans, it was still a preview of transoceanic commercial flight to come, in which Eckener was determined somehow to play a dominant role. Behavioural psychologist by training and expert in early DELAG public relations, he would use ZR3 to restore the bond of the German nation with Count Zeppelin's heritage and reinvigorate the pre-war sense of pride and enthusiasm in a truly national accomplishment. But the times were hardly propitious for such a renascence in postwar Germany. The first frames of the ship were just being rigged as the French began their occupation of the Ruhr in early 1923 and all German attention was focused on the hated enemy. As the ship neared completion over the ensuing year, Weimar policies to impede French exploitation of Ruhr industries led to the manic culmination of German currency inflation and attendant public disorientation. The shock of currency reform in early 1924 (total public loss of savings and a million new unemployed) found ZR3 completed except for continuing unresolved engine problems. How could any zeppelin enthusiasm be reborn?

In the spring of 1924, Eckener's publicity campaign opened judiciously. Gradually it accelerated, skilfully intermixing pride in detailed technological descriptions with cautious prospects for a German commercial ship future. By summer, the campaign broadened into the international press with no resistance to angry themes, originating elsewhere, of Germany's technological victimization by the rapacious Allies. The pre-war symbol of zeppelin pride was in danger of becoming a postwar symbol of German political humiliation at Versailles, but Eckener managed to keep these conflicting images safely apart. In late August, ZR3 finally took to the air, laden with journalists, photographers and radio newscasters, their ears ringing with music from the military band playing *Deutschland, Deutschland über Alles*! Each of the three long test flights gathered demonstrations of increasing public response. The attractive magic of a great airship in flight had lost none of its effectiveness. First was a cruise over all southern Germany, from Munich, where the *Bodensee* had often landed, to the hallowed Swabian sites of Count Zeppelin's life and burial. Next came a repeat of the spectacular Swiss trip of 1908, once again demonstrating a new zeppelin for international acclaim. For climax, ZR3 made a two-day flight over the length and breadth of central and northern Germany. Everywhere the ship drew crowds by the tens of thousands. In its culminating appearance over Berlin, President Ebert and his Cabinet radioed:

> Welcome to the nation's capital! Godspeed for your distant flight! Cross the seas in victorious proof of our unimpaired audacity and as testimony of German accomplishment! Worldwide carry our confidence in Germany's future![31]

From communists and socialists, to conservatives and reactionaries, Eckener again stimulated the psychological dynamics of German zeppelin enthusiasm. Somewhat as in 1908, the zeppelin was again a subject of pride and ardent yearning for a more meaningful future, even though it would soon vanish westward overseas.[32]

And now, with her transatlantic crossing a success, ZR3 achieved her American identity. Already the State Department had had to persuade France to grant overflight permission to the Bay of Biscay, noting the presence of American staff aboard: three naval officers and (still) an Army Air Force major. Two American cruisers took station between the Azores and Newfoundland to assist in rescue if necessary. Dramatic was the spontaneous public reception of the new airship as it circled New York during the early morning rush hour of 15 October 1924. Wrote the *New York Times*:

> Thousands of work-bound halted in the streets, oblivious of all save the glistening shape drumming its way above. More thousands were encamped on the rooftops … Others were summoned to see by their neighbors shouting across air shafts or courts … As the dirigible sailed up the [Hudson] river cheers went up from crowded ferry-boats to aid the din of the harbor whistles.[33]

At Lakehurst the zeppelin could barely move towards her hangar through the congestion of greeting cars and crowds, and here Eckener finally signed her over to America. The German commander and his crew were lionized the next day in New York amidst publicity and entertainment not seen since the Armistice in 1918. A huge throng jammed the Capitol theatre and for the first time in nearly a decade the German national anthem was heard publicly in America. Certainly, it was predominantly a German-American crowd, but the next day was an all-American affair. Eckener was taken to Yankee Stadium for the annual Army–Navy football game and was driven around the great athletics bowl to the wild cheers of 50 000 spectators. The political symbolism was clearly evident – the war was over and there was a new prospect of American–German collaboration for further civilian conquest of the transoceanic skies.[34]

Now America had two rigids to foster the image of naval superiority and to emphasize positive Republican Party virtues. Even as ZR3 established records, ZR1 made aviation history with an impressive 19-day transcontinental cruise during October 1924. Everywhere – through the Middle West, across the southwest to California, up the coast to Seattle, and back – the *Shenandoah* attracted record crowds. It was a realization of psychologist Eckener's practised observation:

> [The airship] was like a fabulous silvery fish, floating quietly in the ocean of air and captivating the eye ... And this fairy-tale apparition, which seemed to melt into the silvery-blue background of the sky, when it appeared from far away, seemed to be coming from another world and to be returning there like a dream.[35]

ZR1 carried an official in-flight journalist who coordinated all publicity by frequent radio contact with earthbound newsmen en route, giving advance publicity on appearance of the airship and full coverage of overflights and departures for further arrivals. On her return to Lakehurst ZR1 was berthed in the hangar beside ZR3, now emptied of hydrogen. Helium then carefully flowed from the older to the newer airship, for there was not yet enough of the precious inert gas for both craft. With that transfer complete, ZR3 set out on her first American flight, to be greeted in Washington by the pride of the naval and Republican establishment. In presence of the president, Mrs Calvin Coolidge christened the new airship *Los Angeles* – allegedly for her civilian status as an angel of peace, but more likely as political identification for naval Secretary Curtis D. Wilbur, who hailed from that pivotal western city that was frequently seen in the Democrat column during national elections. If as yet there was still no clearly practised naval defence role for either airship, it was all great patriotic aviation excitement and political expediency for the US Navy, the Republicans, and the German-Americans.[36]

The half-decade from the Armistice of 1918 to the autumn of 1924 saw a remarkable mixture of failure and progress in the development of rigid airships for commercial and naval service. The German wartime zeppelins lived on in British derivatives, with R34 in the first-ever transatlantic round trip of 1919 and the spectacular loss of R38 in 1921. Of the seven deteriorating war-booty zeppelins, L72 alone survived as *Dixmude* with her flight endurance interim records and loss by explosion in late 1923. German L49 was reborn in a much-improved version as the American ZR1 to scout for the US Navy between September 1923 and 1925. All were overshadowed technologically by the creation of ZR3, with superior size, speed, range and lift. Always flying at the very edge of technological possibilities, the audacious designers and fliers wrestled with their often-faltering vehicles to bring the airship to the threshold of practical transoceanic commerce and naval scouting.

The political uses of this improvement had worldwide resonance. First of all, the Germans, whom it had been intended would be completely divorced from airship development, stood again at a pinnacle of airship achievement. At home, where loss of the war had extinguished any continuity of the pre-war zeppelin enthusiasm, zeppelin-fever and pride soared again with Eckener's nationwide farewell flights of ZR3. An American news correspondent wrote:

> Germany has gone literally zeppelin-mad. Nothing is talked about except the ZR3's thrilling flight … Editorials proclaim a sign of Germany's rise from world-war defeat to renewed glory and power … The Reichsverband Deutscher Industrie applauded the genius of the builders, Luftschiffbau Zeppelin, and praised the work of tireless Germans who fought the mightiest battle the Fatherland has waged for its cultural existence.[37]

In England the socialist government and whatever remained of public airship interest took comfort at the renewed zeppelin achievement by anticipating the promise of the new officially sponsored Imperial Airship Scheme. Secretary of State for Air Thomson had lauded the prospect of two newly designed craft, to be twice the size and range of anything the Germans had done, ready for flight by 1927 and prototypes for others flying worldwide within a decade. Already R101 was in design at Cardington and the contract for R100 was signed with Vickers on 1 November 1924. It had all been unfortunately delayed by internal politics but was now finally on course – or so it was hoped.[38]

In America both the accomplishment and the future could hardly have seemed brighter. ZR1 and ZR3 were in flight whenever there was enough precious helium for one of them. Improved facilities in Texas would soon produce enough gas for both of them, as the Navy, congressmen, and senators were deluged with requests for overflights from every corner of the nation. In late October Dr Karl Arnstein and his 'twelve disciples' – engineers and craftsmen – arrived in Akron to begin work at the new Goodyear-Zeppelin Corporation. Meanwhile, Eckener and his co-pilots toured the German-American scene, with American business and homeland political echoes in New York, Washington, Akron, Detroit and Chicago. Fourteen years of close German and American airship cooperation would follow.[39]

   In late 1924 it was evident that both Dr Eckener and Admiral Moffett understood the essentials of manipulating airship technology for ulterior political objectives: Eckener to stimulate German national pride and confidence, Moffett to keep naval aviation unimpaired at sea. At that point each had complete confidence in the effectiveness of airship technology and understood the basic principles of using it to achieve political propaganda results. Both focused their airships to stand out from any competing stimulus on the public psyche. Each stimulated the sense of national pride to heighten the effectiveness of this technology on public perception; Moffett added a factor of naval service identity and loyalty. Both strengthened the propaganda principle of repetitive presence of the technological stimulus by echoes in the press, film and radio. And for each the technology was an irreducibly simple stimulus in direct public perception on behalf of his cause. For the immediate future, however, both men faced hazards. Eckener had yet to secure the zeppelin future for Germany from the Allies. Moffett could hardly anticipate that his nemesis from the Army Air Force would revisit him within the year at the wreckage of the proud *Shenandoah* in the rolling hills of Ohio.[40]

4
Airships in International Political Competition, 1924–28

The arrival of airship ZR3 in America produced a wave of zeppelin excitement, and almost at once Eckener and his officers began a crowded schedule of receptions and addresses in the major cities of eastern America. After the initial celebrations in Washington and New York, the airshipmen mixed business, politicking and pleasure in Akron, Cleveland and Detroit. The mayor of the Motor City praised the German commander: '[Since 1918] a barrier of ice has lain between the American and German people, which you and your airship have now smashed!' Thereupon followed four days in Chicago, with another fortnight in Washington and New York. Returned to Germany, Eckener was overwhelmed with attention from newsmen and politicians of every persuasion. In contrast to the American acclaim for German technological prowess and the prospects for intercontinental airship travel, Germans celebrated the end of their postwar international political ostracism and claimed a moral victory over the mean spirit of Versailles. At his tumultuous welcome in Berlin the same Scherl publishers who had first advertised Count Zeppelin in 1903 now committed Eckener to six further exhausting public appearances Germany-wide. Thus the now-renowned airship commander stood in the glare of worldwide publicity, which he would intemperately bear for the next fifteen years.[1]

ZR3 had barely landed when German Foreign Office communications began humming with messages about the international politics of airship matters. Paris was adamant in opposition, but attitudes in London were mixed. Americans had rousing enthusiasm for the zeppelin and could easily be further encouraged. Czechs and Poles could barely conceal their disdain. Before long, however, French attitudes began to soften, despite evidence that the zeppelin was now the symbol of postwar Franco-German political animosity. Within a month Italy gave solid support to keep German airship development alive, for Rome already had an airship propaganda coup of its own in mind and could require German expertise and support. Echoes occurred in internal German politics, as at least two political parties used zeppelin motifs in their oversize propaganda posters for two Reichstag elections during 1924. The new airship age seemed to dawn bright and clear.[2]

Now was the time to achieve by airship what earlier explorers had left undone – fully investigating and mapping the interior of sparsely known areas, notably those of the polar regions. Previous attempts by air had failed or come to naught: Andrée by balloon in 1897; Wellman a decade later in his non-rigid airship; Count Zeppelin with others at Spitzbergen in 1910; Amundsen with several planes in 1921–2; and aborted plans of ZR1 for polar flight in 1923–4. Should not the Zeppelin Works be preserved for the noble purpose of building airships to expand human knowledge at the last frontiers of geography? A fortunate meeting of German and Swedish minds soon brought the subject into focus.

It is not precisely clear who began the Swedo-German project to save the zeppelin for polar exploration. Suffice it to say that by early November 1924, members of the German embassy in Stockholm were pressing the Foreign Office in Berlin to encourage efforts by the Royal Swedish Academy of Sciences to mobilize neutral European opinion to preserve the Zeppelin Company. At the Academy, world-famous (and pro-German) explorer Sven Hedin carried the day against an unenthusiastic pro-Allied minority to seek the support of other 'neutral' European scientific societies for a unified appeal to the Allied victors to save the zeppelin for geographical research. When all the results of this démarche were in by early 1925, it was clear that a zeppelin-for-science was quite as politically controversial as any other. Famed polar explorer Fridtjof Nansen (1861–1930) of the Norwegian Academy wrote that this was a matter of international politics, in which scientific societies should not become embroiled. The Dutch and Swiss were similarly negative. Danes, Finns, and Spaniards proposed awaiting the decision of their betters. The German Foreign Office had never warmed to the subject and now cooled down the Stockholm embassy, as it also kept a watchful eye on the broader international political echoes of zeppelin preservation. There matters would have rested, had not new complications arisen that ignited the old Schütte–Zeppelin antagonism and ran counter to Berlin's quiet policy aimed at seeing the Versailles prohibitions removed from all German aviation endeavours.

Accentuating the national and international airship ruckus was an announcement in early October 1924 of the founding of Aeroarctic, an international association of scientists advocating north polar exploration by air. Fifty-eight Germans dominated the membership, with fifteen Scandinavians a distant second. Captain Walter Bruns, an experienced wartime Army zeppelin officer, presumed to lead the German contingent, building on several previous years of popular lectures on airships and exploration. Earlier rebuffed by Eckener, he now had ties with the remnant German Schütte organization, which by late 1924 had designed a specialized airship for polar research. With that prospect in hand, Bruns charmed Scandinavian audiences with grand projects of polar discovery by an airship built to Schütte specifications somewhere outside Germany. Though Bruns' proposals were as visionary as their funding was absent, both Eckener and official Germany worked to dampen non-German enthusiasm for these prospects, thus antagonizing Fridtjof Nansen, recent Nobel Peace Prize winner, Aeroarctic president, and anti-German in the recent war. In March 1925 Eckener spent a week in Stockholm, lionized by official Sweden and the Royal Academy, lecturing wisely about applying his experiences with building and flying ZR3 to plans for polar exploration. Concurrently various Berlin ministries gave Eckener their muted support as they dealt with different members of Aeroarctic. Late in June Eckener wrote to his newly-won friend Hedin:

We have come to an agreement on the terms I proposed. Luftschiffbau Zeppelin will get the funding, will build the ship and take full leadership responsibility. It will make the ship available to Aeroarctic for two polar flights, of course with our experienced flight crews. For the rest, our company can make use of the ship as it sees fit. The ministry agrees, so do the professors [of Aeroarctic], and little boy Bruns will be appropriately relegated to some menial task with the ship's crew. ... In August, right after the holidays, we will launch our campaign to raise the funds. I hope to have success here, even though business conditions are presently quite unfavourable.[3]

Three weeks later he added:

I will postpone my final judgment about the Society [Aeroarctic]. For now I shall direct all my energies toward raising the funds for our airship. I will not wait for some permission from the Allies to begin construction [as Nansen was proposing on behalf of Aeroarctic]. In fact, for basic psychological reasons, and considering the political impasse at home [parliamentary gridlock], I will move to raise the funds from the German people themselves, on the natural assumption that the Entente simply *cannot* deny us Germans the right to build an airship for purely scientific purposes. It would hobble and cast shame upon our whole enterprise if we went trotting off to the Entente for permission. I can do quite well without the indispensability of that 'Study Society' and of Mr Bruns seeking Allied permission through Professor Nansen. I will not submit to that kind of argument, but will start my own campaigning forthwith. The committees for solicitation are being formed, and in the middle of August, when everything is ready, we will step forward to appeal to the German people.[4]

It was vintage Eckener: restoring German identification with Count Zeppelin and his prestigious airship; seizing the initiative from the Berlin politicians; fending off another threat from rival Schütte; and reaffirming the zeppelin as a mighty symbol of postwar German technological aerial achievement. Here Eckener entered forcefully into the international political skyward rivalry for the next fifteen years.

With his publicly alleged objective of building a new zeppelin for polar exploration in a 'scientific' context, Eckener launched his new project to confirm the reawakened airship symbol for German national psychic stimulus, to open the way for German participation in international aviation, and, of course, to preserve his own manufacturing and operating enterprises. Undaunted he pressed forward into new international political storm clouds. French and British memories of wartime zeppelin raids were invigorated by the election of wartime military hero General Paul von Hindenburg, as the new President of Weimar Germany in April 1925. Shortly afterwards Eckener sought to inform Foreign Minister Gustav Stresemann of the planned celebration at Friedrichshafen to commemorate Count Zeppelin's first ascents 25 years earlier, in 1900. Doubtless Eckener could not have known that Stresemann was at the crucial stage of his confidential negotiations with London and Paris that culminated late that year in the Locarno Treaties for German-Allied détente. Stresemann's efforts were already burdened by Hindenburg's election; now any new German zeppelin enthusiasm could further roil the waters. Eckener left this account of his meeting with Stresemann:

I was uncertain about inviting the Foreign Minister to the Jubilee, but decided to ask him personally. It certainly would have given him a favourable opportunity to make some broad political comment in relation to the wonderful reception of ZR3 in America. I was received [at the Foreign Office] with studied reticence. He promptly began speaking in such unfriendly terms about the 'dubious character' of our planned Zeppelin celebration, about which he had had no prior consultation, that I could only regard him with amazement. And when he then said in obvious ill humour that he would have to avoid attending the affair, I became so angry that I bluntly retorted, 'Herr Minister, I haven't even invited you!' With that, of course, the meeting ended.[5]

This episode foreshadowed all Eckener's subsequent relations with Berlin. He had always argued that the government had not contested the Allies firmly enough to emphasize and preserve the airship as an aircraft of peaceful commerce. Then, in 1924, the same government that had contracted and paid for ZR3 had refused any financial guarantee for its safe delivery across the Atlantic. Now its Foreign Office was evidently failing to appreciate what Eckener had done for Germany's aviation and for her favourable image in the still hostile postwar world. Here was a foretaste of another decade of vexation between Friedrichshafen and Berlin.

The dubious mixture of zeppelin enthusiasm with nationalist tensions abroad was evident from various visits of Eckener in eastern central Europe, with its rumblings of German minorities in new postwar Slavic states. Notable thus was Eckener's visit to Prague on 20 May 1925. Here was staged a tremendous public rally, with full trumpets from the German-language press in Czechoslovakia. The Czech daily, *Narodni Politika*, responded in kind, railing at this 'nationalist provocation'. Similar crowds appeared at Brno, with Czech police much in evidence. German-nationalist students at the university there held their own beer hall rally, singing 'Deutschland über Alles!', with pointed exclusion of democratic or Jewish students. Similar problems appeared about a year later, when Eckener visited Germanic Transylvania. Here Romanian police forbade use of a large public hall and were out in force to 'maintain order'. These were hardly responses that Eckener tried to awaken, but the zeppelin did have high appeal as an echo of earlier Germanic domination in those areas or as a harbinger of changes yet to come.[6]

It had been Eckener's intention to use the ceremony and nostalgia of Count Zeppelin's Jubilee as the springboard for his campaign to solicit funds for construction of a new polar zeppelin. For months already he had been organizing a national supervisory committee to prepare the way for his *Zeppelin-Eckener-Spende des deutschen Volkes* (Zeppelin-Eckener-Fund of the German People). Eckener had tried to get preliminary acquiescence from various authorities in Berlin, but encountered either reserved or negative reactions there, the concern being the unfavourable reaction the Jubilee would have abroad. The cabinet strongly urged divorcing announcement of the *Spende* from the Zeppelin Jubilee.[7] Eckener grudgingly accepted the decision, but responded with characteristic defensive vigour:

> As regards alleged unfavourable reactions by the Allies, they should understand that this fund-raising is for purposes of a polar-exploration airship. Even this is just a façade. Actually we are concerned with saving the Luftschiffbau Zeppelin, which after seven years of depression is at the end of its tether. There is the greatest continuing interest in broad circles of the German people for this eminent national and cultural achievement. Prominent men of all parties and diverse social groups have consented to support this effort. This is quite understandable, for the Luftschiffbau Zeppelin is viewed as a national treasure, funded by pre-war popular enthusiasm. I believe that a people must *always* be ready and capable of sustaining its spiritual and technological strength, lest it lose confidence in itself and its future.[8]

Furthermore, Eckener's focus on international politics was as sharp as ever. In personally urging the State President of Württemberg to attend and lend his prestige to the occasion, the airshipman wrote:

> This event is really less a commemoration of our enterprise than an appeal to, and protest against, the Allies for their restraint on the Zeppelin Works, which symbolizes the suppression of the creative power of the entire German nation. I trust that our celebration will command attention and a favourable echo in the whole world.[9]

The celebration of the Jubilee on 21 August 1925 was indeed evocative of nostalgia for Germany's great national symbol – one of the few visible signs that had even partly survived the downfall of the Empire.[10] Most major officials of the Berlin government who had been invited sent their regrets (or some minor bureaucrat), along with their congratulatory greetings. Stresemann dispatched a telegram recalling his own flight of 1909 (with other members of the Reichstag) and expressed hope that airships from Friedrichshafen would benefit the cause of

German culture far into the future.[11] In this atmosphere Eckener formally announced that his company was designing a magnificent new zeppelin, the largest ever, for polar exploration. Soon, he further stated, the German people would again have an opportunity – as they did in 1908 – to give freely of their hearts and purses to foster German aerial technology for the greater glory of their nation. There matters stood in Germany as of September 1925, with Aeroarctic seeking an international identity for polar exploration by air and Germans emphasizing their own national objectives.

Meanwhile in England, the private and government airship teams were beginning their respective programmes for airship design and construction. Chief among the entrepreneurs was Commander Burney, head of the Airship Guarantee Company. Engineer Barnes Wallis, designer of R80, the only somewhat original British airship built by Vickers but too late for its wartime mission, led the Burney teams for design and construction. Together with his chief calculator Nevil Shute Norway – the later famed novelist – the two men spent the first year computing the mathematical principles for their new airship, after which they moved to the abandoned and hurriedly refurbished airship base at Howden in northeast England. The government team reopened its well-maintained facilities at Cardington, where chief designer Lieutenant Colonel Vincent Richmond and others worked with later airship Captain G. Herbert Scott to conceptualize their totally new type of airship for Empire service. Unlike Burney and Wallis, the government team was firmly tethered to the Air Ministry, where Lord Thomson would rule until late 1924 and return in mid-1929. Consistency of purpose at the Air Ministry in London was supplied by the Director of Airship Development (DAD), Group Captain P. F. N. Fellows, through whose hands converged all the strings of both airship programmes.

In early October 1924 both Fellows and Wallis visited Friedrichshafen briefly, to view ZR3 between trial flights. Formally Wallis reported to DAD Fellows at the Air Ministry, but actually the men in distant Howden were increasingly neglected by London, which instead focused on the Cardington team. Indeed, from the very first there was disquieting divergence in the joint Empire airship venture. Wallis meticulously created his airship in a tight economy of effort, but the publicity of anticipation went to Cardington with its costly and long drawn out innovations and experiments. Here was also embedded government suspicion of the well-established wartime company Vickers Ltd, together with a lingering civil-service vs. military bias. By the late summer of 1925 the die was already cast for the ensuing mutual disregard and rivalry between the two sets of designer-builders. Early on, Scott had informed Wallis:

> We have given your ship the number R100, as showing that it will be no more than a rehash of German methods and therefore the last of an outdated form of construction; whereas our ship will be of entirely novel design, embodying the latest and most up-to-date materials and engineering methods, and we regard it as the first of an entirely new series, and have therefore decided to give us the number R101, that is the first of the new series.[12]

For their parts, Wallis and Norway were not sparing in their criticism of the government design and construction teams.[13]

Finally, there was an additional factor that irritated both supporters and opponents of the airship activities – the personality of Burney. Successful in the parliamentary conflicts to rescue at least a part of his vigorous efforts since 1921, he pressed on all fronts to foster sales for successors to his R100. His enterprise and fertile imagination were offset by a salesman's optimism and willingness to take both business and airship risks. Soon anathema to the Air Ministry and the Cardington team, he gradually also eroded his relationship with Wallis and the Howden builders, who soon began to avoid him. Already in September 1925, the pieces were being set for the final end-game of 1930: Air Ministry preference for Cardington; civil-service meddling in procedures and aggressive publicity for R101; relegation of Howden and R100 into relative obscurity; and intensification of leading person-ality postures in gradually heightening competition. Seldom was a technological construction so weighted with political excess baggage.[14]

Public perception of this opening year in preparation for the Imperial Airship Scheme was exclusively focused on the government project. Unlike Wallis, who would concentrate on his single design project, the government lacked focus. At Cardington the designers were busy with in-flight studies, and the surviving airshipmen were relearning their skills in the two surviving airships R33 and R36. Airship R33 was reconditioned for flight to Egypt and testing in tropi-cal conditions there, while R36, the only British airship ever specifically equipped for passenger service, was also refurbished. Then, in mid-April 1925, R33 was torn from its mast in a gale and driven out over the North Sea. For thirty hours the men aboard laboured to bring the ship home safely, while all England was held spellbound by press and radio. When they did succeed in making a successful return to Cardington, it was with tremendous relief that a tired crew disembarked from their badly damaged ship. However, the R33 was now out of service for almost half a year, while R36 was still not up to performance, but during the summer, Karachi was confirmed as the future Indian base for Empire airships, and Indian participation in construction of the hangar agreed. Autumn arrived with both R33 and R36 operable, but now funds were unavailable to experiment with them. They flew for just a hundred hours, while the designers for R101 worked on. Momentarily a journalistic glance focused on Germany. The London *Times* carried a brief account of the Zeppelin Jubilee in Friedrichshafen, noting the presence of the German War Minister there and Eckener's berating the Allies for their anti-zeppelin stance. Then the British lull in airship news was shattered by vivid accounts and pictures of the destruction of America's ZR1 *Shenandoah* over the hills of Ohio on 3 September 1925.[15]

In America, the year after the arrival of ZR3 was filled with more airship liveliness than ever before – indeed, more so than anywhere else in the world. These activities were, however, punctuated by several contradictory elements. First was the inability of helium production to keep pace with all airship needs. With only enough inert gas to fill one rigid airship, ZR3 was favoured in flight for Navy needs and training of her new crew. Since the helium shortage made the gas still six times more expensive than hydrogen in 1925, airshipmen were forced to conserve the gas in helium-handling and airship manoeuvring – a limitation that may have contributed to the loss of ZR1. Second was the continuing need for expensive and time-consuming renovation and technological updating of both ships – for these were still basically experimental aircraft. Thirdly, eager Navy publicity stimulated far more public demand for overflights and visits than could possibly be met. At the same time the airshipmen were pressing to see more operation with the fleet, where scepticism about these aircraft was growing. As a result, tensions developed between the publicity expectations of top naval authorities and the sense of practical limitations on airship use as perceived by the airship commanders. It would all culminate in America's first publicly experienced rigid airship disaster.

By mid-winter 1925, ZR3 – now the *Los Angeles* – was ready for the non-military naval use which the Allies had stipulated as a condition for her construction. Even so, her latitude for service was remarkably broad: training airmen; testing the limits of all her dimensions of flight; experimenting in technological improvements; and, above all, maintaining her public visibility in Navy activities. Striking were the photo opportunities in her manoeuvres at the specialized airship tender *Patoka*, with its towering sea-going mooring mast. With flights to Bermuda and Puerto Rico and several other publicity jaunts, the Navy General Board anticipated a summer of vigorous airship activity – to ceremonies at Annapolis, for a governors' conference in Maine, out to Minneapolis, and even far out to Hawaii. It was too much for ZR3. After inspiring the midshipmen at graduation, she failed en route to the midwest and limped home. The *Shenandoah* was readied to carry on. At this point Admiral Edward W. Eberle issued orders from the General Board, specifying 23 overflights and landings en route to Minneapolis, with a tight schedule for return to duty with the fleet. Now Lieutenant Commander Lansdowne, who had crossed the Atlantic with R34, renewed an earlier protest to the Board, stating that one could not schedule a dirigible like a battleship. The Admiral's testy response expressed doubt whether, therefore, any airship could be of much use either to the Navy or for commerce. Moffett intervened with reasoned consultation. The Minneapolis trip was briefly postponed under new rules of broad discretion for airship commanders to determine exact times and routes of airship operations. Shortly *Shenandoah* was off to the Governors' Conference, with news cameramen aboard, where she ferried various state chiefs about and earned recognition in state capitals from coast to coast. Thereupon followed various duties with *Patoka*. The Navy was still having the best of both worlds.[16]

With autumn nearing, planning resumed for the flight to Minneapolis. Lansdowne was given a list of late-summer state fairs and another dozen sites for recommended overflights. On her return ZR1 *Shenandoah* was to pause at the new Dearborn airport mooring mast, built by Henry Ford with Eckener's prompting – another publicity first, with the motor magnate then aboard to Washington. Lansdowne had full discretion to determine crucial details of the flight, though he preferred service with the fleet to inland barnstorming. Twelve hours after her departure from Lakehurst on 2 September 1925, *Shenandoah* encountered heavy weather. For thirty minutes she experienced turbulence of a violence that not even a German designer could possibly have anticipated. At 4.35 a.m. the next morning, most of ZR1 lay in shards on Ohio's rolling hills, while a 200 ft bow section was still aloft, free-ballooning to a safe landing by Lieutenant Commander Charles E. Rosendahl with six crewmen. Twenty-two other airshipmen survived the break-up, but Lansdowne and other officers were killed in the crushed control car. Newsmen and radio broadcasters were soon on the

114

The wreckage of the US Navy's *Shenandoah*, 3 September 1935

scene, as were thousands of ravenous souvenir hunters who picked the carcass of the airship clean in a country-fair excitement, even to personal effects of the dead. Thus the American public experienced the *Shenandoah* even more vividly in disaster than in flight. And the political repercussions would be just as extreme and dramatic.[17]

For the next four months, almost to the eve of Christmas, the media deluged the American public with details of the *Shenandoah* wreck. First came the immediately reporting journalists who misconstrued their interviews with Lansdowne's widow to the effect that her husband had been obliged to carry out the fatal flight contrary to his own better judgment. Next came the carping of old German wartime zeppelin captain, Anton Heinen, but worst of all was General Mitchell's blast that loss of the *Shenandoah* was 'the direct result of incompetency, criminal negligence, and almost treasonable administration of [aviation in] national defence by the War and Navy Departments'.[18] This outburst precipitated an Army court martial and brought the greater publicity that Mitchell had always sought. The official Navy investigation into the disaster soon ran concurrently with the Army court martial, all of which raised the politics of airship technology and operation – in the context of all service aviation – to a high pitch of public interest. The naval inquiry at Lakehurst was the more professional of the two proceedings, though tempers flared there at Heinen's accusation that Lansdowne was solely to blame by reason of his restriction of gas valves to conserve expensive helium. When the Navy inquiry adjourned to Washington, its further deliberations became entangled in public reactions to testimony in Mitchell's court martial. The daily intrusion of still and movie cameramen, with weekly newsreel screenings at cinemas, were a foretaste of later TV renditions of spectacular murder trials. After Mitchell's dramatic self-defence came a half dozen Navy professionals to rebut the lurid accusations of Navy technological and operational culpability. When the dust finally settled, the American public had had an education in airship frailty and operational hazards that left lingering doubt about the future for airships in national defence or commerce.[19]

Other professional and political aspects of the *Shenandoah* disaster – the third postwar airship to founder – left the cause of airships in America less propitious in outlook than before. The official findings of the Navy inquiry found that the primary cause of the wreck was the violent weather. Emphatic, however, was the court's criticism of Moffett's penchant for publicity flights. These were determined as exceeding the traditional practice of welcoming the public to view the

Navy when it was resting. It was now stated that 'movements [of naval craft] should be limited to essentially naval and military operations in so far as possible, especially in the case of new and experimental types'.[20] Henceforth airships would generally be limited to coastal and ocean areas, where they would still work some of their aerial wonder in the national press, radio and movie news. But the great glamour flights were over.[21]

In retrospect it is clear that ZR1 in her two-year career had established the rigid airship as a viable naval component even though her usefulness for the fleet was limited by her diversion for Navy public relations. Her loss weakened but did not destroy Navy willingness to develop airship scouting for the Battle Fleet. Curiously, new developments in carrier aviation even raised airship potentialities for the fleet. Quite contrary to anticipation, carrier aviation was developing away from its early assigned exclusive scouting mission towards more aggressive fighting characteristics: dive-bombing, torpedo-launching, and fighter protection for the carrier itself. As the 'Gun-Club' admirals tried unsuccessfully to curb these new carrier developments, they could still rely completely on airships as their own integrated components in strategies of seeking out the enemy in the Pacific and bringing him to confrontation in climactic battle. Though many decision-makers in the Battle Fleet now had grave misgivings about airship effectiveness – questions of high unit cost, limited range with helium, low speed, and extreme vulnerability to weather – there was still tolerance enough for airship experimentation. But even this slight edge of acceptance would be hostage to long delays in new naval airship procurement and likely revisions in the fundamental strategic conception of war plan ORANGE.

Thus matters stood at the end of 1925. In Germany, Hugo Eckener was launching his campaign among Germans in all Central Europe to raise funds for the building of his new polar airship. In Britain, the two competing teams of airship builders were moving from technical blueprints into the early phases of construction at their respective sites. Only in America was a single rigid airship in frequent flight: the sturdy 'civilian' *Los Angeles*: training crews, conducting experiments, just hovering at the outer margins of naval fleet exercises. For the immediate future her unglamorous role would be eclipsed by two other airships, the semi-rigids *Norge* and *Italia*, technologically born of Italian creativity and pressed on international public attention by Italian fascist propaganda.

In midsummer 1925, as Lansdowne was completing his planning for *Shenandoah*'s fatal flight into the midwest, sustained efforts of the Aero

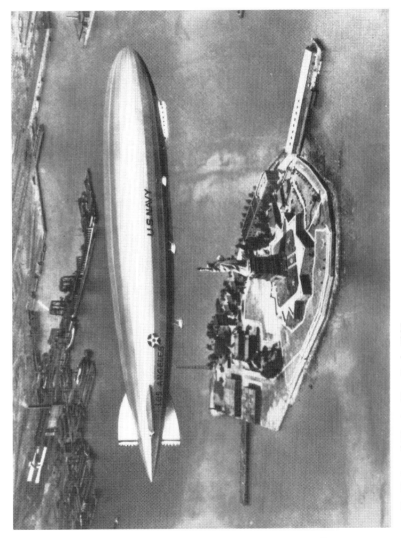

Los Angeles over the Statue of Liberty, New York, 1925

Club of Norway to foster arctic exploration finally bore fruit. Three men primarily contributed to that success. First was Roald Amundsen, experienced Norwegian polar explorer, who preferred the longer range and lift of a dirigible to the still uncertain performance of an airplane in the vast polar region. Second was American Lincoln Ellsworth, who continued earlier American dreams of polar airship exploration. And, finally, there was Umberto Nobile, Italian designer and builder of semi-rigids that did yeoman wartime service for Italy against Austria. Between 1919 and 1925 he built a further two dozen improved semi-rigids, of which half were sold to Britain, Spain, Argentina and America – including the ill-fated *Roma* of 1922. His willingness to sell his semi-rigid N1 below cost met fortuitously with Amundsen's thrifty planning for a polar airship and Ellsworth's financing. During the next eight months, semi-rigid N1 was rebuilt from a relaxed pleasure traveller to a scientific workhorse meant to withstand the rigours of cold, long-distance polar flight. About one-third the size of ZR3, the N1 would carry 16 scientists and crew. On 29 March 1926 she lost her formal Italian identity and became the *Norge*, an airship symbolizing Norwegian pride and hope, just twenty years after Norway's independence from Sweden.[22]

From the very beginning the polar airship venture acquired heavier burdens than those of anticipated arctic icing. These were the excessive political expectations heaped upon the ship and its flight. Amundsen strove to realize the scientific confidence of the Norwegian Aero Club, but he was further pressed by the arrival at Spitzbergen of the American naval flier, Lieutenant-Commander Richard E. Byrd, with a big Fokker airplane that dramatized aviation's rivalry of airplane with airship. Like Amundsen, Nobile had his own personal and national agenda. He strove to raise public perception of the semi-rigid airship up to rigid airship quality in technology and performance, another facet of aviation technological skyward rivalry. Nobile also carried with him echoes of the wartime Italo-German conflict, which, in turn, heightened the sensitivities of Italian inferiority that sought compensation. Mussolini himself was present at Ciampino airfield to preside at transferring N1 to Norwegian sovereignty. Theatrically he grasped the Italian flag just lowered from the ship and gave it to Nobile, ordering him to drop it at the North Pole. For the rest of *Norge's* flight, Italian propaganda blared forth the superiority of fascist technology and Italian navigation; it would redouble these activities with the sistership *Italia* on a further polar flight in 1928.[23]

The flight of the *Norge*, 11–14 May 1926, from Spitzbergen over the Pole to Teller, Alaska, was notable for several reasons. First was the undeniable accomplishment of this arctic first: basic photo-mapping of 3000 miles traversed in 70 hours, which only an airship then could accomplish. There were, however, the facts of barely coping with serious hazards en route and it was a wonder that the ship made it. But none of these matters dampened the enthusiasm of the Norwegian populace, upstaging the reserved Swedes, enjoying the admiration of the Americans, and enduring the ecstasy of the emotional Italians. In Germany, however, the zeppeliners echoed their pre-war disdain of non-rigid competitors Gross-Basenach and Parseval, wrinkling their noses in suspended disbelief. The French, still experimenting militarily with non-rigids, gave their Romanic cousins a paternalistic pat on the back. Worldwide the best of airship expectations were buoyed again.[24]

Diametrically opposite were the reactions of the two expedition leaders. It was all a bitter disappointment to Amundsen, for Commander Byrd claimed to have flown to the Pole just three days before the *Norge* ascended for her own trip of greater pioneering significance. Furthermore, so shaken was Amundsen by the scrapes with near-calamity en route, that he vowed never to board an airship again. Vehemently he also resented Nobile and all the Italian hulla-baloo about the flight. For their part, Nobile and his airshipmen were exhilarated by their own sense of accomplishment. They had flown their small craft, originally intended only for short service between Rome and Sardinia, all the way from the Eternal City to the Pacific Ocean – nearly five thousand miles. The Italian government, press and public went ballistic with excitement. Mussolini, they said, had finally brought Italy confident and triumphant into the twentieth century, in this Year IV of the Fascist Era. It became a brilliant demonstration of political manipulation of an aircraft technology then briefly and uniquely identified with Italian engineering.[25]

Nobile returned to enthusiastic reception at home. *Il Duce* confirmed his status as an Air Force officer and promoted him to General. Plans were soon under way to build a new semi-rigid thrice the size of the *Norge*. Mussolini, however, now discounted further polar flight in preference for a bold thrust across the South Atlantic to Argentina and Brazil, where millions of Italian immigrants were a loyal foreign support for fascism at home. Other forces were also at work to destroy Nobile. Enter General Italo Balbo (1896–1940), young and charismatic leader of the rapidly developing Italian Air Force. As the first Minister of Aviation, Balbo carried forward the dreams and enthusiasm of the pre-war aeronautical futurism of Marinetti and d'Annunzio with a succession of swift postwar fighting craft and strategies. These were the intended stuff of fascism's future, not Nobile's lumbering gas bags. In characteristic lethal political infighting behind smooth totalitarian façades, Balbo soon won Mussolini to his more adventuresome aviation and undercut official sponsorship for Nobile's next all-Italian polar thrust. Still, given his wide popular support, Nobile readily found other sponsorship from the Royal Geographical Society of Italy and the City of Milan, raising enough funds for a sister ship of the *Norge*, now to be properly named *Italia*, together with a supply-ship for Spitzbergen harbour named *Città di Milano*. Direct Soviet interest developed with Russian scientist Rudolph Samoilovich (President of the Leningrad Institute of Arctic Studies), who sought further use of Italian airships for Russian polar exploration. All the while, Italian propaganda whipped up public enthusiasm and expectations for the venture at home, seeking also a broader worldwide appreciation of Italian airship endeavour.[26]

The flight of the *Italia* went from overblown expectation to hyperbolized calamity. Fully provisioned for the now-understood rigours of the arctic, cheered on by the Pope, the King, and *Il Duce*, *Italia* left Milan on 16 April 1928 for a flight to Spitzbergen and met the *Città di Milano* at King's Bay three weeks later. After delays in final preparations, and a two-day trial flight into Russia's southern arctic, the

The *Italia* landing at Seddin, near Stolp in Pomerania, on 16 April 1928, after cruising over Austria and Silesia en route to Sweden and the north

airship took off towards the Pole on 23 May. Aboard were twelve airmen, four scientists, and a requisite journalist from Mussolini's daily *Popolo d'Italia*. Just after midnight, on 25 May, *Italia*'s contingent circled the Pole, dropped proper flags and a papally-blessed cross, and sang the fascist anthem. Almost back to Spitzbergen the next half day, disaster struck: lift was lost, an engine failed, and the ship crashed on the pack ice. The passenger car was torn from the hull which soared away with six men aboard, never to be seen again. For the next two months, the survivors wrestled to overcome their grim stranding. Several were lost as they tried to trek for assistance. Planes of several nations flew long search patrols. Amundsen overcame his aversion to Nobile and was lost on his own aerial search mission. At last the remaining survivors were found near their famous red tent by Professor Samoilovitch aboard the Russian ice-breaker *Krassin*. It all made for spectacular feats of irresponsible journalism. Correspondents backbit and undercut each other in claiming national prestige for the search and rescue. The large Italian press contingent, at its forward base with the *Città di Milano*, notoriously mangled the issues and reputations of personalities. Nobile returned home in public disgrace, was cast out of the Air Force and shorn of his rank by rigged court martial. Altogether it was a livid drama of failed technology interacting with flawed personalities and individual fortitude.[27]

The wreck of the *Italia* had immediate engineering and political effects. Technologically it was the death knell for semi-rigid airships. Italy, which had been with Nobile in the van of postwar development of these craft, gave them up completely. Now Italo Balbo swept into prominence with a succession of swift, successful seaplanes. Soon they would fly in military precision across the south and north Atlantic in *formazioni di stormo* to Brazil in 1931 and to the Chicago World's Fair in 1933. Semi- and non-rigid airships would survive experimentally in Europe and Russia. The American Navy alone systematically continued developing non-rigids for coastal anti-submarine service, which it maintained until 1962. Thereafter only the popular Goodyear 'blimps' remained vehicles for aerial advertising and television filming. Rigid airship advocates in Germany, Britain and America re-emphasized the strength of their craft and joined in censure of *Italia*'s frailties. The day of the poor man's large dirigible was over.

The case of the *Italia* was a textbook example of heavy-handed political manipulation of airship technology by a modern dictatorship. First had been the excessive publicity and over-reaching expectations about the ship, its Italian participants and the planned flight. Next came an orgasm of excitement when the ship was at the Pole, followed then by eight weeks of lurid journalistic exploitation of the disaster. Forthwith, Italian officialdom, from Mussolini downward, furiously backpedalled from association with the venture to escape its political fallout. Italy's aerial reputation was salvaged by the shift to Balbo's airplanes, while Nobile was harried out of his country to spend much of the next decade building a few of his craft for the Soviet Union. In Italy and abroad Nobile and his ships were soon forgotten, except for that one sensational disaster.

Meanwhile, notable advances in airplane technology and operation were extending overland air routes – and national prestige – from Cairo to the Cape, between Britain and Australia, and from Europe to the Far East. Increasingly, airplanes were also attempting the hazardous transatlantic crossing. In fact, between 1925 and 1928, in contrast to Lindbergh's feat, more lives were lost cumulatively in these airplane efforts than perished with the *Shenandoah* and *Italia* together. But the compelling psychic attractiveness of the airship held for their disasters as well as their successes. Public awareness of an airship crash simply had greater endurance than the momentary notice of any individual plane lost over the Atlantic. Much more than the little planes, the great skyships carried the pride and burdens of national prestige. Thus the mitigating circumstances of hazardous arctic operating conditions, and even the stereotypical discounting of Italian frailties, could not fully offset the negative impact of *Italia*'s crash. The disaster added its quantum of doubt to airship awareness.

During the three years from autumn 1925 to 1928, rigid airship developments held great public attention in Germany, showed troubled technological progress in Britain and lagged in all respects in the United States. Major personalities affirmed their own importance and recognition. Eckener became a consummate showman for the new zeppelin cause in Germanic middle Europe. In England, Lord Thomson was out of office, but as 'shadow' Air Minister was active in lectures and private advocacy. Richmond and his Cardington team enjoyed continuing publicity. Wallis was overshadowed at remote Howden. Burney was ever travelling, talking and writing on Britain's aviation future. In America, Admiral Moffett continued advocate development of *all* naval aviation, with strong visibility for the two new giant aircraft carriers just beginning their trials. Rosendahl put the *Los Angeles* through her paces. Garland Fulton at BuAer oversaw the design of two naval super-airships and endured four years of negotiation for their construction contracts. From Goodyear-Zeppelin at Akron, Litchfield worked the Washington political scene to gain support for the final naval airship plans developed by Dr Karl Arnstein and his Zeppelin Company team from Germany. It was a time of busy airship preparation amidst widespread general aviation enthusiasm in all three nations.

In these mid-1920s German public aviation awareness broadened beyond its nostalgic memories of zeppelin technology, recently reinvigorated by the transatlantic flight of ZR3. Sailplane enthusiasm grew and spilled over into excitement for motorized sport flying – both still subject to the politically irritating surveillance of the Versailles Interallied Aviation Control Commission. Several small struggling commercial airlines flying only within Germany sought federal support for extension of their networks beyond Germany. Additionally, Eckener orchestrated a continuing publicity campaign about Allied threats to destroy the Zeppelin factory and German airship research. Here was a trio of German complaints and ambitions that helped stimulate several Allied statesmen to negotiate with Stresemann to normalize Germany's postwar peaceful aviation.

These deliberations developed in the more relaxed political milieu of the emerging Locarno Era (1925–9), marked by the efforts of Stresemann, British Foreign Secretary Austen Chamberlain and French Foreign Minister Aristide Briand, who sought to restore Germany and Europe to postwar political normality by an Anglo-Italian military guarantee for Franco-Belgian security against a possibly rearmed Germany. Still, the negotiations for the aviation accord were difficult. France resisted abolition of the Aviation Control Commission, expansion of German motorized sport flying, and restoration of zeppelin construction and flight. Britain shared the French memories of wartime zeppelin raids but trusted the Allied monopoly of military aviation to keep the Germans in check. As for airships, Britain reflected the confidence of its new generation of skyship research that promised to relegate 'outdated' zeppelin technology to the past. All Allied nations sensed the increased competition from German commercial aviation and some potential loss of political prestige but hoped to gain from German technological expertise and general improvement in aviation business. France at last settled for the evident Allied military supremacy and sought the crucial advantages of German concessions on French overflights of the Reich to her east European allies at Warsaw, Prague and Bucharest. When it all finally came together, the new aviation treaty of 8 May 1926 marked *in effect* the first significant revision of the Versailles Treaty. Forthwith German commercial aviation was gathered in a federally financed air service, newly called Luft Hansa (after 1935 Lufthansa). And herewith the zeppelin was fully preserved, again a symbol for German transoceanic political prestige.[28]

As it later turned out, the French were proved to have been more accurate in their evaluations of German policies than the trusting British. Almost a year before conclusion of the new aviation treaty, as Eckener was launching his campaign for funds to build a new polar research airship, his colleague, Claude Dornier (1884–1969), received a remarkable research-construction grant from secret official funds for a giant seaplane. Count Zeppelin had in 1910 brought Dornier into his expanding company. This venture flourished in the wartime expansion of German aviation, where Dornier built the giant Staaken winged bombers that destroyed more targets in 1916–18 than the vaunted zeppelins. At the end of the war Dornier moved his airplane-building to Switzerland, Italy and Spain – thus eluding the watchmen of the Aviation Control Commission. Indeed, much illegal German military activity had found refuge abroad, mostly in the Soviet Union. Here were based experiments in artillery, tanks, aviation, poison gas, and other military ventures forbidden by the Versailles Treaty – all staffed by German military personnel and funded by concealed subsidies of the Weimar government. In this context Dornier in mid-1925 personally received a commitment of five million marks from clandestine naval funds to develop a new flying boat for mine-laying or transport – a project realized in 1929 as the giant twelve-motor Do-X passenger plane. By then Dornier, though nominally subordinate to company-chief Eckener, was virtually independent in his operation and doubtless Eckener and Colsman privately fumed at the ease of Dornier's funding while they had to undergo all the prodigious effort of airship fund-raising that ultimately yielded only half as much and still left the Company prodding Berlin for further resources.[29]

In the milieu of German aviation enthusiasm Eckener undertook to rescue and expand zeppelin building and flying in Germany. The intervention of the Swedish Royal Academy to foster zeppelins for polar exploration gave Eckener his opening for manipulating some favourable Allied opinion to maintain his enterprise. Forthwith he planned the gala Jubilee of 1925 in Friedrichshafen to commemorate Count Zeppelin's first ascent in 1900. Concurrently he made prodigious efforts to establish a nationwide organization of sponsorship for a popular fund-raising drive to build an airship for polar research and other commercial use. But here he was caught in a triple dilemma. First, he had to move swiftly with fund-raising in order to capitalize on revived German zeppelin enthusiasm before it might languish. Secondly, however, was the stubborn fact that the Versailles aviation restrictions were then still in effect and that the German government perforce could not be seen as approving or fostering solicitation. Crowning it all were the speeches and illustrated lectures of Eckener and his four top airshipmen (Flemming, Lehmann, von Schiller, and Wittemann), who criss-crossed central Europe and included Switzerland, Austria, Czechoslovakia, Hungary, and Romania, and the Baltic states – for crowds of thousands to little groups in schools, cafés and pubs. Voices were uniformly favourable, even with Communist deputies. Kurt Tucholsky, a prominent Communist author, however, was hostile. He condemned the zeppelin as a symbol of discredited militarists and reactionaries and ridiculed the plans for polar exploration; it was all just wasted money denied for aiding the suffering proletariat. In sum: the *Spende* was an incredible effort that faced serious economic odds in countries just barely emerging from the ravages of postwar business adjustment and ruinous inflation.[30]

If postwar German economic difficulties were troublesome, Eckener's more immediate problem was the state of international and internal German politics. Just at the moment the *Spende* was being proclaimed, Germany's negotiations for détente with her former enemies were reaching their climax at the League of Nations in Geneva. Simultaneously, negotiations for removal of the Versailles aviation restrictions were delayed well into the spring of 1926 – precisely the time that solicitation for the new zeppelin was most intense. On several occasions in these months the Weimar cabinet debated the impact of *Spende* propaganda on foreign relations and domestic circumstances. The Foreign Ministry, of course, wished for the complete disappearance of the subject. The Army and Navy, technologically disdainful of zeppelins after their wartime failures, opposed any kind of government advocacy for the *Spende*, lest their own future aviation funding suffered. The Treasury was strongly negative on grounds that eventually it might have to bail out the faltering enterprise. Other ministries with responsibilities for financial support in public welfare believed that Germany was still too poor to be involved with these money-devouring skyships. The Interior Ministry, responsible among other things for fostering technological progress, was divided in its counsel. Only two ministries were clearly supportive: Transportation and the Post Office, the former easily juggling heavy subsidies for Luft Hansa and favours for airships, the latter anticipating enhanced revenues from transoceanic mails. And all these federal doubts were strongly echoed in the internal policies of the Prussian state government.[31]

It all seemed a bizarre, exaggerated rerun of Count Zeppelin's problems with Berlin two decades before – with this crucial difference: the drive to build a new airship in 1908 was self-generated from public enthusiasm for the Count, whereas the *Spende* was an elaborate propaganda instrument to preserve the enterprise that unsolicited public generosity had built before the war. Treading a careful path between rekindled public zeppelin enthusiasm and foreign-policy hazards, the various government agencies expressed grave caution about the impact of such fund-raising on the slowly reviving German economy and on prudent fiscal policies. Both the federal and Prussian administrations moved quietly to impede the venture. Agitation and solicitation were prohibited on official premises. Unions, employee social groups and comparable organizations were 'advised' to down-play participation in *Spende* activities. Public schools and universities were declared off-limits for solicitation and their personnel 'advised' to neglect the *Spende* and its motivations.

However, campaigning proceeded officially in all German states except Prussia, which accounted for about 40 per cent of the population of Germany. As the *Spende* expanded, notions of a polar airship faded into the background. Instead there developed other themes: zeppelins as the great international fliers of the future; Germans as technological benefactors of mankind; and the mean-spirited enemies of the recent war denying Germans their inherent right to make the airship a symbol of freedom, progress and peace. But still the Berlin restrictions hurt. In late April 1926, Eckener pleaded with President von Hindenburg to remove government checks on *Spende* solicitation. Almost at once, all restrictions were removed. It was an easy accommodation. By now the Locarno Treaties were safely ratified, Germany was admitted to the League of Nations, and Allied-German negotiations on full sovereignty for German commercial aviation were almost completed. For Eckener and the *Spende*, however, it was an empty success. Public attention had indeed waned and the zealous campaigning tapered off. By year's end the total financial results were registered – 2.6 million marks, less than half the requirement to build the airship, not to mention costs of her trial flights and subsequent operating expenses.[32]

Now, at last, zeppelin construction could begin. As of early 1927, plans for the new LZ127 were complete and the great structural rings began assembly in the largest hangar. Like LZ126 – as ZR3 was known in the USA – the new airship also was built very much in public view. News releases almost weekly kept Germans informed as the new skyship slowly took shape. Friedrichshafen again became the *Zeppelinstadt*. Visitors streamed to the site for guided tours and purchase of zeppelin mementoes. Additional stimulus came from positive echoes of the great Amundsen–Nobile polar flight of 1926 and from US Navy publicity about the *Los Angeles* in service with the American Fleet. On the surface, it was all a very positive scene.

Accentuating these sureties, Eckener travelled to Spain and Argentina in July-August of 1927 to promote the prospects of airship service to South America. After years of negotiations with officials and businessmen in Spain, the Colon Compania Transaerea Espanola (founded on 16 September 1922 with a capital of 10 million pesetas) was formally authorized by royal decree in February 1927 to 'establish a line of airships between Seville and Buenos Aires'.[33] Now Eckener sought to lock Argentina into the Spanish enterprise that would use German zeppelins and operating expertise. But it was becoming clear to him that the nebulous qualities of the Spanish negotiations were replicated in Argentina. Then, after a perfunctory resolution of details in Buenos Aires, Eckener returned home with a stopover in Rio. Here he found Brazilian officialdom eager to accommodate Colon Compania at a new airship port to be built outside Rio, with all the requisites for a modern transoceanic airship terminal: mast, hangar, passenger-handling accommodation and zeppelin maintenance, together with a speedy suburban rail service to the heart of Rio de Janeiro. As he departed for Germany, Eckener had a firm impression of Brazilian determination to make Rio the major entry point of transoceanic air service into all South America, a marked contrast to the leisurely complacency of his Hispanic partners. Soon Brazil would win the airship advantage.[34]

Underneath, however, Eckener had his continuing problems. Greater funds would still be required to finish LZ127, even though the Reichstag had voted a subsidy of four hundred thousand marks in 1927. Berlin still troubled Eckener's days, now with periodic reminders that the new ship was (by earlier agreement) due for participation under his command in two polar voyages for Aeroarctic, which was also encouraged by the polar flight of the *Norge*. At its first official public convocation in November 1926, Aeroarctic presented a new, more European image, with France now supporting its Norwegian president Nansen to give the airship venture a more international scientific cachet, as contrasted with Eckener's all-German zeppelin. But when Aeroarctic pressed for international – and German – funding, it had even less luck than Eckener. Though Nansen's society was not part of Nobile's second polar venture with the semi-rigid *Italia*, that airship loss in May 1928, together with the notorious publicity about the subsequent four-week search for survivors, thoroughly dampened public enthusiasm for airships in the Arctic. Now Eckener could readily demonstrate that *his* ship was clearly of *German* quality in design and construction, intended for more important and versatile use than ice-pack rummaging.[35]

Unlike Aeroarctic, Eckener's prospects for funding his ongoing airship construction were not hopeless. Just as in 1924, he had the strength of the entire Zeppelin Company to draw upon. Under Colsman's pragmatic management that company, by 1928, was a far cry from the legendary 'pots-and-pans' makeshifts of 1919. Within Germany's first 'economic miracle' of 1924–9, the now diversified conglomerate developed successful new strategies of production and marketing: sophisticated light metals, industrial gases and fabrics, and a broad variety of high-quality drive-trains and engines – even a luxury automobile to compete with Mercedes-Benz, the glamorous 12-cylinder Maybach-Zeppelin. Momentarily prospects darkened in 1928 after the *Italia* disaster, when the earlier Reichstag subvention had been used up and before a further allocation could be voted. Here the dour prediction of the Treasury minister became reality: the government would have to foot the bill to complete the airship that public enthusiasm – but not its purse – had carried for two years. Again Eckener mobilized his contacts and influences to promote a final Reichstag subsidy of a further seven hundred thousand marks to complete and test-fly LZ127.[36] All these stresses, together with those of preparation for the coming transatlantic flight of the airship, now named *Graf Zeppelin*, irritated Eckener to the very eve of his departure for America. When a journalist of the prestigious *Vossische Zeitung* then asked him in the course of a long interview about his view of the *Spende* fund-raising three years before, Eckener growled, 'The German people are swine; they were more interested in throwing their money away on wasteful non-essentials than in supporting their Zeppelin heritage.'[37] In subsequent years of Germanic and international public acclaim Eckener's momentary embitterment of 1928 subsided. Still, his determined efforts of the next decade to make the zeppelin an essential factor in international communication and a tribute to German technological genius were always tinged with an underlying note of wary scepticism about the reliability of governments or of popular enthusiasm.

In England, as elsewhere, the 1920s were a decade of burgeoning aviation technology. Multiple improvements rapidly expanded commercial airplane use, making these craft far less expensive and more feasible for service than the unwieldy airships, notably on short and intermediate service. This was not lost on the design-building teams at Cardington and Howden. The research and experimentations dictated by the failure of R38 inevitably produced ever-increasing delays and costs as Cardington sought by zealous design change and experimentation to correct the alleged failures of zeppelin ways. The Vickers Burney–Wallis team at Howden worked with simpler design innovations and stricter financial curbs. But still the complicated process could not be readily curtailed.

By early 1926 the latent hostility between the two airship teams was becoming evident. Soon Air Vice-Marshal Salmond gave up his efforts to arrange continuing consultations between the two groups, though there remained some informal talks and occasional visitations. Cardington's 'scientific' disdain for 'conventional' Howden stiffened Wallis's aversion to sharing his own innovations with the government team. Wallis considered himself a successfully established professional, and (based on his achievement with the R80) an engineer personally resolving problems on his own drawing boards. At Cardington, by contrast, Colonel Richmond was supervising manager and coordinator of several different developing research-construction sub-teams under his purview. Thus grew there the self-satisfying image of a progressive Cardington research organization in contrast to the older Howden builder with his alleged outdated zeppelin derivation.[38]

All the while, other bureaucratic forces pressed upon the entire Imperial Airship Scheme. As Cardington sought ever-greater funding for its diverse research and experimentation in every major aspect of airship design, the British Treasury became increasingly critical. Its invasive inquiries met Cardington's resistance to revealing 'secrets' that might accrue to the benefit of Howden or elsewhere. The British Army and Royal Navy still hovered in the background with their nagging thrusts to weaken the RAF and return its planes to their respective services. These irritations spilled over into airship matters, with Army inquiries on dirigible usefulness for troop or supply transport and with the Admiralty concerned with airships as reserve naval scouts. Lord Thomson, either as Air Minister, or later in private, supported Cardington against the Treasury. With the armed services, the Air Ministry vigorously defended the RAF against incursion, while also quietly assuring the soldiers and sailors that the new airships would be readily adaptable to either service in wartime. Given the enormous expense of the Imperial Airship Scheme, it was an unpredictable game of probe and parry from one bureaucratic sector to another, seldom benefiting the airship venture.[39]

Finally, British airship designers and builders had to contend with a unique characteristic of British socio-political behaviour, as expressed in the conduct of allegedly socially superior amateurs and socially inferior professionals. Senior members of the Civil Service prided themselves on being creative amateurs, whereas the professionals, as graduates of technological colleges, had the taint of tradesmen. Conflicts were inevitable and in matters of airship development, as well as the development of civil aviation during most of the 1930s, the odds soon became insuperable – to the detriment of British commercial air development, notably across the North Atlantic.[40]

And what was the British public now perceiving of these airship matters? Few echoes of bureaucratic bickering reached the press, but far more important were the effects of Air Ministry publicity. Airship R33, based in the second Cardington hangar, was a necessary training resource and made some flights over the countryside and London. In autumn 1926 she briefly pioneered equipment for in-flight launching and recovery of planes. These were her final publicity moments, for she then soon followed R36 into disuse and break-up.

But now the Air Ministry could sound new trumpets for the future of Empire airships. For a second time since the war, the prestigious Imperial Conference met in London during October 1926. Sir Samuel Hoare, now Air Minister, submitted his department's carefully crafted study on the future of aviation in the Empire. With detailed analysis of all aviation development, both imperial and foreign, it elaborated on the promises of airline routes worldwide. Keynote of the presentation was the Imperial Airship Scheme, with arguments nicely focused to counter memories of earlier airship failures. Now were stressed the wide-ranging scientific research into aerodynamics, the improvements in structural design and building materials, and the development of diesel engines thought safer for tropical flight than petrol motors. Notable also were the advanced studies in Empire-wide meteorology. It was undeniably a fine example of Air Ministry research.

More flamboyant were the releases from Ministry publicity offices which explained in great detail plans for the R101. Here were seen luxurious accommodations: spacious lounge, elegant dining room, promenade decks and cabins for a hundred imperial passengers. More than just plans, the conference members saw a silvery eight-foot model of the airship and were taken by special train to Cardington to view a test section of the airship in the gigantic hangar. Construction of the innovative mooring tower rising near to the hangar was visibly impressive, the model for other masts to be built at Ismailia and Montreal. It was a *tour de force*, but focused on only *one* Empire airship. R100 was barely mentioned at the conference or in publicity, given no technical elaborations, no interior plans, model or site visits. The government and the public had just one airship type in view for the future of the Empire.[41]

Though delegates to the Imperial Conference may have been impressed by prospects of the Imperial airship future, the public response remained lukewarm. In late 1926 came more airship negativism. Aviation commentator and retired Royal Naval Constructor E. F. Spanner published the first of several anti-airship studies. In his book, *This Airship Business*, he revisited the whole spectrum of airship negativism: insufficient buoyancy for the planned skyships, lack of adequate safety measures, as in the case of the doomed R38, inability of the craft to survive adverse weather, and various inadequacies of both construction teams. Furthermore, he denied the favourable financial prospects for building and operating these gigantic airliners, as indeed he questioned their appeal to future travellers. Though Spanner correctly anticipated several factors that would later contribute to the failure of R101, many experts considered him an intrusive crank, hostile towards other engineers. Still, he was the first to sound public concern about the secrecy and rivalry developing between the two airship teams, as his works certainly touched that nerve of residual British animus about airships.[42]

As if in counterpoint, Lord Thomson soon after published his exhortation, *Air Facts and Problems*, a plea 'to organize aviation and make it the factor that it should be in a national and international sense'. It was his conviction that the British people could and would acquire 'the habit of the air'. Indeed, Thomson feared that England might soon lose her best aviation opportunities if she did not intensify research and experimentation, establishing a creative government–business partnership to avoid the likely penalties of world market loss and deficiencies in air defence. But for all his concern for aviation generally, his heart was still with the airships. Here he wrote some of his most rhapsodic prose as he envisioned the Empire strengthened and reaffirmed in a worldwide network of airship travel and communication.[43]

During 1927 and well into 1928, publicity about the airships subsided to a low murmur. Within the Air Ministry, however, the Imperial planners refined and expanded their proposals for all aviation development. Notable here were projects for airship service to South Africa and Canada. Capetown would be served via the east African coast, through the new intermediate base and mast at Ismailia near Suez. Projects for an alternative west coast route required leasing a base in the Canaries from Spain for an intermediate mast and constructing another on St Helena. The West African alternative offered a climate far more temperate than Suez and the possibility of then further flying safely non-stop overseas from Capetown to western Australia during the torrid middle-eastern summer. The fears of some route partisans that India might be neglected were allayed by the fact that both British airships would be pressed to the very limits of that alternative range and would not likely risk that venture. Still, the planning went on, for airship travel to Capetown would cut the two-and-a-half weeks liner trip to just three days. Much more likely was the service to Canada, where base and mast construction were begun at Montreal in early 1928. Indeed, the Canadians moved with enthusiasm and had their imported British tower completed within two years. This would be the only one of the several projected Empire routes to be briefly realized in mid-1930.[44]

Concurrently the Howden group was not idle in its own planning endeavours. Burney was constantly plaguing Wallis with suggestions and directives to improve R100, while visualizing even greater projects. Wallis responded to Burney's proposals for a South African service in 1925 with a design for a 140-passenger liner, from which he derived variations for a bomber carrying 20 tons of explosives and for a fast naval scout with an 11 000-mile range. In 1927–8 Burney prepared improvements to R100 to meet various anticipated needs of purchasers abroad, primarily in the United States where Burney spent much time and effort parading his airship business plans before President Coolidge, Commerce Secretary Hoover, and various naval and postal officials. Most promising was his contact with Juan T. Trippe, a young entrepreneur with an airplane service to Cuba and great ambition for his just-founded Pan American Airways, destined for the Caribbean and onward down the coasts of South America. Trippe was introduced to airships when the US Navy let his specialists board the *Los Angeles* to calibrate radio communications for his (then) Colonial Air Transport, flying between New York and Boston. Now he was open to discussions with Burney for airships of his own. In the spring of 1928 these talks scanned a wide horizon for Anglo-American airship construction and operation: 48-hour London–New York service via the Azores and Bermuda; interlocking schedules from the Caribbean south to Rio;

expansion of airship construction at Howden; parallel American building of enlarged R100s; and development of bases with masts at various crucial points of operation. Burney's climactic cachet was his expressed conviction that:

> The future political stability of the world depends largely upon the close cooperation in international policy between the United States and the British Empire. Anything that tends to draw these two great political entities closer together must be for the good of civilization – a commercial development that inherently contains an idealized political goal as well as a financial prize.[45]

Soon, however, Trippe chose the far less expensive and operationally more flexible Sikorsky flying boats for his ambitious Latin American and subsequent first transoceanic trials. Once thus committed, he became a hard, slippery opponent of German and American commercial airship developments, while circumspectly still wooed by Eckener and Goodyear-Zeppelin. Burney continued to press his airship hopes onward, towards his pyrrhic success with the first – and last – transatlantic flight of R100 to Canada two years later.[46]

In contrast to the promising prospects in governmental and private anticipation, progress in building both British airships faltered increasingly after the Imperial Conference. While Howden could show engineering advance, there were still disruptive interruptions by strikes each year from 1927 to 1929. At Cardington, despite a larger workforce and few labour troubles, costly delays developed in other ways. Materials and sub-assemblies from afar were often late. The wide-ranging research and design innovations required frequent pauses for interim testing. Item after item, each manageable in itself, cumulatively delayed the estimated delivery date for R101. Newly developed ballonette discharge valves were fitted in duplicate with special ship-length servo-systems. Extra servo-motors were installed for the rudders and elevators of the ship. An ingenious new system was devised to secure expanded lift of the ballonettes to the airship frame – again time-consuming. Finally came the constant vexation with the diesel engines. These were adapted directly from service in heavy Canadian railway locomotives, and required further strengthening of the airship frame. With all these changes it was realized in late 1927 that R101 was becoming so seriously overweight that it must reduce her payload and cruising radius. Howden struggled with comparable but far less serious problems: the great engine-weight dilemma was there resolved by limiting the flights of R100 to temperate zones and using much lighter petrol engines. But R101 was still burdened by the heavier diesels because of then-feared petrol fire in tropical areas. By late 1928, just as the new German *Graf Zeppelin* was taking to the skies, British inner circles faced the grim fact that their two new airships, inching towards much-delayed completion, were falling seriously short of their glowing anticipations just three years before. Indeed, Director of Airship Development Wing Commander R. B. Colmore confided that R101 would probably have to be cut in half for insertion of an additional bay to raise her lift to an acceptable minimum.[47]

American public awareness of the airship between 1925 and 1928 was caught between the *Shenandoah* disaster and the equally publicized loss of the *Italia* in the Arctic. The undoubted popular hero of that era was Charles Lindbergh with his daring solo transatlantic flight of mid-1927. As 'Lucky Lindy' toured the adulating nation over the subsequent year, creative engineers sought to make early transatlantic passenger flight more feasible by designing floating airfields to be strung across the ocean at 300-mile intervals. These 'seadromes' and the inspiration of Lindbergh's audacious skill, seconded by other pioneering airplane flights, seemed to wrest the future of transoceanic flight from the airships for the planes. For both the US Navy and for commerce the cause of the airship was in temporary shadow in America.

At the Bureau of Naval Aeronautics, airplanes and their pilots were also in the ascendancy, especially as they anticipated the early commissioning of the two new giant aircraft carriers. But Admiral Moffett still kept an even hand in developing all types of naval aviation. In the face of exasperating delays in authorizing, funding, and contracting for construction of the two new super-airships, the sole surviving *Los Angeles* did yeoman service in every way that her 'civilian' status permitted: testing and developing new equipment and techniques of flight; facilitating radio compass calibration for all aviation; searching for lost fliers in the western Atlantic; and further flying to Caribbean islands and Panama, usually to moor with supply ship *Patoka*. While publicity flights were now curtailed, the *Los Angeles* still managed to make the news and the cinema newsreels. She overflew an Atlantic City beauty contest. She saluted hundreds of departing veterans en route to Paris for a decennial reunion with their French comrades-in-arms. She celebrated an American Legion convention at Fort Worth, Texas, near the productive helium plants. But in all these efforts she was still a constant hostage to time-consuming and expensive maintenance of gas cells, engines, structure and hull covering. It was a struggle for survival until new designs, new materials, and new enthusiasm for the anticipated super-airships could breathe life again into the naval airship programme.[48]

In naval publicity and popular attraction the airship was now over-shadowed by the imminent arrival of the two new fleet aircraft carriers, *Lexington* and *Saratoga*, each twice the size of the pioneer *Langley*. But this ugly duckling had been the cradle of American carrier aviation. Here naval crews learned the intricacies of shiphandling unique to carriers. Here airmen perfected their techniques of hazardous take-offs, sighting and landing their fragile planes on ever-moving decks. Initially the fleet admirals had been confident of controlling the careers of their airmen in conformity to a century of seagoing tradition, while the carrier itself was restricted to scouting for the fleet. Inevitably, however, the practice of their aerial arts brought the pilots and their shipmates into confrontation with the fleet limitations. Should not the carrier develop its own aerial fighter defence, rather than relying on its feeble gunnery and that of accompanying warships? Should carrier planes not take the initiative to seek and destroy its enemies with its own bomb- and torpedo-carrying planes? Lindbergh's solo audacity only strengthened the dash and initiative of these young naval airmen. When the two new super-carriers were commissioned half a year after Lindbergh's flight, it was already disturbingly clear to some 'Gun-Club' admirals that carrier aviation would not easily be held just to scouting for the fleet.[49]

With naval and public attention diverted to the new carriers, developments for the airshipmen were further obscured by the delays of congressional action in awarding construction contracts for the two planned giant scouting zeppelins. As naval and Goodyear designers virtually marked time, the captain of the *Los Angeles* tried to attract renewed attention to the airship. His heroic expertise in the *Shenandoah* wreck had established Lieutenant Commander Rosendahl as America's best-known airshipman, a role that he carefully manipulated for the next two decades in a waning battle for airships in the US Navy and in worldwide commerce. Early in 1928 he got official permission and carrier sanction to land the *Los Angeles* on the new *Saratoga* to test possibilities for airship refuelling and regassing at sea. The attending propaganda photography only confirmed the incompatibility of two ships, each rolling in its own native element, the *Los Angeles* almost colliding on the surging deck of the carrier. This event became curiously symbolic of circumstances in government and business decision-making about naval airships during 1925–8.

Much as was the case in Britain, too many cooks were participating in devising the naval dirigible menu. Within the Navy itself there was clear agreement about the need of scouting units for the fleet, but sharp disagreement about fewer scouting vessels vs. more airships. When the dispute sharpened to suggest elimination of rigid airships entirely, the Army Air Force was ready to reassert its exclusive claim to fly the rigids, and *that* in turn threatened the whole justification for separate naval coastal and seagoing airship aviation, as laid down in the agreement of 1921. In Congress and at the Bureau of the Budget, the strong postwar stance of thrift was still evident, readily curbing expenditures, especially when agencies disagreed about their needs. Such funding underwent two processes of congressional action: an initial struggle to assure authorization for the expenditure and a second following to secure the necessary appropriation of required monies. In each of these two phases the whole carefully built structure of decision could become unglued when new personalities or different political forces materialized to press for other alternatives of action. When, finally, the needs were both authorized and subsequently funded, individual congressmen stood forth to foster the interests of specific businesses or geographical areas that sought to profit from the newly available public projects. It required four years of political jockeying between all these participants and interests finally to realize the new naval airship plan.

The airship designers of the Navy – notably Commander Garland Fulton, the man behind the scenes of all naval airship decision-making – had their project well in hand by early 1926. Together with the new German zeppelin construction contingent at Goodyear, they studied the lessons from the wreck of the *Shenandoah* and incorporated greater strengths and design revisions into the new dirigible plans. Unlike the British, with their experimental studies of the R38 disaster, the American–German naval zeppelin designers built confidently and swiftly on their previous experience. Once the Navy had its other priorities in order, Admiral Moffett wrestled for months through a maze of congressional committees to secure passage of BuAer's comprehensive new five-year aviation programme. This contained provision for two giant naval airships and a new west-coast base for them. Already at this stage Moffett's airship plan was muddled by the intrusion of a demand for construction of a small Ford-related experimental metal-hulled rigid. To assure his Michigan votes, the Admiral accepted the idea, which eventuated in the airship ZMC-2 *Metalclad*, a project of no enduring significance. Moffett's major focus was, of course, on the two new zeppelins, which he praised for these advantages: wide radius of action, high speed relative to surface ships, ability to hover protract-edly, prompt reception and transmission of information, and unusual capabilities for long-range reconnaissance. These new airships would greatly enhance the scouting requirements for western Pacific naval operations as long as war-plan ORANGE retained its singular fleet-thrusting impulses of the later 1920s. At the end of 1926 Moffett finally had his BuAer five-year programme in hand, with provision for two super-airships, their new west-coast base, and a tiny appropriation to fund the call for bids on the new dirigibles.[50]

During 1927 other congressional committees dealt with a separate but intimately related matter – the security and abundance of helium for American airships. Ever since the destruction of the hydrogen-inflated Army semi-rigid *Roma* in 1922, helium became a requisite for any American airship operation. America's monopoly of this safe non-flammable lifting gas became a subject of popular national pride and a perceived benefit for the country in commerce and defence. Professional airshipmen were less enthusiastic. When *Shenandoah* first flew in 1923, helium cost six times more than hydrogen, had 7 per cent less lift, and imposed awkward operational limitations on the airship. There had been constant pressure ever since to reduce the cost and lighten limitations by increasing production from the natural gas fields of Texas. The helium legislation of 1927 enhanced cooperation from the Interior Department (which nominally controlled such natural resources) and entitled a private enterprise to produce more gas than the government plant was delivering. The law also placed rigid limitations on any export of helium. The Goodyear Company fully supported these measures and lobbied energetically to realize them. Its well-known publicity agent, Hugh Allen, was reported as boasting, 'Only the United States has the God-given monopoly and advantage of helium for its airships in peace and war and should never relinquish it!'[51] That was the American position for the next decade. It would con-tribute significantly to the ultimate demise of all great rigid airships for whatever purposes in any nation.

Meanwhile, Moffett had anticipated that Goodyear-Zeppelin would build the ships, but politics required the Navy to solicit competitive proposals. Surprisingly, in May 1927, half a dozen American and foreign bidders submitted 37 different designs, none as competent as Goodyear's. Soon other politics further muddied the waters. Several congressmen supported claims of an American naval shipbuilder to adapt its workplace to airship construction, employing the techniques of an experienced foreigner – none other than ever-ambitious Johann Schütte. The bid-wrangling went on for months, as Congress also deliberated funding the BuAer bill it had previously authorized. In that process one of the two authorized super-airships was dropped. Now Goodyear was faced with an unacceptable business cost dilemma and undertook heavy lobbying to restore the second airship to funding.

Goodyear, it will be recalled, had been active in developing an American enterprise for construction and operation of commercial airships since 1920, when it first began negotiating with the beleaguered German Zeppelin Company. Nothing then came of these matters. In 1921, William C. Young joined management at reorganized Goodyear, with new emphasis on dirigible aviation. Here he formed close ties with later CEO Paul W. Litchfield and the crucially important Harry Vissering. With these circumstances he had developed influence with the Republican leadership in Washington, the Navy, and renewed negotiations with the Germans at Friedrichshafen – which altogether produced the Goodyear-Zeppelin Company at Akron in 1925. Henceforth Goodyear was tied into various aspects of naval airship maintenance and design. Now Litchfield and Young entered vigorously into the arena of Republican politics at Congress and the White House on behalf of naval aviation legislation, with eyes also on future commercial airships. At Washington they both excelled in the delicate mechanisms of lobbying, while not neglecting party politics at home in the Republican stronghold of Ohio. Indeed, Young claimed major credit for seeing the two new Navy rigids through both authorization and funding, stating that at one crucial legislative juncture a weary Moffett had told him that he had gone as far as a military man could and that Young would have to carry the ball from there – which he did.[52]

Late in 1927 the Navy terminated the whole entangled bidding game for new airships and stipulated a new competition with deadline for midsummer 1928. Bidders now emerging were only three: Goodyear, Schütte, and the American shipbuilder (with pirated earlier Schütte designs). While these bids were under Navy consideration, Goodyear lobbying continued unabated. In March 1928 the Akron builder outflanked opponents in Congress by a direct appeal to the White House, where Young convinced Coolidge to intervene on behalf of naval aviation and thus successfully secured funding for both new naval airships. The bidding wrangle went on for another half-year. By summer's end it was clear that the shipbuilder had adaptable facilities but no adequate designs. Schütte's bid in his own right was of high professional quality, but he had no construction base. Americans and

Germans breathed with relief when the contract finally went to Goodyear in early October 1928. Just a week later, the new *Graf Zeppelin* lifted off for its memorable transatlantic flight.[53]

Thus matters stood just a decade after the last Imperial German Zeppelin raid on Britain. The years 1924–8 had opened with a strong upsurge in airship enthusiasm. In both Germany and America the transatlantic crossing of ZR3 excited powerful emotional responses. For Germans it was the sweet international recognition of their reborn zeppelin prowess, offset by the bitter loss of their skyship to a recent enemy nation. Hovering overall was still the threat of termination of German zeppelin skills by other recent enemies. Americans rejoiced as the only nation with functioning naval airships and the promise of their commercial versions to come. The flights of the *Norge* and *Italia* roused enthusiasm among Norwegians and Italians alike, each finding technological evidence for their political superiority in these voyages of polar exploration. But with airships still so expensive and still so few in number, their disasters – like their successes – had the same multiplier effects on emotional public attention. The continued, relatively humdrum, service of ZR3 at the margins of naval operations could not offset public distraction at the loss of ZR1 and its lurid publicity exploitation in interservice rivalries. The far more intensive Italian political manipulation of its two semi-rigids produced excited fascist political highs and an emotional low so intense that Italians gave up airships of any kind for ever. Still offstage in the international skyship drama, bold new British design ventures and flight plans barely offset wartime memories of zeppelin raids. The ever-delayed project for Imperial airship linkage was poor competition for the excitements of the jazz age in Britain. Comparably in America, years of delay in political negotiations for the new generation of naval airships gave free rein to public enthusiasm for planes of the Lindbergh era and newly arrived naval carrier aviation. However, in Germany in late 1928 it was still a question of airship expectations all around, with the country finally at the threshold of her new zeppelin age.

Within the restricted margins of airship design and construction other political factors were evident. In Germany the government was initially apprehensive that future zeppelin technology would impede its efforts to normalize postwar international relations with the Allies, and thus Weimar energetically tried to restrict solicitation for new zeppelin funds. Once the aviation treaty of 1926 was signed, however, Berlin avidly pursued promotion of its Luft Hansa airline, leaving zeppelin development to private enterprise bolstered by parliamentary subventions. In Britain, the earlier decision for government to foster both a private and a state airship for Empire-wide commerce remained intact. What wavered and worsened were the technological-political relations between the two design-construction teams, intensified by Treasury interference in the government ship as delays and cost overruns steadily increased. In America, once the political fallout from the ZR1 crash had subsided, the fate of future naval airships was at the mercy of an intra-naval dispute about airships per se, of constant congressional delays in legislation, and of interminable posturing in the politically-dictated design competition – until the final positive decisions of later 1928. In all these circumstances, in all three nations, the earlier appeal of the glamorous airship image receded with more realistic public knowledge of airship fragility.

In contrast to some waning public enthusiasm, the building teams in all three nations continued their devotion to the technological attractiveness of their skyships. The men at Friedrichshafen had for long nurtured their quiet loyalty to the heritage of the old Count and had a solid, matter-of-fact confidence among themselves in their technology. Indeed, theirs was a sense of superiority to the apparently faulty Anglo-Saxon designs and flights, and of disdain for the Italian semi-rigids. In England, engineer Wallis and his Howden team worked in assurance comparable to the Germans'. At Cardington, the government team was immersed in design theory, interim experimentation, highly innovative engineering applications and showers of Air Ministry publicity. The commitment of American design-builders was no doubt influenced by their intimate contact with the German Zeppelin Enterprise, first at Friedrichshafen and then at Akron with the Goodyear-Zeppelin merger. It was in naval operations that airshipmen began developing self-persuasiveness in their technology and its operation. Initially this stance was in contrast to the seaborne Navy, later in competition with carrier aviation. And in both Anglo-Saxon nations there was occasional willingness to justify risk unto death for the nobility of scientific technological progress – an attitude hardly shared in Germany.

Thus the half-decade of the mid-1920s saw the fortunes of airships and their political manipulation constantly whipsawed between technological success and operational failure. Delays in construction of more advanced skyships were evident in all three major nations, while the losses in extant airships raised uncertainties for the future. Overall, public excitement surged in airplane enthusiasm and promise, unshaken by successive small accidents. Yet, the best for airships was still to come, climaxed by spectacular events in all three nations between October 1928 and October 1930.

Hubris and

In just two years, between October 1928 and October 1930, the high international airship hopes of the previous decade attained both resounding achievement and ill-starred misadventure. The new *Graf Zeppelin* crossed the north and south Atlantic and flew spectacularly around the world. The Americans completed their own ultra-modern airship construction works and began building their first naval super-airship. Britain finally launched both of its state-of-the-art airships. One completed a round-trip flight to Canada. The other foundered three months later en route to India. All these events quickened national enthusiasms and fostered international political posturing, both positive and negative. It was the brief culmination of global skyward airship rivalry.

The month of September 1928 saw a great flurry of publicity as the new German LZ127 made five trial and demonstration flights over Germany and neighbouring North Sea areas. Here was acclaimed a new triumph of German technological achievement, the largest zeppelin ever built and until completion of the two new British rigids the largest airship in the world. The first flight, staffed with eager German and American journalists and cameramen, retraced Count Zeppelin's journey of 1908, now with even greater public acclaim and enthusiasm. The last trial flight was an operational feat: all over Germany, across Holland, touching Britain's east coast, and calling on President von Hindenburg in Berlin – 34 hours aloft for nearly 2000 miles. And here the first international political repercussions were heard. France protested vehemently about illegal overflight of her occupation zone along the Rhine. Worse yet, Eckener was accused, probably falsely, of deliberately taking the zeppelin over the castle at Doorn in Holland to lift the spirits of the exiled German Kaiser, once so closely tied to the

141

Count and alleged perpetrator of wartime zeppelin raids over Allied nations. Thus, from the beginning of postwar zeppelin commerce, renewed German technology would continue to contend with old antagonisms.[1]

Buoyed by revived German airship fever, the *Graf Zeppelin* left Friedrichshafen on 11 October 1928 for the new world. American anticipation was more subdued, but still built upon the aviation enthusiasm exuberant since Lindbergh's solo flight the year before. Only the American Navy equalled German anticipation, placing its Lakehurst air station and communications network in service for the flight. Indeed, two naval cruisers were dispatched at equidistant thirds across the ocean to assist in some unforeseen dirigible distress. The German Foreign Office negotiated overflights across France and Spain. Eckener pressed his publicity with newsmen aboard the flight from the Scherl Verlag, Count Zeppelin's old newsmaker since 1903. America was there with the Hearst network featuring attractive Lady Drummond Hay and her companion, Karl von Wiegand, who fifteen years earlier had interviewed the old Count on prospects of transatlantic flight. Always at ease with sophisticated dimensions of experience, Eckener engaged the artist Ludwig Dettmann to paint the airship at various points on the voyage between heaven and ocean. Thus zeppelin propaganda covered a broad spectrum of media and objectives.[2]

The political goals of the new German air venture were evident in the roster of its distinguished passengers. First, in honour of the Old Count, there was his son-in-law, Count Alexander von Brandenstein-Zeppelin, an obligation of honour that Eckener readily paid. Then followed the men of future significance: chief of civilian air service Erich Brandenburg, whom Eckener needed to convince of the sound prospects for commercial airship development; Colonel Emilio Herrera, director of the Spanish airship enterprise Colon, representing German-Iberian hopes to make Spain the crucial take-off point for zeppelin service to South America; and finally, Lieutenant-Commander C. E. Rosendahl, most recently commander of the *Los Angeles*, who solidified Eckener's ties with the US Navy and its involvement with naval airship construction at Goodyear-Zeppelin. Out over the mid-Atlantic the airship encountered unexpected severe weather that posed a threatening hazard and then produced sensational news reports. When the zeppelin finally cruised majestically over Washington and New York, the *New York Times* headlined: AIRSHIP HYPNOTIZES CITY GAZING UPWARD, and wrote:

Thousands of cars p..
Throngs of journalists, officials, and well-... ...must
impossible to process immigration and customs at the air station.
Zeppelin fever gripped America.[3]

Eckener, his crew and passengers had a rousing welcome in New
York City. Admiral Moffett rode with him in the open car that led a
long procession up Broadway, showered with ticker tape and public
acclaim. Next day the airshipmen were received by President Coolidge,
later by President-elect Hoover, all resoundingly echoed in radio broadcasts, news cameras and rhapsodic journalism. Since the zeppelin
required professional maintenance at Lakehurst, Eckener had to forego
invitations for mid-western overflights, but he and his staff visited half
a dozen major cities as far west as Chicago. Chairman Paul Litchfield of
Goodyear-Zeppelin initiated discussion with bankers and business
circles, probing the future of commercial airships. When the *Graf
Zeppelin* left on its homeward trip, there was popular anticipation of
early transatlantic travel, replete with political symbolism of world
cooperation and peace. And the airshipmen of the US Navy celebrated
German-American technological and operational partnership in
profitable commerce and far-flung naval defence.

Among aviation experts and others, however, there were as many
doubts as bouquets. Lindbergh cordially helped welcome Eckener to
New York but thought that zeppelin transatlantic commercial flight
was still far off. Soon he would become technical adviser to PanAm's
Juan Trippe, who in turn would become an obdurate opponent of all
commercial airship development. Critics asked: what about the structural frailties experienced on the flight, and the great overall costs – all
to make a trip slower than ocean-going speed-queen *Mauritania*? All
congratulated Eckener on his skill, but Britain's Major Scott, no doubt
mindful of his own airship venture, said that much larger and more
powerful airships were needed. British press comment was brief and
matter-of-fact, but reminded readers that it was their R34 which had
been the first airship to cross the Atlantic – a decade earlier! France
gave grudging recognition of Eckener's feat in the sense of sportsman-

ship well done. But many other citizens and their east European Slavic allies saw mostly a spectre of resurgent German air power and aggression. Possibly some of them were reading the words of young Dr Joseph Goebbels, leader of Berlin's emerging Nazi political movement and editor of its aggressive mouthpiece, *Der Angriff* (The Attack):

> In all of us there wells with elemental strength that surge of pride [about the zeppelin trip] in belonging to a people expressing the primal power of its vitality and its unimpaired, unbroken determination to live.[4]

Now began a new spate of positive political manipulation of the zeppelin image in Germany and abroad. At home, and five days later in Berlin, the airshipmen received tumultuous popular acclaim. President von Hindenburg proclaimed that, thanks to them, Pan-Germany's [*Alldeutschlands*] heart beat more proudly, thus pointedly including the Teutons in divided middle Europe and farther abroad. Eckener himself, sceptical though he might personally be, valued the crowds in the streets and especially at airports, where the zeppelin itself gave emphasis to the excitement. These friendly enthusiastic masses became a standard measuring stick for reportage of political significance. Henceforth zeppelin officials tried only to guard their ship and personnel from crowd-surging; otherwise they encouraged the fervour of the masses to benefit Germany and the fortunes of the Zeppelin Company.

More pointedly than with the crowds, Eckener focused his attention on the person and functions of Erich Brandenburg, who had become civil air chief, notably to develop the new Lufthansa, lauded by later Air Minister Hermann Goering as 'the stronghold of the Luftwaffe spirit during the years of darkness'. Though a devotee of airplanes, Brandenburg had no anti-zeppelin animus and was quite won over to commercial airship prospects by his flight with Eckener and continued as a strong zeppelin advocate until the Nazis dropped him in 1934. He was superseded in commercial aviation at the new Nazi Air Ministry by Luft Hansa chief Erhard Milch, seconded by the continued zeppelin support of ministerial advisers Fisch and Mühlig-Hoffman. These were the men and functions that Eckener diligently engaged between 1925 and 1939.[5]

His relations with the German Foreign Office were often less felicitous. Eckener had always been at odds with the Allied disarmament authorities, the most recent being the wrangle about zeppelins in potential service with the Aeroarctic organization. Always, it seemed,

Dr Ludwig Dürr, Reichspresident von Hindenburg and Dr Hugo Eckener, Berlin, 1928

some niggling internal foreign policy tiff about the zeppelin, even when it triumphed. In 1929, a zealous German journalist would shout that Eckener had done more for Germany's worldwide image in a year than Weimar diplomacy had achieved in a decade. In 1931, a prominent Italian correspondent would write that Eckener was the world's third-best-known German, after Hindenburg and Hitler. Eckener always made the requisite contacts with Berlin to arrange for overflights and landings abroad, but various individuals and organizations at home and abroad frequently came to Eckener directly, thus bypassing official channels. And when the zeppelin was in flight, Eckener might make a quick touristic decision that would 'violate' some boundary. When protests then arrived from the Foreign Office, it was usually the quirks of weather that were used to explain the deviation. But in its heart Berlin would seem to know that again it was being upstaged by Friedrichshafen, that the zeppelin was again making political waves.[6]

Now Eckener forged ahead with new plans for airship construction and flight. The *Graf Zeppelin* was proving its mettle, but it was still an experimental ship, built within the confining walls of a vintage wartime hangar. A much larger facility was needed to construct the next generation of transoceanic skyships. Barely a fortnight after his return from the USA, Eckener sent an appeal to the Württemberg state government for a subsidy of two million marks to construct a new hangar – quadruple the subvention already promised by Brandenburg at the Transport Ministry. The request was partly to match the generous support for rival Luft Hansa. It was the German variation on commercial aviation development around the Atlantic rim: gasbags vs. wings, private endeavour vs. state enterprise.[7]

Finding German officials reluctant to increase zeppelin financing, Eckener redoubled his attention on leaders in government, finance and journalism. After the coldest winter in half a century, he took the zeppelin on two Mediterranean trips in early 1929. Present on one or another of these flights were Transport Minister von Guérard, Reichstag President Löbe, several Reichstag deputies, postal chief Sauter, Württemberg governor Bolz, Reichsbank chief Schacht, and a spate of German and foreign journalists. Eckener's memoirs rhapsodically recount the flights from the icy north, down over the palms of the Riviera, above the classic monuments of Rome and Greece, to the warmth of a descent to the surface of the Dead Sea. Captain Flemming thought the guests were well impressed, but quoted Eckener's doubts: 'With these politicians you never know how long their momentary enthusiasm will last; well, we shall see.'[8]

postwar Near Eastern politics. In England, fears for the implications of the flight for British aviation prestige had already been aroused and there was sensitivity over the military installations of the Egyptian Canal Zone being surveyed by foreign craft and the zeppelin's political impact in Cairo. What if Eckener suddenly turned south towards Kenya to replicate the wartime flight of L59, then seeking to succour Berlin's embattled colonial army in German East Africa? Worse yet, would the newly completed British airship facilities at Ismailia, awaiting R101 en route to India, first have to entertain the rival zeppelin? Unmistakably word reached both Eckener and the German Foreign Office that no flight permit for Egypt would be approved. By that time, however, Eckener had already invited Egyptian correspondent Mahmoud Abdul Fath (of Cairo's prominent daily *Al-Ahram*) for the trip. Fath then sent a glowing report of gazing down over Jerusalem upon the Dome of the Rock and Haram al-Sharif bathed in silvery moonlight. At the end he wrote:

> The Egyptian people, through no fault of their own, are being prevented from witnessing a magnificent spectacle [the zeppelin]. It is due to [British] envy of the thoughtful, hard-working German nation, which is developing so quickly and out-classing most other countries, particularly in aviation. As a result, the [Egyptian] people cannot see the *Graf Zeppelin* and it will not see the Suez Canal.[9]

The French would continue to nurse their political apprehensions for the next decade in all three continents where they governed subject peoples or pursued their own commercial aviation interests. The British attitudes, by contrast, would change dramatically after 1930.

New political stimulation at home and abroad came from near-disaster with the next airship flight. Eckener, together with American interests, was feverishly preparing for a global flight of the *Graf Zeppelin* in the summer of 1929. Preliminary to that was a trip to Lakehurst beginning on 16 May. The next day, when engines began failing one by one near Barcelona, Eckener turned back and barely reached the French naval air base at Cuers. Here the Germans found technical succour and warm compassion. Of course the event made surpasses everything else to date. No doubt the French have given prudent aid and their bit of *Schadenfreude* [at German expense] is quite understandable. Our newspapers gloss over this publicity fiasco [*blamage*] as a fortunate coincidence rather than as proper comeuppance for Eckener's arrogant posturing. At any rate, we can now more effectively downplay all this business here at home.[10]

That process of competition for federal funds and public attention in Germany would become ever sharper and more politically strident through the Depression years of 1930–2, until the Nazis came to power in early 1933.

Funding and politics: these would be the crucial factors in months of preparation for the global zeppelin flight and its realization. Already Eckener knew that little could be expected from the government. Luft Hansa was swallowing nearly twenty million marks of subsidy in 1929 and would need more for its widening network of European air service. The Foreign Office and Reichstag had to wrestle with the far greater financial demands of the upcoming Young Plan that might double or triple Germany's annual quarter-billion-dollar payments to the Allies on wartime reparations. So Eckener, left to his own resources, widened contacts with publishers, intensified public relations, and expanded his airship travel and express goods service. These efforts soon bore fruit in negotiations with the Hearst newspapers in America, which paid half of the quarter-million-dollar costs of the flight on condition that it officially depart from Lakehurst and terminate there. Eckener then negotiated other journalistic income and propaganda for a German-European flight designation originating and ending at Friedrichshafen. The balance of the funding came from the postage on mail sent by thousands of collectors worldwide, seeking commemorative cancellations at landings in Germany, Japan and America. For that flight, the zeppelin again had its own postal service aboard the ship itself, yielding more philatelic treasures. During most of the ensuing decade this postal revenue would yield the equivalent of nearly five million dollars – all through the Depression years – for flight expenses of the zeppelins.[11]

Political aspects of preparations for the global flight were in varied evidence. The German Foreign Office negotiated requisite overflight and landing permits. Yet this service seemed almost superfluous, for Eckener had already made far-reaching arrangements with various agencies in nations en route. Intense was his research with Soviet authorities about weather and topography in Siberia, hitherto only sparsely observed and mapped. On the leg to Tokyo a Russian geographer was often in the control car for consultation. As regards Japan, ever since Germany had shipped a wartime hangar there for re-erection at the base at Kasumigaura, Eckener had nurtured thoughts about Far Eastern zeppelin prospects. In anticipation of the global trip, he conceptualized a zeppelin construction and flight subsidiary in Japan, making inquiries with Nipponese naval, governmental and aviation experts. The presence of journalist Kitano and Admiral Fujiyoshi en route to Tokyo affirmed these prospects. The welcome in Japan was tumultuous, emphasized with festivities by Japanese scientists, military–naval receptions, and meetings with businessmen and politicians. As one commentator observed:

> Here were heard in clear tones the voices of two peoples, expressing a common determination to work together in the image of the zeppelin. The *Graf Zeppelin* is in every sense a wonderchild of politics. It descends from out of the blue in minutes, banishing fog and hazards to illuminate Germany's name with luster and significance. German foreign policy must move swiftly to capitalize on these circumstances!

Subsequently in America, German associations with US Navy and Goodyear-Zeppelin were firm. Lieutenant-Commander Rosendahl flew the entire circuit. This airship flight matured aviation journalism, radio, and film reporting worldwide. International enthusiasm soared as news and photos appeared rapidly, following the zeppelin around the world. Praise for German endeavour whetted national zeal elsewhere to surpass the zeppelin feat and reap its own rewards of image and achievement.[12]

Prodigious indeed were the new records set by the *Graf Zeppelin*: non-stop Germany to Japan, 6800 miles in 101 hours; first Pacific crossing, 5800 miles non-stop in 79 hours; first American transcontinental non-stop airship flight, 2900 miles in 50 hours. Worldwide it was a trip of 21 000 miles in 20 days, with 20 passengers and the crew of 36 aboard, plus 30 tons of supplies, goods and mail. No wonder the airship seemed the only transcontinental and transoceanic carrier likely to fly for the next aviation generation.[13]

The crowds and political reactions to the flight surpassed anything else to date. At the outset Lakehurst was inundated with cars and spectators. Russian officials had lent full support for the flight across Siberia, but when adverse weather dictated a route far north of Moscow, the wrath of Soviet journalism was vented on decadent capitalist arrogance slighting the vibrant new society being built in Russia. The reception in Japan exceeded anything hitherto experienced; Germany renascent shone in contrast to memories of alleged Allied disrespect of Japan and her interests at Paris in 1919. Jubilation awaited the zeppelin in western America, especially when psychological behaviouralist Eckener delayed briefly in order to cross the Golden Gate in the rays of the setting sun. Forty thousand people overwhelmed naval security personnel at Los Angeles in a Californian outburst of zeppelin fever. On the east coast, the greatest ticker tape parade ever in New York City and a great reception by President Hoover seemed to affirm that world airship travel was on the brink of realization. Eckener then remained to talk with men of American industry and finance (at the peak of the Wall Street boom of 1929), while the zeppelin flew on to finish her 'German' global journey. Britain, now just about to launch her own two giant airships, displayed scant interest in the zeppelin achievement. As the zeppelin flew over France, the cartoon in a prominent Paris journal expressed French pique: Eckener seen in the control car, looking down on the Eiffel Tower, asks his helmsman for the time; the response caption reads 'Twelve years late, sir'![14]

The *Graf Zeppelin* arrived in Germany for a tumultuous welcome. A few negative comments were still heard. German Communist papers echoed the earlier anti-capitalist diatribes of *Pravda*. Goebbels' Berlin *Angriff* ignored every phase of the global flight, instead focusing its venom on alleged Weimar betrayal in agreeing to renegotiated reparations payments to the Allies. But these were still only minor irritations in waves of journalistic euphoria, lauding a season of superlative accomplishments for German technology. An all-metal Junkers plane had recently completed the first westward plane crossing of the Atlantic. The new liner *Bremen* began its record-breaking ocean crossings. All summer long there were expanding trial flights of the gigantic twelve-engine Do-X flying boat by Dornier. But round the world the *Graf Zeppelin* surpassed them all in notoriety and acclaim. Five days after the airship return Gustav Stresemann spoke to the League of Nations Assembly in Geneva, heralding that technological accomplish-

German election poster, 1924

ments, so often tied to war, now gave way to those of peacetime significance, where the victories of mankind over nature gave better awards for heroism and dedication to ideals. It was all a climactic expression of technology in interaction with propaganda and politics.[15]

Visiting Akron in later October 1928, Eckener found Goodyear-Zeppelin and the whole city agog over the prospects of becoming America's prime centre for rigid airship construction. For Akronites it seemed the dawning of a new clean industrial era at a city long ill-reputed for its grimy rubber and tyre production. All was bustle and anticipation, including plans for a new Akron international airport to serve zeppelins and their passengers. Naval designs for the two new super-airships were finalized. Goodyear played it all very cool, momentarily seeming to consider other sites like Los Angeles for its new industry and related airport. In September 1928, Jerome C. Hunsaker was brought aboard at Goodyear-Zeppelin, resident in New York but frequently at Akron, as general supervisor for adaptation of naval designs to commercial ships and related matters of commercial airship planning. With his strong background in previous American dirigible design and construction, Hunsaker worked hand in glove with zeppelin designer Arnstein and Commander Fulton, now the guiding naval spirit of airship design and its future civilian versions. It was Hunsaker also who was the mainstay for Eckener's opening conversations with American industries seeking participation in future commercial airship enterprise. Concurrently, Arnstein completed designs for an advanced new construction hangar – which Litchfield named an Airdock – while Goodyear still played its siting game to prise major benefits and contributions from Akron city. Such suspense and such euphoria![16]

Meanwhile at the US Navy, other aspects of naval aviation were maturing. The aircraft carrier was about to demonstrate its independence. For seven years the naval airmen and their carriers had been held in subordination to the Battle Fleet, to act primarily as its eyes and defence. But now they were ready to go it alone. During Caribbean manoeuvres at Fleet Problem X in January 1929, the commander of the carrier *Saratoga* got grudging approval from the Problem Chief quietly to break formation with the fleet and launch an amazing left-flank simulated bombing attack on the Panama Canal. The result was judged as knocking out the vital link between America's coasts and precipitated consternation and controversy in top naval circles. For airships a new question loomed: if a carrier could thus act on its own, or in groups, what would be the impact on continuity of warplan ORANGE? What was the significance for the scouting airships about to be built at Akron? Moffett no doubt found the two naval aviation types still experimentally compatible. More urgent business took him to London for three months of renewed international naval conferences, where he argued for more US carriers and a hybrid type of flight-deck cruiser. Were the growing numbers of carrier pilots likely to engulf the limited roster of airshipmen? Now the hitherto latent rivalry of airship with airplane became openly evident.[17]

While Goodyear jockeyed for advantage and Moffett parleyed in London, the airshipmen were not idle. All through 1929 the *Los Angeles* continued as maid of all work. Notable was the continuous experimentation with the hook-on and take-off of airplanes by trapeze mounted on the lower airship hull – work towards perfection of the process for its later adaptation in the *Akron* and *Macon*, where it promised vastly to enlarge the scouting range of the new naval airships. Public presentation of the dirigible was still foremost in naval minds. President Hoover's nomination and victory in 1928 had been significantly influenced by Goodyear's activities with Ohio Republicans; no wonder the *Los Angeles* and Goodyear blimps cruised over his inauguration parade in 1929. Shortly thereafter Litchfield and Hunsaker met with Hoover at the White House to outline their preliminary plans for commercial aviation, based on passenger ships derived from naval airships. They were prepared to commit ten million dollars to the venture, but they must be assured of revised long-term airmail contracts and of government legal and financial commitments comparable to those already available to American maritime shipping. Hoover was especially impressed with plans for the Pacific and gave his assurance for executive support in all matters of potential legislation. In late August 1929, circumstances were even more favourable, when the *Los Angeles* flew to the National Air Races at Cleveland to give the first public performance of its airplane trapeze at work in the presence of 100 000 spectators. In the course of the festivities all the key men were there: Moffett, Litchfield, Arnstein, Fulton, Hunsaker – and Hugo Eckener, who had just completed piloting the *Graf Zeppelin* around the world. It was a high-point of America's anticipation of an airship future.[18]

Americans, their airshipmen, and Goodyear-Zeppelin all revelled in the burst of worldwide publicity generated by Eckener's global flight. The sponsoring Hearst press, the news weeklies, radio broadcasts and cinema newsreels affirmed a promise that transoceanic flight would soon be regular and that there America's political image would loom in significance. The genial zeppelin commander stayed on in America for a month to strengthen these potentialities. With the assistance of the Goodyear team he consolidated his association with American enterprise most likely to benefit from the new airship era. But none of these potential partners could then know that they were negotiating in the last brilliant month of Wall Street's five-year bull market. And Hunsaker would shortly announce plans for Atlantic and Pacific commercial airship companies that would derive their passenger airships from the naval zeppelins about to be built.

By mid-autumn of 1929, all was ready to open the practical phase of America's new airship venture. Litchfield had wrested most of what he needed from the city of Akron. In one sector of the expansive area dedicated to the new international airport, Arnstein's monumental Airdock took shape during the summer: a hangar enclosing 45 million cubic feet, wherein sudden changes of outside temperature could induce interior cloud formation and rainfall. In early November the Airdock was completed. Simultaneously with its dedication Admiral Moffett appeared with other naval dignitaries, businessmen, politicians, and 30 000 spectators to drive a golden rivet into the first structural component of the new naval airship ZRS4, later to be named *Akron*.[19]

In the summer of 1928, it had appeared to the popular British press that R100 would be launched a month before the *Graf Zeppelin*, thus winning what had been described as 'a feverish and secret two-year battle' showing keen competition between Howden and Friedrichshafen. To Burney it appeared as a matter of honour:

> We must be in the air before the Germans, if for no other reason than to maintain our national prestige. We could not contemplate the possibility of being beaten by Germany in civil aviation after having beaten her militarily.[20]

When it became clear, however, that Germany's craft would be operational long before either British ship emerged from its hangar, little further was heard in the press about that alleged Anglo-German race. Indeed, when the Germans completed their epoch-making global flight in September 1929, the popular press paid scant attention, focusing instead on Britain's victory over Italy for the Schneider Trophy seaplane races. Instead, the battles fought in the daily press involved Howden and Cardington, one widely read paper reporting:

The end of one of the most remarkable struggles ever seen between state and private enterprise is well in sight. The two parties wait with dramatic intensity for completion very quickly now of the two giant airships that are twice as large as any previously constructed. When these airships come out of their sheds, the battle will begin. Which will win: the product of government design and workmanship or the product of private enterprise?[21]

In the summer of 1929, the British airship programme entered its final preflight stage. The images of R101 blossomed in Air Ministry propaganda with bold claims for luxury and performance but R100 was lost from public attention. The great new masts were ready at Montreal and Ismailia, while a third was begun in South Africa. With these technological accomplishments came also a new political impulse. In the July elections Labour emerged as Britain's largest party and took office, with Ramsey MacDonald again Prime Minister and Lord Thomson back at the Air Ministry. Trials of both dirigibles were scheduled for autumn. In Parliament airship questions increased in frequency and some politicians sought opportunities to identify with the new airships.[22]

The broader political milieu also seemed propitious for the new airship venture. Though quite in the shadow of the booming American economy, Britain seemed to be mastering some of the negative economic consequences of the war. Much of industry appeared stable, an uneasy labour peace was welcome after disruptions of the earlier great strikes; and the international balance of payments was momentarily favourable. Matters of Empire were more exciting. All British aviation was making good strides, notably on the routes to Africa and India. In South Asia events were reaching a crucial turning point. The interim report of the Simon Commission on India in October 1929 foresaw important progress by mid-century for Indian political reform and even possible dominion status. Anticipation grew for the next Imperial Conference, planned for October 1930, and already constitutional pundits predicted greater self-rule for the Dominions. MacDonald himself gave the tone for a more cooperative political climate when he urged the Commons 'to consider ourselves more a Council of State and less as arrayed regiments facing each other in battle'. What symbolism the new airships could project: daring technological innovation, economic enterprise, progress in India and in the entire Empire![23]

In early autumn, airship enthusiasm alternated with sobering news. Both ships had in-hangar trials of their potential lift and engine thrust. R100 made out well in context of her technical specifications, but the trial results for R101 were much below par. She was reported in the popular press as 'underpowered, overweight, deficient in speed, unprovided with a satisfactory system [of in-flight management], and unable to carry the hundred passengers for which accommodation has been provided'.[24] Opponents of airships rushed into print with their condemnations. These deficiencies had, however, already been privately noted by both Burney and the Air Ministry. Burney's proposals of 1928 to Trippe at PanAm contemplated larger and more powerful ships and in early 1929 design was already under way at Cardington for R102, a third larger than R101. For the interim, various remedial steps were under way for R101. Her luxurious accommodations were cut back in size and quality. Various structural areas were reduced in weight. Her gas bags were expanded to provide more lift within their wired networks. Still, the government propaganda drove on to cultivate her public image as before. When the colossus finally emerged from her hangar in mid-October, public interest was intense. The London *Times* reported:

> One million people travelled from all parts of the country to gaze in awe at the giant silver airship as she went through her final trials at the mooring mast today ... The scenes at the air station were unequalled in the history of airship flying. Battalions of police, stationed every hundred yards along the four miles of roadway leading to Cardington, were powerless to deal with the congestion. Hundreds of omnibuses arrived here all day, travelling from Newcastle, Leeds, Cardiff, Swansea and Nottingham ... The predominant impression made by the State Airship R101, as she now swings at the masthead at the Royal Airship Works, silver in colour and imposing in her size, is the way she looks right and in a way which the elongated cigar ships [zeppelins] of the War Period never did.

R100 would arrive at Cardington two months later.[25]

Just as R101 first ascended, Burney published his widely-read study, *The World, the Air and the Future*. Though claiming that the British airships were significant steps forward in aviation, he soberly indicated that neither British dirigible, nor the *Graf Zeppelin*, were more than experimental craft, just preliminary steps in the evolution of transoceanic commercial transport. But, given the limitations of winged aircraft of the time, airships held the key to Britain's imperial future. They would shorten the distances that separate the various parts of the imperial system ... weld it into a solid economic and political structure, and so give it sufficient power such as will enable the Empire to compete on level terms with a continental organization like the United States ... The future of the Empire lies in the air. It is no exaggeration to say that not only its political and economic development but also its continued existence depend on our capacity to establish within the next generation an efficient system of Imperial air communication.[26]

With the advent of 1930, national pioneering aviation was becoming international commercial flight. Spectacular as were the achievements of the *Graf Zeppelin*, in its shadow the airplane was advancing steadily from its continental limits towards the mid-East, Asia, Africa, and Brazil. America's PanAm planes circled the Caribbean and thrust southwards towards Rio. Ever-increasing frequencies of flight prompted the standardization of all European service schedules. Rapid improvements of airplane technology put this craft, and especially its flying boat types, at the threshold of transoceanic flight. These advances produced their own muted instances of international political contest. But the airship still exemplified the strong impulses of politically-tinged competition among the world leaders: Germany opening commercially towards South America, America seeking strategically to command the Pacific, and Britain thrusting towards Canada and India. And as a contest between airship and flying boat developed, so did worldwide negative economic conditions, which would then especially impact upon the enormously expensive airship development. Seldom would global aviation stand again at such a threshold, both promising and threatening.[27]

During 1930, the airship further invigorated its impact on the public psyche in Europe and the Americas. Most prominent was the role of Eckener, who rose from his image as the flying Columbus of 1924 to become the aerial Magellan of 1929. At home he continued to emphasize the zeppelin as a work of German technological superiority and symbol of Germany's re-emergence to world stature. Abroad he pressed for urgent zeppelin development in transoceanic commerce, symbolizing postwar international conciliation. He accepted the airplane, but only as a short-flight provider on routes impractical for airships. His only international equal was Lindbergh. These two men personified the competition between their respective aircraft, where maturing airplane technology challenged the competitive long-distance advantage of the airship.

Opening the new decade, Eckener strengthened his dominant role in the zeppelin enterprise. First, he did not impede the departure of Managing Director Colsman, whose policies had produced the profits that helped foster the postwar zeppelin, but whose business successes were quite overshadowed by zeppelin achievements. Secondly, Eckener intensified his personal political activities in venues at home and abroad, fostering the zeppelin as Germany's showpiece. During a year of declining German prosperity he still coined rewards from the sale of Company properties. He attracted further attention and funding with a notable South American flight, half a dozen other international voyages, and fifty short zeppelin jaunts with doubled passenger capacity at high fares. Finally, Eckener contained the threat of flying-boat builder Dornier within his own larger enterprise. The giant Do-X plane, which had originally been funded secretly by the German Navy, was kept off the Company balance sheets, as its own highly advertised technology and promise faltered in the face of crippling developmental costs. In these three aspects Eckener's business acumen and manipulation of the airship seemed to bode well for the coming zeppelin decade.[28]

At the opening of the new year, activity buzzed down at the Lake: completing plans for LZ128 (half again larger than the *Graf*) and finalizing planning for the triangular voyage to Brazil and the States. In late March Eckener was again briefly in Washington, now to receive the Special Gold Medal of the National Geographic Society. Six thousand guests, officials, diplomats, and officers attended this gala celebration. Admiral Moffett was there, as were Litchfield, Fulton, Hunsaker and all the other airship notables. Prominent also were Senator McNary of Oregon and Representative Parker of New York, who would soon initiate the first congressional legislation for a Merchant Marine of the Air. His name now inscribed among the notables in geography and exploration, Eckener conferred further with various American backers for airship development; they were bruised by the Wall Street crash, but hoped for rescue with government subsidies. Memorable was his brief negotiation with Postmaster General Brown, which resulted in issuance of the most famous set of special zeppelin stamps ever, whose use would soon yield over a hundred thousand dollars for zeppelin flight expenses. Meanwhile, Captain Lehmann took the *Graf Zeppelin* on a celebratory cruise to Bonn, where crowds of a hundred thousand rejoiced in the zeppelin, again chorusing 'Deutschland über Alles', just as throngs had greeted the old Count along the Rhine twenty years before. The next month, on return from America, Eckener was splendidly received in London to address the Royal Aeronautical Society on developments for transatlantic airship service. Two days later the *Graf Zeppelin* arrived at Cardington for convivial shop-talk with Britons from both airship teams, then carried Eckener and a complement of British notables over the rooftops of London back to Germany. Singlehandedly he seemed successfully to be ignoring the gathering clouds of the Depression.[29]

Plans for the voyage to Brazil and America took the zeppelin enterprise a solid step beyond the earlier experimental trips. Now Friedrichshafen could verify the dirigible as a reliable, all-weather transport in differing world temperature zones. Here were also reaffirmed the ties with Spain. Seville celebrated its potential role as European turn-around gateway to Latin America. The zeppelin would further prove its commercial worth on this course, where it was only three to four days en route, as compared with nearly three weeks by most liners. Once arrived at Recife (Pernambuco), passengers and mail would transfer to the South American air networks already developed by the Syndicato Condor with German Luft Hansa expertise. It would be a profitable saving of precious business time.

Just as tempting were the potential political rewards. Eckener burnished Iberian pride by taking prominent Spaniards aboard for the inaugural voyage, all to mark the importance of developing Seville for zeppelin operations. Brazil was even more significant as a political objective. Germans were the most important European immigrants there, especially south of Rio, where their influence was radiating outward into the rest of South America. The reception of the zeppelin at Recife and Rio was tumultuous, far more resonant than the brief episode of French aviator Mermoz's pioneer airplane crossing ten days before.[30]

Both French and American commercial aviation were contesting Eckener's triumph in Brazil. Paris had developed its service down the west coast of Africa to Dakar, while its Latécoère enterprise had a growing foothold in South American aviation. Now it only remained to close the South Atlantic gap, previously serviced by fast destroyers between Dakar and Recife. Unfortunately, Mermoz was lost on a subsequent survey flight, while Latécoère's business would soon founder. Washington was actively represented by the expansion of Juan Trippe's PanAm, thrusting from Miami down both the east and west coasts of South America. And both of these business-political competitors of the zeppelin were featuring the threatening technological rivalry of the flying boat.[31]

From Rio the zeppelin flew northward freighted with influential personalities, two American naval airshipmen, and its lucrative European, Brazilian and American mails. Over Cuba and PanAm's aviation center in Florida, and up the east American coast Eckener cruised to evoke airship resonance with the citizens below. As he later wrote:

> The mighty airship, matched by its lightness and grace, its beauty of form modulated in delicate shades of colour, never failed to make a strong impression on the public psyche. It was like a fabulous silver fish floating quietly in the ocean of air. And this fairy-like apparition, when it appeared from far away, lighted by the sun seemed to be coming from another world and to be returning there like a dream.[32]

Along the Washington–Boston corridor, and at Lakehurst again, the crowds were as massive, awe-struck and excited as before. But that was no longer the response of Eckener's potential backers for airship development. While Hunsaker moved ahead with studies and plans for Goodyear, American business was caught in the enveloping anxiety of the Depression. As Eckener flew back across the Atlantic, other negative prospects loomed: revolution was threatening in monarchial Spain, while economic conditions in Germany were also rapidly worsening. These portents indicated that Eckener was mostly alone in Europe further to develop overseas zeppelin service, although Goodyear remained optimistic for American potentialities.

Withal, the summer of 1930 still fulfilled some of the year's earlier promise. Planned zeppelin flights were fully booked with loads of mail in sight. In June yet another honour came to the veteran airship commander. Fridtjof Nansen had died and now Eckener became the President of Aeroarctic, that irritating international group for whose explorations the zeppelin had ostensibly first been built. In July, France relinquished her postwar occupation of the Rhineland. The zeppelin promptly overflew the liberated zone, celebrating another breach in the hated Versailles Treaty. Late in the summer Eckener mollified Soviet resentment over his failure to visit Moscow on the global flight by making a special cruise to the Russian capital. Earnest discussions ensued there about Zeppelin Company assistance for Russian dirigible construction and training of Soviet airshipmen – deliberations that soon produced a secret Politburo decision to establish a bold airship programme in the next five-year plan, comprising four different dirigible types in eleven airships of various dimensions. *Pravda* exulted over German recognition of superior Communist aviation technology and thousands gaped in the streets of Moscow at the symbol of Soviet–German airship friendship overhead. The French ambassador reported his concern to Paris about the Soviet–German collaboration. It was in fact an important step in fostering Stalin's programme of Soviet aviation spectaculars that marked the 1930s. In an ironic historical circumstance Eckener returned to Germany just as the September elections produced a ninefold increase of the Nazi deputies in the Reichstag, thus establishing his one significant competitor for German emotions and turning Germany's future upon an ominous new course.[33]

The autumn zeppelin season opened reassuringly with a flight to Görlitz, in south-eastern Germany on the Czech frontier. Airship crowds overran the local airport, augmented by a hundred thousand Sudeten Germans from Bohemia, streaming in by every conceivable conveyance to celebrate German togetherness. This portent would be confirmed eight years later with a new zeppelin, but across the frontier at the then Nazi-liberated city of Reichenberg. Eckener returned to Friedrichshafen to learn how that very morning the British R101 had been destroyed in northern France. Promptly he and Captain von Schiller set off to England to march in the funeral cortège of the British airship victims. Shortly after his return to Germany, Eckener met for discussions with Hunsaker, visiting from Goodyear-Zeppelin, to plan for German–American airship developments in the coming years. It was a momentous time for the Zeppelin Company, as the decision was made that all future ships should be inflated with helium. More than ever, Eckener was tied internationally to his close association with the Americans.[34]

During 1929–30, the city of Akron and Goodyear-Zeppelin contributed to the continuing momentum of American aviation enthusiasm, technological confidence and assured government naval airship funding. Here developed a regional flood of dirigible publicity and souvenir kitsch, reminiscent of zeppelin gadgetry in pre-war Germany. Widespread and impressive were the pictures of a zeppelin mooring-mast audaciously poised atop the new New York Empire State Building, the highest structure in the world. And not far from its shadow were the Wall Street offices of the National City Bank and the nearby suites of Jerome C. Hunsaker with his Goodyear-Zeppelin planners. Here in mid-October of 1929 were created the two Delaware corporations that marked Goodyear's bid for commercial airship services across the Atlantic and Pacific: International Zeppelin Transport (IZT) and Pacific Zeppelin Transport (PZT) companies.[35]

Both new business entities were solidly all-American, though Eckener and (later) von Meister were board members of IZT. The two new companies were 'study' corporations, to analyse operational needs, likely problems, to update technological and meteorological information, and to estimate costs and financing. Had plans developed successfully, IZT would have become the holding company for three subsidiaries, responsible respectively for flight operations, airship terminal management and possibly a company to purchase ships from Goodyear and lease them to the operating firm. The new directors of IZT were recruited from the boards of major American industrial and financial powers – Goodyear, United Aircraft, Aluminum Company of America, Carbide and Chemicals Corporation, General Motors, and several New York financial stalwarts. National City Bank was the principal stockholder of the group. PZT was set up on similar subsidiary assumptions. Its governing board had the same New York firms already noted for IZT, together with prominent west-coast enterprises like Dollar Steamship, Matson Navigation, the Los Angeles *Times*, Transcontinental Air Transport, Western Air Express, Standard Oil of California, several California and Hawaiian banks *and*, later, Juan T. Trippe of PanAm. All told, the two new Goodyear-sponsored study corporations represented impressive rosters of American business expertise and industrial power, confirmed in airship endeavour just a fortnight before the Wall Street crash of late October.[36]

Now Hunsaker and his staff set out to work up various detailed studies: updating data on basic airship technology, continuing meteorological tracking across the Atlantic, designing passenger accommodations for the ships to be derived from naval blueprints, and estimating operational balance sheets for profit or loss in the enterprise. Most exciting were the 'war-gaming' imaginary airship flights that brought the sense of the various studies together into practical business formulation. The airship then favoured was a 'stretched' version of the *Akron*, about 25 per cent larger, with a payload of 80 passengers and 12 tons of express goods. Eckener joined the Hunsaker group in examining terminal sites at various points south of Philadelphia. Most favoured was the Hybla Valley south of Alexandria, VA, with a likely intermediate stop at New York's new Floyd Bennett airport. Airdocks on the Arnstein model were planned at either end of the transatlantic route. Early in 1930 Goodyear announced plans for its projected Pacific service, beginning with a California–Hawaii leg, later to be extended to Manila. PZT's longest flight would take six days (with intermediate stops at Hawaii and Tokyo), thus bettering two weeks by liner. Goodyear planners understood that the service most likely to be realized first would be with IZT, but their planning favoured PZT, for that would be an 'all-American' project, with airmail receipts locked in both ways and without dealing with the German partner and his nation's potential overflight and financial problems. Far superior to the limited accommodations of the *Graf* were Goodyear's designs for spacious passenger cabins, public rooms and promenade decks. If only the financial prospects could soon be realized ...[37]

Indeed, American airmail subsidies were at the very heart of profitable aviation operations on domestic and international routes. It was here that Juan Trippe had so constructed his Caribbean routes for PanAm. He had played a crucial role in 1925–7, devising the original federal airmail legislation. Its success vaulted Trippe from a minor domestic airline operator to become America's premier international airline entrepreneur – so much so that he soon became the State Department's 'chosen instrument' in fostering American aviation foreign relations, all in publicity linkage with Lindbergh as his most prominent pilot and close adviser. The Foreign Air Mail Act of 1928, engineered by Trippe, favoured the airplane against the airship and indeed a 1929 amendment specified payment for mail carried in a 'plane', but which (on a Post Office interpretation) excluded an 'airship'. This was the problem that Goodyear sought to remedy with new federal legislation for airship mail, express and passenger services.[38]

Building on the assurances of President Hoover in 1929 and the gala celebration at Washington in 1930 for Eckener, Goodyear enlisted Republican Senator McNary of Oregon and Republican Representative Parker of New York to introduce identical bills in the new Congress in April 1930 to obtain government support for its commercial airship enterprise. This proposed legislation funded 75 per cent of airship construction costs, upwardly revised airmail contracts, and provided merchant-marine-type limited liability for these 'common carriers engaged in foreign commerce'. Linking these craft to their naval parentage, the bills authorized use of naval airship facilities nationwide and assigned the ships to naval duty in case of war. It was a bold beginning. A Goodyear lobbyist was active in Washington and a Goodyear blimp stationed there made regular Capitol overflights for congressmen with undecided political attitudes. Hearings before various committees in both chambers ground tediously ahead. Naval authorities and Goodyear followed this slow progress with cautious optimism. But the mills of these gods ground too slowly and not very fine at all. The legislative session ended before any effective action was taken on either bill. After the upcoming mid-term elections were done, a new Congress would have to begin the work all over again. It would become a long legislative journey until a surprising climax three years later.[39]

The slow legislative procedure in Washington did not impair the enthusiasm among Akronites and naval airshipmen. Each anticipated new beginnings in their respective spheres of action. Goodyear news releases buzzed with reports of airship building and expectation of IZT and PZT. So far the Depression had touched Akron only marginally. If tyre sales were down, the offset was still robust optimism about developing America's only airship industry. Naval airshipmen there could see their future literally taking shape inside the huge Airdock. Though their *Los Angeles* was but infrequently on public view, she was busy experimenting with the trapeze for airplane hook-on and release that would become the heart of operation for the new aerial giants. Yet, theirs was still the sense of a mission only partly achieved, especially when other naval authorities threatened to remove *Patoka* from her unique sea-going mooring function because she was under-used. It was the bane of America's political compromise with her allies in 1921 (in which the Germans could build the airship for Washington, but only in a non-military configuration and just for 'civilian' use), which still constrained the effective participation of the dirigible with the Navy. Since the loss of *Shenandoah* in 1925, no rigid airship had performed its essential scouting duties in fleet exercises. In late 1930 the Allies relented, to permit *Los Angeles'* full use in fleet manoeuvres. Now she was docked for intensive overhaul, for her service in the next naval exercises of early 1931. At long last the airship could try to achieve its delayed promise as an integral factor in naval operations, though now it would confront the competition of fully matured aircraft carriers and their planes. Overall, it was still a time of promise and anticipated fulfilment.[40]

In late 1930, American naval airshipmen sympathized deeply with the British at their loss of R101, but felt secure against comparable harm by reason of their own experience and use of helium. Hunsaker promptly went to London to pursue IZT's interests in seeking transport advice from Cunard and potential use of the Cardington base for stopovers on IZT's transatlantic route. For several days he then met with Eckener at Friedrichshafen. Here he insisted that any German ships flying with IZT must use helium to assure safety for its passengers and facilities at terminals. En route back to America he paused in Paris to examine the former French airship base at Orly for possible IZT use and to stimulate French support for the service. Upon arrival at New York he felt secure for the future of commercial airships and confident of IZT guidance for the hitherto more independent heroic Eckener.

All in all, the months of 1929–30 were the most propitious times for American airship prospects since those of 1924–5. *Los Angeles* was finally being readied for work with the fleet. IZT and PZT were moving ahead in planning, despite evidence of faltering investment for these bold ventures and of the shadows of improving flying boats. Indeed, Dornier's American subsidiary (with General Motors) was already seeking to distort the slowly moving congressional legislation for the Merchant Airship Bill by special provisos for the 'common carrier' with airplane giants like the Do-X and their own mounting operating costs. Secure, however, was the visible presence of the first naval super-airship at Akron, with its sister-ship assured forthwith. Beyond these craft were the carefully developing plans for commercial versions of the naval airships, one each destined for IZT and PZT. And here Hunsaker shared Eckener's determination 'that we will only know by doing, and the sooner we get busy, the better'.[41]

1930 was to be the year in which transoceanic flights of the two great British airships would finally begin to establish a global network to reinforce Imperial economic and political ties. The Labour government also hoped thereby to divert attention from mounting economic distress at home and soon to enlist substantial Dominion financial support for the next phase of the airship programme and its exorbitant expense. Prior to the new year, R101 had already completed seven trial and publicity flights over various parts of Britain. Reports in *The Times* indicated widespread popular enthusiasm for the ship: 'Steamers blowing sirens ... trains whistling ... a large crowd in Trafalgar Square ... at most villages the schools were turned out to see us pass ... a spectacle for thousands.' But the effect was dissipated when the great skyship was absent from the skies for the first half of 1930, needing time-consuming attention to detailed technical check-ups, structural alterations, and work upon weight-reduction. R100 made a 54-hour endurance flight in January, mostly unseen in cloudy skies, noted in detail by *The Times* but quite unreported by Air Ministry publicity. These were still highly experimental craft, engaged in all the harrowing details of proving flights and corrections – facts that Thomson emphasized on several occasions, all the while expanding on the glowing future of the airships in Empire service, and took pride in the fact that R101 was 'purely British, not an imitation of the zeppelins [cheers from the listening Peers in the House of Lords]'.[42]

Expectations for the craft in late spring were disappointing and alarming. R100 was in the final stages of preparation for a flight to Canada when she suffered structural weakening during a burst of speed in trial flight. The ensuing delay was publicly justified by a request from the Canadians to postpone arrival of the ship at Montreal. Even less felicitous was the experience of R101 at the annual RAF display at Hendon in late June. Just the week earlier the ship had been test-flown to verify results of the months-long work to lighten her structure and enhance her lift. Since these efforts were not fully successful, it was now necessary to proceed with an earlier-contemplated insertion of a new section at the centre of the ship to provide the required additional lift. Furthermore, the outside cover was showing rot and splits. Emergency repairs made her ceremonial flight possible, but en route her plodding heaviness and an alarming tendency to dive suddenly forward gave indication of trouble to come. Both public and political patience were wearing thin.[43]

Lord Thomson, however, had overriding enthusiasm and confidence for the airship venture. Addressing the Imperial Press Conference the day before the Hendon celebration, he praised the achievements of the RAF and Imperial Airways. And he put special emphasis of expectation on the airships:

> The final tests will take place this year and I hope to be able to submit to the Imperial Conference in October some tangible results. I do appeal to you to lend a sympathetic ear on behalf of airships because ... they represent the most scientific of experiments and their success is a matter of incalculable significance. ... If we get the support of our Dominions and Colonies, we shall soon be able to make civil aviation 'fly by itself', and we shall put a veritable girdle of air communications around the earth.[44]

Indeed, the Dominions and Colonies had now become the crux of the political and economic future of the whole long-delayed Imperial Airship Scheme. Their financial assistance was essential to construct and maintain new intermediate airports in maritime Canada, at Malta, and en route to the Cape – not to mention support for the next pair of airships already in design. This was the crucial aviation matter that Thomson would present to the up-coming Imperial Conference and for which emphasis R101 *must* dramatically complete her round trip to India before mid-October. When informed by Cardington that insertion of the new bay on R101 must be delayed until it was certain that R100 could make the announced Canada flight, Thomson replied:

> So long as R101 is ready to fly to India by the lst week in September this further delay in getting her altered may pass. I must insist on the programme for the Indian flight being adhered to, as I have made my plans accordingly.[45]

All through the month of July the airship was in her shed at Cardington, for the work of reducing leakage in the operation of her gas valves and installing large-scale padding in her structure around the expanded gas bags to prevent loss of lift by chafing. On 29 July her frame was parted to begin insertion of the new bay.[46]

That very same morning R100 set forth on her Canadian flight, without Lord Thomson who had pressing business at home. In contrast, Burney was very much there, bustling with projects for further Anglo-Canadian airship development. Ironically, Wallis was not aboard, by now having quit airships for a new career in airplane development. Relationships between the two still-competing crews had developed into professional respect during the previous months, but morale on the Canada flight was impaired by inept disagreement between Major Herbert Scott, on board in his role as Assistant Director of Airship Development – Flying and Training, and R100 Captain Ralph Booth about priorities in flight command, and by Scott's decision, while over the Gulf of St Lawrence, to advise piercing a threatening weather front instead of circumventing it, later described as a 'reckless manoeuvre' that the ship just 'got away with'. Once arrived at Montreal, it was fair weather and great popular excitement. Thousands visited the ship moored at its St Hubert mast; multitudes saw, admired and hailed R100 on a thousand-mile cruise around central-eastern Canada. As she sailed majestically over Parliament Hill in Ottawa the carillon played 'Rule Britannia!' and an estimated hundred thousand spectators cheered. Moffett, Fulton, Rosendahl, Arnstein and Hunsaker were among the many Americans who came to Montreal to meet the British airshipmen. American film-maker Howard Hughes offered a quarter million dollars to have R100 fly down to circle New York for the opening of his spectacular movie 'Hell's Angels', about zeppelins and aviators in the recent world war. Canadian politicians pressed to be seen aboard or at least near the 'Argosy of Dreams', as Imperial Oil's

R100 at St Hubert, Montreal, August 1930

advertisement rhapsodized. Tight-lipped were the French-Canadians, who dismissed 'the monster' as an instrument of British imperialist repression. Reserved, too, was new Canadian Prime Minister Bennett about Burney's thrust that Canada should bear two-fifths of the cost of building his design for a new airship, necessarily twice the size of R100. Overall, however, the flight was a tremendous political success for Canada, which saw itself at last a coequal with the United States as a participant in transatlantic aviation.[47]

In contrast to her triumphant reception in Canada, the return of R100 to Britain occurred in virtual obscurity. Among the very few to welcome her at Cardington was Thomson himself, who praised the flight as 'a contribution to our imperial communications that will be of incalculable significance', in which he also expressed 'my high appreciation of the work of all who have been responsible for the design and construction of R100'. But his words were unheard in the absence of government publicity and as public attention focused on the deciding 1930 cricket Test against Australia. The intense interest generated a year before with the launch of R101 seemed to have evaporated. Little was done by the Air Ministry to generate public awareness of this rival airship success. Indeed, the British Post Office prohibited R100 from carrying any mails on the Canada flight, evidently disdaining Eckener's remarkable financial and propaganda successes with zeppelin mail as 'of practically no value whatsoever in establishing and developing an airmail service', or stimulating public awareness of the airship at work. Now that R100 had completed her Canada trip, the necessity for the India flight of R101 became paramount. The fate of Labour's nationalization thrust was seen to be in the balance, not to mention that of the Royal Airship Works itself.[48]

Meanwhile, R101 was completing her enlargement. Details of the India flight were in final preparation, and now prospects for future airships focused ministerial attention on the upcoming Imperial Conference. Two aspects held major significance. First was the need for improved facilities to support a 1931–2 programme for use of both ships in flights to Egypt and Canada. Thus would be met some service demand, and, above all, the airshipmen, still far less practised as compared with the Germans or even the Americans, would develop more flight experience. Both ships would require further technical attention: enlarging R100 with a new bay for added lift, and full renovation of both ships after their demanding international trips. New masts and facilities were required in Malta and maritime Canada, together with improved meteorological and navigational aids. But these were just intermediate steps toward the fully-developed airship future. Now, as of late August, DAD Colmore presented a project for two new ships, R102 and R103, each 60 per cent larger than R101 but sensible with a payload of only 50 passengers and doubled cruising range. The ships would be built at Cardington, though Howden was still on minimal stand-by. With Treasury support for the new ships tentatively approved, though crucially dependent on successful completion of the India flight, the Air Minister withheld preliminary notice of future construction, so that he could submit it personally to the Conference upon his triumphant return from Karachi. It was an audacious strategy.[49]

Thomson's political subtlety was respectfully disputed by the Ministry's new Permanent Secretary, Christopher Bullock. In correspondence with the equally new Air Member for Supply and Research (AMSR), Air Vice Marshal Hugh Dowding – later to distinguish himself in the Battle of Britain in 1940 – Bullock recorded his troubled thoughts, quite different from the enthusiastic submissions of Colmore. In his judgement neither ship was suitable for the work for which it had been designed six years before, and flights should be limited to the Egypt route alone, with new facilities in Malta, seeking regularity of operation before any new construction began. He opposed Colmore's wish to build the new ships at Cardington, arguing that they and their operations should be transferred to commercial interests. As to financial assistance from the Dominions, Bullock doubted that even £100 000 from Canada could fill the gap, while Australia (if she could find any money for air development) would only favour extending Indian plane service to her country – not to mention that political upheaval in India had so weakened revenues there that even new internal services might not be funded. Thus new construction would overburden the anticipated Air Estimates and weaken the National Exchequer.

> My primary objective [he continued] has been to ensure that, if the Secretary of State insists on a gamble, he does so with his eyes open and realises that he is making a radical departure from the wisely cautious policy he has hitherto pursued.

It is not clear that this draft memorandum for Thomson, which Bullock discussed in mid-September with Dowding, reached the Air Minister in final form before his departure. But in any event, no matter how successful the India flight, hard new times were closing in upon Thomson.[50]

Reconstruction of R101 was complete by 1 October. Her gas bags were renovated, new padding was added against their chafing, and a new cover was installed from forward centre to the stern of the ship. Now time was of the essence. Dowding himself was aboard for a brief trial flight, which he described as smooth and uneventful, but as an experienced RAF pilot the new AMSR knew little about airships. He relied upon the assurances of Richmond and Colmore as to fitness of the virtually new ship, but later bitterly rued his role in officially issuing the new certificate of airworthiness.[51] In optimism about the improved lift, four men were added at the last moment for the flight, including RAAF Squadron Leader William Palstra, Australian Liaison Officer at the Air Ministry, officially pressed upon Thomson as the symbolic presence of Canberra in anticipation of extended airship service to Australia. R101 left Cardington early in the evening of 4 October 1930 in what would become rapidly worsening weather. The ship had barely three tons of spare static lift to rise from her mast. She had been further burdened by several tons of extra fuel taken aboard to give some hours of respite from the noisy and odorous refuelling at the mast of Ismailia during a ceremonial dinner party on board – which was to be embellished by an additional half-ton of blue Axminster carpeting over the workaday airship floor. The flight seemed to proceed uneventfully until the early morning of 5 October over northern France. Then, in now punishing stormy weather, the ship suddenly pitched, dived twice and crashed near Beauvais. The resultant hydrogen explosion killed all but six of the fifty-four men aboard, including Thomson, Sefton Brancker (Director of Civil Aviation), Richmond, Colmore, Squadron Leader Michael Rope (designer), and Scott – much of the cream of Britain's airship builders and fliers. It was a devastating blow to airship optimism worldwide, so buoyed by zeppelin successes and American anticipations.[52]

A week later the funeral cortège of R101 victims moved silently through the streets of London, with a memorial service at St Paul's Cathedral, en route to final rest at Cardington cemetery. Over a million citizens lined the streets to watch the solemn procession, which included Eckener and American naval personnel. It was London's largest public outpouring between celebration of the Armistice in 1918 and the coronation of King George VI in 1937. In disaster R101 commanded public attention never previously attained either by her psychic attraction or by all the Air Ministry publicity.[53]

The cause of the misfortune was not fully understood at the time and has only recently been clarified by careful research. Factors in the

The two patriarchs of R101, prior to departure of a flight to the Midlands, 4 October 1930, Lt Col. V. C. Richmond, Assistant Director of Airship Development, and Lord Thomson, Secretary of State for Air. Both were lost in the disaster at Beauvais

accident were multiple. Rebuilt R101 was insufficiently tested due to her hurried departure. Aviation meteorological expertise at the time was in its infancy. Continued chafing of all the gasbags during the unexpectedly worsening storm caused loss of normal (static) lift. That loss required flying dynamically – steering the airship upward under full power at about an 8-degree angle to produce an additional aerofoil lift like an airplane wing. As the increasing storm beat upon the top of the uplifted prow of the dirigible, the unrenewed cover was ruptured, thus exposing forward gasbags to further damage and diminishing the vital dynamic lift. In the final sudden dives of the ship there was a quick control-car decision to reduce speed by half and thus was lost what little remained of dynamic lift. When the ship made an abrupt landing from low altitude, flares were accidentally ignited and these set off a violent explosion of dangerously intermixed hydrogen and air. For all its glamour and proven superiority of comfortable long-distance flight to date, the airship was still in experimental development, fraught with risk and requiring intensive operational skill, which so far only the Germans had sufficiently acquired.[54]

What accounts for the British undertaking such a potentially hazardous flight? This was still an era of pioneering enthusiasm and romance for all aviation. Toleration of risk was high among all aviators and seen by the public as heroic – splendid in success, tragic in failure. All airships lost some lift during flight by seemingly unavoidable gas leakage. Flying dynamically was an accepted practice, though Eckener insisted that the Germans avoid it by more intricate management of gas and ballast. Unexpected or tempestuous weather was seen as the airman's unavoidable lot. Just before take-off, Lieutenant Commander Noel Atherstone, First Officer on the flight, wrote in his detailed diary:

> Everyone is rather keyed up now as we all feel that the future of airships very largely depends on what sort of a show we put up ... Let's hope for luck and do our best.

And Thomson had expressed a layman's excitement when he wrote to Princess Marthe Bibescu a month before the departure:

> To ride the storm has always been my ambition and who knows but we may realise it on the way to India but not, I hope, with undue risk to human lives.[55]

What, more precisely, were the likely political pressures on the men of R101 to make the flight on Thomson's tight schedule? No doubt there was a strong desire to achieve at last the consummation of six long years of government experimentation and development, despite some doubts expressed privately to Brancker by some experts about the technological readiness of their ship. This impulse was narrowly focused upon team loyalty, which deceptively shored up their technological confidence. This group motivation was largely untested by regular and intimate professional contact with other British airshipmen or interaction with the Germans and Americans. Indeed, despite some friendly professional and social association between the two teams, there was a bizarre inequality in the formal testing of their respective processes and product. The technological development and construction of R100 were constantly checked, step by step, by the Cardington team; but Cardington never formally consulted Howden – or any other airship authority – about its own development.[56] There was a prideful sense of maintaining the continuity of British airship progress since 1917. All along, the evident competition with R100 was felt as favouring their side in that contest. Then, still further delays opened the way for the rival to make the Canada flight. Now, no matter what needs might still be felt for their ship, the officers of R101 could not plead, as Bullock did, that they were still not ready to take off for India. Nevil Shute later put it thus in his critical memoir:

> The success of our Canadian flight undoubtedly was instrumental in bringing about the disaster to R101. Up to that point it was still possible for the Cardington officials to declare that neither ship was fit for a long flight. But when we came back relatively safe and sound from Canada that last way of escape was closed to them: now they had to fly to India or admit defeat.[57]

Thus, trapped competitively, still harbouring numerous doubts, just moderately experienced with R101 but with a strong commitment to Britain's Imperial airship cause, these men rode R101 into the storm.

As with the airshipmen, one can at best speculate cautiously about Lord Thomson's personal urgency to make the India flight when he did. Leaving aside allegations that Thomson sought to become Viceroy of India, all evidence confirms his strong career ambitions and wish to strengthen the sinews of Empire with a network of fast airships. No doubt he also felt strong pressure to bring the years of costly airship expenditure to obvious fruition – and where better than in a closer link with the Jewel of the Empire? He sought then to influence the Imperial Conference to support the Imperial Airship Scheme with hitherto-lacking subsidies for an intermediate sustaining flight programme and then for the new airships envisioned by Colmore. With such successes he might deter the thoughts of his senior civil servants to turn airship activity away from socialist government sponsorship towards conservative capitalist enterprise. In a larger, Imperial sense he quite likely expected the dirigible to make a significant psychological impact on the Indian subcontinent. Possibly he thought of an internal cruise between Karachi and New Delhi, much like R100 in Canada, to strengthen British prestige in offsetting Gandhi's troublesome activities and countering the appeal of strident opposition at the Indian Congress. Similarly significant was the occasion for the ceremonial state dinner aboard R101 en route, at the mast in Ismailia. Here the airshipmen would be aligned with the RAF, recently responsible for controlling unrest in the Middle East and supporting the governments of Iraq, Persia and the newly-independent Saudi Arabia – all by concentration of its forces in Egypt. And like India, the Nile Kingdom was in political transition towards some relaxation of British rule, in negotiations for which it was wise to impress the Egyptians with all forms of British aviation prowess. Royal Engineer though he was by training and identity, Thomson still had too much confidence in the work of his technological subordinates, for whose calculations and experiments he failed to seek competent appraisal. Thus he embarked on the flight to India with self-deceptive enthusiasm and a kind of self-assured innocence, an ambitious leader resolved to see it through with other airshipmen.[58]

Finally, how might a successful flight of R101 have played into the political fortunes of the Labour Government? Recall, first of all, that the worldwide popular image of the airship was riding the wave of German zeppelin achievements, American naval airship-building, and British imperial sentiments. Success for R101 would only have confirmed that optimism, though Wallis's biographer J. E. Morpurgo goes too far in writing that 'Thomson could bring off a great coup, face-saving to the Government, to the Party, and ultimately of genuine advantage to the nation'. In fact, fifteen months after coming to power with a slim majority, Labourites were depending frequently on the uncertain support of Liberal members to pass their legislation in Parliament. The growing Depression and escalating unemployment were weakening public confidence in Labour as it wrestled with little effect to meet these problems. Given the magnificent public presence in London at the funereal return of the men of R101, there could comparably have been some upsurge of public sentiment upon their arrival crowned in success. In Parliament the question of India's future was growing in importance and indications were that Labour leniency might seek to confer Dominion status upon New Delhi. Conservatives vigorously opposed Labour here, with Churchill splendidly in the oratorical lead. Here a psychological boost from R101 might have aided Labour's cause. As a party, however, the Labourites were fracturing over various issues, and the ageing MacDonald was weakening under the strain. Thomson was his protégé and close personal friend; his triumphant return with R101 could have invigorated party cohesiveness and brought strength and prestige to its faltering leader. Funding would at least have been found for the intermediate flight programme, but new airships? It is unwise to conjecture beyond these possibilities.[59]

The R101 disaster was the beginning of the end for twelve years of British political conflict over rigid airships for Imperial commercial flight. Initial discord with the Royal Navy in 1918–19 gave way to five years of harassing dispute between government groups and commercial interests. The resolution of 1924 injected ideological strains that transformed normal technological competition into an unnecessary contest for political prestige and influence. It was the psychological appeal of that technology which gave this contention such a fervid quality – a foretaste of international rivalry in supersonic aircraft development half a century later. So, for the British, it all came to a crashing end. Airship R100 remained thereafter gradually deteriorating at Cardington in face of the rapidly worsening Depression and exchequer deficits. In August 1931 the MacDonald government fell and soon afterwards R100 was scrapped, as were all further plans for airship development. During those years the other kind of aircraft competition had impinged on the vaunted superiority of airships in long-distance flight. The airplane, notably the flying boat, became technologically feasible for transoceanic flight. For the immediate future, however, the airship still had a strong, if now flawed, popular appeal and influence in Germany and America. World airship attention would now focus upon Friedrichshafen and Akron.[60]

6
A Buffeting for German and American Airships, 1931–35

Five sets of circumstances affected developments in the airship between 1931 and 1935. Never absent was the impact of the great worldwide Depression. In remarkable counterpoint came the astounding success of the German zeppelin, both in commercial service to Brazil and in undertaking a new generation of advanced airships for North Atlantic operation. A disappointing third series of events produced the failure of the American airships by naval neglect and adverse winds. Then, by mid-1933, both the German and the American dirigibles were subject to manipulation or victimization by strong political forces: the National Socialists in Berlin and the hard operational prejudices in the American Navy. And finally, as of early 1935, only Germany was left to continue zeppelin expansion, which now faced the rapidly maturing flying boats.

In the early 1930s, millions in Germany and abroad still yearned to have the thrill of 'experiencing' the *Graf Zeppelin*; invitations for the ship flooded in from a wide variety of localities and agencies. Though some observers considered these trips mere 'circus flights', Eckener felt them to be crucial in advancing the zeppelin dream, which he needed to foster his enterprise and saw as aiding German spiritual development. During 1931 the zeppelin made more than twenty national and international flights, covering a remarkable total distance of nearly eighty thousand kilometres – an aviation achievement hitherto unparalleled. Six of the international flights achieved notable political impact.

The first of these politically significant journeys was back to the Middle East, and this time directly to Egypt. In 1929 Britain had refused permission, reserving the first airship visit to the Pyramids for England. However, with R101 no longer in contention, Eckener quickly secured Britain's reluctant agreement to a zeppelin flight to Egypt. He also soon offered discreet technical consultations on safety for R100, still awaiting its fate at Cardington.[1] While apparently no such contacts occurred, Squadron Leader Booth, captain of the R100 Canada flight, was specially invited to fly with the zeppelin to Egypt. Abul Fath of Cairo's daily *Al Ahram* was again aboard. He described the great enthusiasm of thousandfold Egyptian crowds en route to Giza. British soldiers secured the airship at its landing, all very proper for technical safety but otherwise not felicitous. Wrote Abul Fath:

> What shocked us when we got off the airship was that all the people around were British – not an Egyptian in sight … [They came] later, but only after a time, long enough to leave the passengers with a certain [British] impression.

And a later correspondent reported:

> In cruising majestically over Cairo, the *Graf Zeppelin* captured the Egyptians' imagination, their enthusiasm also fired by the belief that the spectacle was somehow symbolic, auguring well for their rising national aspirations after centuries of alien tutelage. Recollections of the airship were passed on to successive generations, and in the local language, the phrase '*zayy al-zeppelin*' (like the zeppelin) came to signify anything that was large, impressive and almost mythical in character and proportions.[2]

Somewhat as happened in Egypt, the flight to Vienna in early July nurtured repressed feelings among many Austrians, from socialists to right-wing nationalists, for closer association with Germany. Since 1918 Austria had been forced by international treaties to maintain its artificial independence from ties with Germany. But change was in the wind. In March 1931 Vienna and Berlin had announced plans for an Austro-German customs union. France and her allies vigorously fought this likely forerunner of an *Anschluss*, brought the matter into the World Court and pressured Vienna to withdraw its participation. The zeppelin visit coincided with these negative events and much resulting Austrian frustration. Crowds streamed into Vienna by special trains to join top officials of the government and a hundred thousand citizens in celebrating the zeppelin symbolism of their long-denied national consummation. News and radio accounts of the occasion were fulsome, despite a frightening mid-European banking crisis. The

Austrian 'Zeppelintag' celebration was a bold public response to French efforts to keep the German cousins apart, and a widely-felt relief from other grim economic and political realities – all with an implied promise of a brighter day ahead.[3]

In contrast to the localized political impact of the zeppelin in Egypt and Austria, the polar flight of July 1931 had worldwide resonance in verifying the airship as an instrument of geographical exploration and scientific research. Furthermore, the flight tested the zeppelin in extreme climates, touching the Arctic before venturing a bit later into tropical climes. As financial plans were made for this expensive project – at long last achieving the aerial objective of the *Zeppelin-Spende* of 1925–6 and beyond, the woes of the Depression became evident. Initially news magnate William Randolph Hearst had thought to underwrite an elaborate scheme to have a polar submarine meet the polar airship at sea level inside the Arctic Circle, but when prospects for this stunt failed, Hearst's support also died. German publisher Ullstein partially filled the financial gap; for the rest, Eckener approached German makers of all conceivable kinds of instrumentation used on the flight. As this search faltered, philatelists came again to the rescue. Six hundred pounds of German and Russian mail were carried, much of it featured in a dramatic exchange of post with the Soviet icebreaker *Malygin* at Franz Josef Land. Here also appeared veteran Italian polar flier, Umberto Nobile, virtually banished from Rome when his semi-rigid *Italia* crashed near the North Pole in 1928. Worldwide publicity for the polar flight, actually just to the edge of the Polar Circle to meet insurance limitations, brought welcome news relief into the deepening shadows of the Depression. The study of geography reaped a small reward and the frayed political confidence in man's ability to cope with challenge enjoyed a momentary respite.[4]

Eckener's most important airship and political venture now promised to bear fruit. Throughout 1931 work at Lake Constance focused on opening regular commercial zeppelin service to South America. To this end Eckener visited Paris in June, seeking permission for repeated overflights of southeastern France. In a feature article in the *New York Times*, he expressed his hope for a spirit of mutual cooperation that could grow out of the linking of individual economic interests and gradually reduce the poisoned atmosphere between Paris and Berlin. While awaiting the slow French response, Eckener continued to fly the *Graf* roundabout Germany, to Iceland, to Russia, and again to England. All the while he kept a weather eye on the progress of the flying boat Do-X that was slowly, and in financial distress, making its way from Lisbon to New York with many stops in West Africa, Brazil, the Caribbean, and east-coast American cities. Just three days after Do-X finally thundered over Manhattan, the *Graf Zeppelin* opened four-day service to Brazil.[5]

Contrary to Eckener's plea for mutual understanding, French political omens for approving regular zeppelin overflights were not good. The earlier experimental trips had brought various complaints that the Germans were cruising low and slowly to photograph the Schneider-Creusot armament works or other sensitive localities. The French consul at Tangiers had complained that the zeppelin made a great impression on the natives there, hardly to the benefit of France.[6] More important, the zeppelin was now a threat to French commercial aviation interests in South America, where Aéropostale was hitherto dominant and whose presence fostered French prestige there. In Brazil, the zeppelin connected with the developing Brazilian-German airline Condor that flew to much of South America. Thrice during 1931 the airship landed at Recife, testing the hazards of tropical service and requiring a specially negotiated French overflight permit for *each* trip. Brazilians cheered, Germans celebrated their technology and its political advantage, and the French nursed their frustration at the loss of business and prestige. In the following years all three kinds of response grew in intensity.[7]

In Germany itself, by the end of 1931, political power was moving from the Reichstag to the streets, where paramilitary bands of right- and left-wing extremists fought each other weekly. The disintegration of Germany threatened. Like other prominent spokesmen, Eckener was swept into the maelstrom of political controversy. In January 1932 he participated in a radio series on 'German Crisis and Hope', calling on fellow Germans to unite behind a government trying its best for the nation, and favouring Hindenburg's continuance in office. Although he did not intend his speech as campaigning for embattled Chancellor Brüning, for whom he had already refused to put his airship on a vote-catching flight, public response was mixed and often rude. Private correspondence poured in upon Eckener, both praising his courage and urging him to stick with flying his zeppelin rather than trying to pilot the ship of State. In July he firmly established his anti-Nazi position by refusing use of the huge Friedrichshafen hangar for a monster south-German Hitler demonstration. In November he stood with the German National Association in another effort to rally the varied forces of the German political centre. This venture, too, was a failure. Wrote the influential *Deutsche Zeitung*: 'Dr Eckener is building castles in the air ...

The centre is politically dead. And a miracle of its reawakening cannot be achieved, even with the name of Dr Eckener'. As 1933 opened, the shabby journal *Neues Deutschland* featured a front-page sensation:

1933: Danger for Hitler?
Is Soviet Germany Coming?
Will Hindenburg be Followed by Hitler or Dr Eckener?

Portraits of all three men graced the purple prose. Though just a yellow-press shot in the dark, Eckener later said that this article, more than any other event of 1932, made him an enduring target of Nazi hostility.[8]

For the Zeppelin Enterprise itself, 1932 was barely a prosperous year and initial construction of the LZ129 slowed as funding faltered, even though the cash position of the business did benefit from the sale of its interests in Dornier. Flights occurred to Holland, England and Danzig, but effort was mostly focused on developing the South American operation. Eckener made some headway in difficult negotiations with Brazil to ensure more frequent direct service to Rio by having Brazil build a fully equipped terminal at nearby Santa Cruz with luxurious passenger facilities. Eighteen times that year the zeppelin crossed the equator on nine round trips, always featuring festive ceremonies derived from maritime tradition. Brazilian-Germans gave their enthusiastic support as the zeppelin began cruising further afield over areas with pro-German citizens. Less positive political notes were still evident. As before, Eckener had to negotiate delicately with the ill-disposed French for each overflight and, as before, the PanAm flying boats at Rio gave Eckener pause for reflection on the future of airship legislation in America. All Germany continued in political tumult. The zeppelin was in hangar for its annual renovation when Hitler came to power in late January 1933, being greeted enthusiastically at Friedrichshafen by many Company workers. It was a momentous turning point in the fortunes of zeppelin enterprise and an ominous harbinger of a grave non-political crisis that would soon burst upon Goodyear-Zeppelin in America.[9]

Meanwhile, the Soviet Union was plunging full force into manipulating the psychological attraction of airships for Communist political propaganda and advantage.

The Russian venture into airship designing, building and flying was a distinct aspect in the Soviet ideological thrust to use science, engineering and technology to manipulate the forces of social change towards Marxist-Leninist political goals. Accordingly, scientists and engineers

'Who comes after Hindenburg? – Hitler or Eckener?' German press speculation, 1933

held a prestigious position at the top of the Soviet societal pyramid, where they enjoyed optimum preferment in the Communist Party. With their planning and forecasts these so-called 'objective' thinkers and practitioners set the pace for Russian industrial development by way of extravagant and bureaucratically detailed five-year plans. In every way Russians were pressed and motivated by these ideological and allegedly doable drives to develop their Eurasian continent as leader of world Communism. It was seen that these ideological emphases could be intensified by using the inherent psychological impact of huge airships, as already noted worldwide.[10]

During the Stalinist 1930s, aviation was especially favoured to demonstrate and advertise Soviet technological achievements and thus also to prove the political correctness of Communism. Here great airships were assigned to play a major role. More than vast industrial complexes, huge dams and deep subways, aircraft could bring these evidences of Soviet superiority into every town and collective farm. Furthermore, giant airships appeared (as of 1930) to be the key to developing more widespread and rapid communication and transport over Russia's nine time-zones and thus could more readily be opened the great undeveloped resources of distant Siberia and the remote southeastern Muslim regions. Of course, plans and pictures appeared far more quickly than actual airships. All these prospects for Russian airship development were spread wide by the mass media of books, news stories, films, posters and radio prophecies. Notable was the use of postage stamps to carry images of great Russian airships at work into every corner of the USSR even before the first construction site had been developed. Eckener's visit to Moscow occasioned the opening gun in a philatelic media campaign over the next four years, showing an impressive rigid airship (the unidentified *Graf Zeppelin*) against a background of massive industrial construction and featuring an idealistic Communist worker speeding up the first five-year plan to complete it in four years. These phantom airships were credible factors in the vast euphoric propaganda of the Soviet Union.[11]

Into this world of excited planning and naive technological optimism came Italian airshipman Umberto Nobile, virtually banished from Italy, to achieve the great projects of Russian airship development decreed by the Politburo in later 1930. Just prior to his arrival, Soviet philatelic propaganda had set the sights for him with a second issue of widely distributed propaganda stamps. These featured zeppelins over steppes and industrial centres or above routes linking all Russia together; characteristically the highest value featured Russian science at work. When Nobile arrived in Russia for his longer residence in July 1931, he explored a part of Siberia by plane and met the *Graf Zeppelin* near the Arctic Circle, an event advertised in a new set of philatelic praise that again used the zeppelin for Communist propaganda. Thereupon Nobile settled in at Moscow for five years of airship work for the Soviet Union.[12]

His memoirs convey a tragicomic chronology of high hopes, incredible technological missteps and some successes. Initially he was

1931 Russian poster advocating an Airship Building Programme

instructed to begin with a revised grandiose plan to build several hundred airships of different types and sizes. Yet here the factories themselves had still to be raised from sites in muddy fields, and eager, half-educated men and women had to be trained and worked into cadres of airship builders – not to mention training airship crews. Enthusiasm was rampant, as were the bureaucratic mix-ups and continuing incremental technological mistakes. In May 1932, another revised five-year plan projected 50 different semi-rigids up to 3.5 million cu. ft and eight rigids from 4 to 9 million cu. ft. If Nobile was aghast, not so the propaganda. In 1934, new stamps rhapsodized the Soviet rigids in full glory. Airship *Pravda* (truth!) was pictured emerging from the Akron Airdock placed in a Russian landscape. Airship *Lenin* (of course!) was poised over another map of Siberian routes, while the name of Stalin's faithful paladin Voroshilov graced yet another zeppelin giant. It was enough to puff the breasts of many a comrade: these highly visible gigantic aerial manifestations of Communism's thrust to catch up and overtake the West.[13]

It is important, however, to indicate what Russian science and workmanship did indeed accomplish, both before and with Nobile's direction. By late 1932, four small non-rigids were built at Leningrad and Moscow. These were the initial construction and operational schooling for Soviet airshipmen that Nobile then developed into the more sophisticated builders and fliers of his own ships. Between 1933 and 1936 five Nobile semi-rigids were built and flown with varying success, while detailed plans were completed for an additional major rigid airship. As all airshipmen learned by doing – and sometimes not doing well – so did the Russians. All five ships made flights of various distances over different regions of Russia; one, in fact, achieved a world flight duration record in 1937. Yet two of these ships were destroyed by fire in hangar accidents; two others crashed with loss of life in accidents. The propaganda hyperbole and images went on; the failures were concealed in repressive silence, with death or disgrace for the participants. Nobile later praised his Russian designers, builders and fliers but complained bitterly about the immense unnecessary complications for his work: the incredible expectations and beliefs as to what could be accomplished in shortest time; the appalling conditions of construction and of workers' incompetence; the constant interruptions of work by sudden endless meetings for technical disputes or internal propaganda exercises; the abominable quality of materials from subcontractors and their chronic delays in delivery. Always threatening was the sudden loss of qualified personnel (at long last trained), either by abrupt appointment elsewhere or, increasingly after 1935, by disappearance into the jaws of Stalinist purges. Indeed, it appears that every Russian airshipman or builder who had contact with European experts had vanished by 1939 – including the prestigious Professor Samoilovich, who had rescued Nobile in 1928 and been with Eckener on the polar flight of 1931. Meanwhile, the publicity went inexorably forward in newspapers, trade journals, engineering shows and whatnot. An airship still soared above Russain cities on one postage stamp of 1938, but by now far more spectacular achievements had been marked by Soviet planes at home or in some international competition abroad. Thus Russia's airships, their political propaganda, and their most notable personnel quickly disappeared into impenetrable silence.[14]

In America there would be seen the culmination of dirigible enthusiasm in the achievement at long last of two technologically state-of-the-art airships with long airborne endurance for wide naval scouting and the promise of their early adaptation for commercial airship operations.

The opening phase of America's anticipated naval airship vitality began with an obvious link with the recent past. In February 1931 the *Los Angeles* was ready for her first and only operation as a fully participating naval unit. Flying in from Lakehurst to moor with *Patoka* off the Pacific entry to the Panama Canal, she was sent to scout for her side of Fleet Problem XII against an opponent manoeuvring with a diversified force, including two aircraft carriers. Although she early discovered her adversary, her operation was at such short range that she was soon targeted in tactical hazard – and was then 'shot down' by carrier planes. Officers and men in every sector of Fleet Problem XII promptly engaged in heated controversy about the effectiveness of the naval airship. 'NAVAL MEN DOUBT AIRSHIP WAR VALUE', proclaimed the *New York Times*. While airshipmen found her round-trip participation from Lakehurst a record in time, distance and endurance, much of the Navy Admiralty and all the carrier men disdained her performance as negligible, if not outright ridiculous. This dispute would endure for the next four years. With *Akron* and *Macon*, from 1932 onward, the training and development of on-board scouting planes began in earnest, though *Akron* did not survive to participate in a formal Fleet Problem. *Macon* participated in various naval exercises between late 1933 and early 1935, but all these assignments were in the same kind of limited scouting area and always tactically proximate to the carriers. Here the Fleet Problem judges were more realistic in their evaluation of durability for a helium-borne airship, but still ZRS5 (*Macon*) was soon judged destroyed, though then reinstated in service as 'ZRS6' or 'ZRS7'. In all, *Macon* and her devised sisters were 'shot down' at least eight times during these fifteen months. She did not survive her accident of early 1935 to participate as planned in Fleet Problem XVI, which was staged west of Hawaii, where, for the first time, a naval airship would have had the broad area and manoeuvring scope to justify the scouting function for which all American naval airships had originally been designed.[15]

As a result of these naval misuses of the scouting dirigibles, American airshipmen developed an animus towards top Admiralty decisions about their ships in general and towards the aggressive carrier fliers in particular. Britain had already earlier had a comparable experience. Historian Hartcup recalls:

> 'In the RAF', wrote T. E. Lawrence [of Arabia] after the R101 disaster, 'there exists a jealous and ineradicable feeling against the lighter-than-air ships. We are so pinned to aircraft that we cannot bear a good word of the gas bags'. This feeling may have made the Cardington team more stubbornly determined that their airship must succeed.

No doubt a comparable circumstance was emerging in American naval aviation. Admiral King's biographer indicates that the Admiral had no particular bias for airships and felt, like Moffett, that they should be given full opportunities for experimental development in fleet exercises. He noted how carrier pilots had 'shot down' *Los Angeles* almost immediately in Fleet Problem XII and had done so 'with singular pleasure'. He disliked the contemptuous way in which airships were often dismissed as 'gasbags' or 'pigbags' and their fighting men called 'helium heads'. Forty years after the naval misuse of airships, Admiral Rosendahl still recalled that era with singular bitterness. During a long discussion in 1974, Rosie's conversation was peppered with frequent references to naval participants of that time as 'sons o' bitches' (men of carrier aviation) and 'horse's asses' (Admiralty officers positioning airships in tactical combat situations). Vice Admiral Scott E. Peck, navigator of the *Macon*, reminisced with less rancour in 1978: 'We were made sitting ducks out there – huge targets, slow manoeuvrability, and unable to use any of our five onboard scout planes in self-defence. Those carrier flyboys just loved it!' No wonder that already by 1932 American rigid airshipmen were developing an in-group defensiveness which tended to isolate them from broader aviation trends. No wonder that they welcomed their professional association with the German airshipmen (zeppelin swastikas later notwithstanding) and nurtured a passionate devotion to their ships which replicates among a new generation of enthusiasts today.[16]

If the carriers and their fliers were becoming a bane of the airshipmen's lives, it was no less so for the senior officers of the 'Gun-Club'.

Their concept of naval warfare was still derived from Mahan's vision of a climactic encounter between warring battle fleets. The Jutland clash of 1916 had only partly realized that concept, since the Germans contrived to slip away from the British Fleet. Here was born the momentary myth that scouting German zeppelins had alerted the Germans to escape the British grasp. Though soon belied by valid German evidence, this explanation appealed to some Allied naval experts and was still heard as late as 1926 in Congress to justify building two new super airships as scouts for the American Battle Fleet. At that very moment, however, the experimental aircraft carrier *Langley* was developing her unique independent expertise. Initially conceived as a seagoing airfield for planes to scout for the Battle Fleet and defend it in action, the carrier fliers were rapidly developing their own fighting initiative with bombers and torpedo planes. This aerial prowess threatened the monopoly of heavy seagoing artillery, worse yet of the in-line structure of the Battle Fleet, and – worst of all – of the authority of the 'Gun-Club' admirals alone to determine the course of battle action at sea. By 1932, with four carriers in service, their captains and fliers were increasingly restive in their roles subordinate to 'Gun-Club' decision. They had fully developed their own fighting skills to determine and initiate action against the enemy, as demonstrated in their strikes at the Panama Canal in 1929 and at Pearl Harbor in 1932. But in one crucial respect the 'Gun-Club' Admiralty still held a possible trump card. The carriers and their planes (as of 1932) were limited to an action radius of about a 150 miles from the moving fleet. The airship as a battle-fleet scout, however, had far greater range and endurance and, although vulnerable to enemy action, could provide crucially important intelligence for the fleet before probably being destroyed at a far distance. Here the airship could function to maximum advantage of the Battle Fleet alone as it sought the enemy in the western Pacific in pursuit of warplan ORANGE. No wonder that Navy propaganda posters of 1931 showed *Los Angeles* with trapeze plane ready for release, 'going everywhere' as eyes of the battleships in line at sea below – and not a carrier in sight. In this image the battleship was supreme, with the airship as its far-ranging informer, each beholden to the other. But the image was deceptive, for by 1932 few naval leaders had much confidence in the airship that was developing so slowly.[17]

In another and decisive respect, the fate of naval airships was being determined quite apart from contemplation and later engagement as naval scouts. From 1929 onward, warplan ORANGE was fundamentally

US Navy recruiting poster 1931 – not an aircraft carrier in sight!

changing in its essential character. All through the 1920s, the warplanners working under successive commanders-in-chief, the General Board and with the constant testing of anticipated campaigns at the Naval War College, had postulated a quick war. The American Fleet would press directly across the Pacific to liberate the Philippines and then proceed to defeat Japan in her own waters. Endless re-fighting of the Jutland battle in war-gaming at Newport gave promise of climactic victory. By the end of the decade, however, accumulated wisdom indicated less likelihood of success in the fast-moving version of ORANGE.

Various kinds of attrition inherent in the 7000-mile thrust westward, plus the effects of anticipated Japanese strikes on the American naval flanks, reduced the estimates of success to uncertainty. From 1930 onward, the warplans were increasingly adjusted to advise sequential capture of Japanese mandated islands in the central Pacific and their conversion into forward American naval bases. Now the carriers would acquire new operational sites from which to operate with the fleet in whatever mode the Admiralty would order. Since 1925 the war-gamers at Newport had been relating carrier tactical engagement with fleet activities. In succeeding years these studies constantly intensified to become a series of interrelated strategic reviews, always interacting with broad plans for Fleet Problems and studies of their results. Since there were no airships with the Fleet in those years, there was little consideration of airship possibilities in these war games. When some of these students later became fleet commanders, they had thus little inclination to consider airships belatedly available for their use. It was, indeed, as though the Navy was now encumbered with an expensive and complicated ship of no tactical value and uncertain other use.[18]

Into these rapidly changing technological and operational circumstances the two new super-airships were born. ZRS4 *Akron* was built between November 1929 and August 1931. Goodyear and the Navy had few of the vexations experienced by the builders of R101. Temptations for further technological experimentation abounded but were restricted by close Navy discipline. America's version of unfavourable construction was caused, as historian Smith wrote, 'by a farrago of trivial events that made the *Akron* an object of public controversy and harassed the airship even beyond her tragic end'. Then came rumours that *Akron* was a victim of inferior materials and shoddy workmanship. These, and other media airship squalls, were welcome news diversions for editors swamped in a flood of Depression stories about economic woe and social distress. But it was also evident that airships in America still generated a wide scope of public interest and identification.[19]

In design and construction, *Akron* and *Macon* were essentially twins. Their postulation assumed that very wide-range scouting was essential for effective naval deployment over the broad seas, notably in the western Pacific, focus of warplan ORANGE in a conflict with Japan. Here was developed a unique technological and operational improvement of these naval scouts. The trapeze (already mentioned above in experimentation with *Los Angeles*) was the device to launch and recover pairs of four Curtiss F-9C observation planes. These would be launched on dual divergent flight patterns, at left and right 90-degree angles from the airship, on a radius of about 125 miles outbound and return, at a speed of 100 knots. Meanwhile, the airship proceeded forward on a steady course at 50 knots, at the centre of the moving diamond pattern, retrieving the duo a hundred miles or so further on for pilot rotation and refuelling. Then a second pair would fly out on the same pattern for subsequent retrieval. A maximum of five pairs could be launched and retrieved during a long summer day and could scout an astounding area of more than a hundred thousand square miles. Thus *Akron* and *Macon* were to function as flying aircraft carriers for the planes that would do the scouting. It was a bold and remark-ably innovative plan to improve aerial scouting for the fleet. But would the fleet now make use of the innovation?[20]

Akron was launched in early August 1931 and christened by Mrs Herbert Hoover in full attendance of naval leaders and fliers and Goodyear builders. In what was probably the greatest day of Akron industrial history, 200 000 citizens and visitors enjoyed the carnival-like celebration. Admiral Moffett invoked airship pioneers and sounded his keynote for the future: America now led the world in airship devel-opment, with peerless naval scouts arriving and commercial ships soon to follow. Radio and newsreels carried the message to all America and the world beyond. Especially heartening in the developing Depression weariness was news that a delaying Congress had finally approved funding for the sister ship. But too much was publicly expected too soon. Instead of soaring off to scout for the fleet, Rosendahl kept the ship hangar-bound for two months of rigorous testing before *Akron* emerged from the Airdock. Subsequent trial flights were cautiously brief and the first long naval flight in early 1932 produced no sensa-tions. More rumours were spread among an impatient national public, alleging further airship inadequacies and reviving earlier naval derision about these 'worthless' weapons. After several months of troubleshoot-ing and trials, *Akron* took off in May 1932 on a transcontinental flight, with west-coast extension north towards Canada, in the familiar role of naval publicity appearances. But there was little news of planes on the flying trapeze. After Rosendahl went off to required sea duty, his suc-cessor put the ship through her paces to prepare her as an effective fleet participant. This effort required much tedious and repetitious practice to integrate *Akron*'s scout planes, by way of the complicated and ever-troublesome trapeze mechanism, into the working of the airship. At the same time it was necessary to devise the whole new dimension of scouting flight patterns for the planes and the in-flight relationship of the dirigible navigation to its winged brood. Moffett constantly pressed for acceleration and perfection of these efforts and made several flights with the *Akron* to urge the training forward. It was thus no surprise when he appeared for a flight in early April of 1933 to take the ship up towards New England on a routine exercise to assist in calibration of seaboard RDF stations. Tragically, and again with still imperfect weather predictions, *Akron* unexpectedly encountered the worst storm front in a decade. Five hours into her last flight, in the early morning of 4 April 1933, *Akron* was beaten downward into the raging Atlantic. It was the beginning of the end for American naval airships and for Goodyear-Zeppelin's bold commercial anticipations.[21]

All the foregoing events of naval airship use and development were doubtless considered by Goodyear and Hunsaker in their endeavours to establish commercial airships, from the role of *Los Angeles* with the fleet in early 1931 to the perfecting of *Akron*'s planes for participation in fleet exercises by the spring of 1933. But apparently the IZT-PZT team efforts were hardly touched by awareness of the carrier–airship conflict and certainly not by the changes slowly developing in warplan ORANGE and their potential impact on the future of airships in the Navy. Much more immediate to Goodyear attention was an emerging political struggle to complete the congressional legislation that would assure the future of commercial airships.

Quite unexpectedly Goodyear had been thwarted in achieving its promising legislative goal in 1930. Despite diligent lobbying, the Akronites were quite surprised in late 1930 by a sudden upsurge of opposition from Juan Trippe of PanAm. Hunsaker had evidently assumed that Trippe's membership on the PZT board, which had given him full access to airship technical and political data, would have secured PanAm's support for the commercial airship enterprise. However, Trippe felt quite free to develop covertly his own strategies on several fronts in the international business skyward rivalry.[22]

Trippe with PanAm was fighting three interrelated campaigns. The first was to achieve participation – preferably preponderance – in Latin-American, transatlantic and transpacific commercial aviation. The second was to use incremental business advances in one or another of these areas to foster far-sighted preliminary exploration of flight routes, notably with the assistance of the Lindberghs, and at the same time to press relentlessly for technological improvements of the flying boat so that it could at last fly point-to-point among islands between continents. Thirdly, while incremental victories were being won in the first two campaigns, it was necessary for Trippe to delay or even defeat the full political-economic realization of commercial airship enterprise by whatever means possible. These campaigns were an epic struggle, fraught with political hazards and great financial risks.

Trippe's incremental successes by the end of 1930 were already remarkable. As of 1927, he had engineered legislation to guarantee a sound income for his domestic airline and extended that to favour his foreign expansion. By late 1929, he had State Department support, which facilitated his control of Central American and Caribbean aerial commerce. Early in 1930, he compromised with west-coast South American shipping magnate W. R. Grace to establish the Panagra enterprise from Florida to Chile. Shortly thereafter Trippe began PanAm flights to Rio. By late summer, he had ruthlessly annexed the earlier established east-coast NYRBA airline, with its fleet of superior Consolidated Commodore flying boats. Concurrently he was pressing his aircraft builder Sikorsky to complete development of the more advanced S-40. Late in 1930, Trippe finalized the initial stage of his negotiations with British Imperial Airways and French Aéropostale to conclude a gentleman's agreement that would solidify their control of north-Atlantic commercial aviation with firm exclusion of Luft Hansa and Italian aviation commerce. As the year closed, he was in discussion with the Lindberghs about their aerial exploration of the northern Pacific circle route between America and Japan, and on to China. It was all clear evidence of Trippe's constant quest for political power to secure PanAm routes and the powerful aircraft to service them. This was the foe that American airship interests faced from the autumn of 1930 onward.[23]

Congress reassembled in early December 1930 for a 'lame duck' session that extended to early March 1931. By then House hearings had indicated that Goodyear's search for federal subsidies to construct their commercial airships might not survive in an era of tightening financial stringency. Now Hunsaker scheduled an impressive array of talent and data before the House Committee on Interstate and Foreign Commerce. Here was presented the full glamour of airship potentialities: impressive size of the ships, their power, their speed and their safety with helium – all accentuated with brilliant conceptual illustrations of luxurious passenger accommodations. Goodyear's President Paul W. Litchfield and Hunsaker both testified at length on all the positive aspects and noting the implications of American prestige with airships in international commerce. A week later these presentations were repeated before the Senate Committee on Commerce, chaired by the redoubtable Hiram Johnson, Senator from California. For his benefit those data were focused on prospects for Pacific airship service, whose benefits would largely accrue to the Golden State. Rather muted in these several enhanced presentations was Goodyear's crucial aim: to revise the existing weight-per-mile formula of mail compensation to a space-per-mile basis, provided the airship carried no less than five tons of regular mail on a minimum range of 2000 miles without refuelling. This provision hit the heart of PanAm's profitable system of federal funding for small amounts of mail at high airmail surcharge rates. Near the end of the Senate session Trippe struck, to thwart the progress of Senate hearings. As Hunsaker then phrased it:

> Trippe represented that he had great influence in Congress and would join us in pushing for passage of an amended Bill. He was invited to do his best, but there was no result. He was also quite frank in stating that, if not amended, he would do his best to kill the Bill. ... There was evidence that several Senators had been approached by Pan American agents to prevent action on the original Bill. An earnest effort was made by us to get together with Pan American on a program. Several meetings were held both in Washington and New York and an agreement was made by us to accept their amendment and by them to use their full force to get an amended Bill reported out. No bill was reported out [before the session ended].[24]

That situation was bad enough, but worse was yet to come. Goodyear could already anticipate that naval airship *Macon* would be completed by the late autumn of 1932. Time was therefore of the essence in moving the Merchant Airship Bill towards enactment into law, so that work could begin in the vacant Airdock on the first commercial derivation from the naval airships. Once the 'lame duck' session of Congress was over in early March of 1931, the House needed to reorganize its procedural structure to conform to the election results of the previous November. These had produced the first Democrat majority in a decade by a very tiny margin. The ensuing political struggle was fought with primitive partisan intensity and remained unresolved until the following November, when a Texas by-election produced an additional Democrat seat and the House could finally organize under new political leadership. In retrospect it seems incomprehensible that in a year when the Depression was sinking millions of Americans into distress, the nation staggered downward *for nine months* without a functioning national legislature. And in the interim, Goodyear lost almost half the time remaining before the Airdock would stand empty.

Once the House was in session again, Hunsaker undertook tortuous negotiations to find new Democratic sponsorship for the Bill, to help arrange a new set of hearings and generally to win the procedural cooperation of the Democrat organization. Simultaneously he pressed for reintroduction of the same Bill in the still-Republican Senate, but he held off hearings there until a favourable vote in the House had been achieved. Further delays ensued in obtaining the grudging assent of the Postmaster General (still beholden to Trippe), the Budget Bureau (which asserted a thrifty fiscal programme of the President), plus the War, Navy and Commerce Departments. With these assets in hand, Hunsaker turned to House procedure itself, only to find a legislative calendar now clogged with hearings on railroads, buses, public utilities and holding companies – all beset with grave financial difficulties or spectacular bankruptcies. Given the popular media emphasis of such distressing news, Goodyear sought some journalistic trump cards. It played one with an announcement in late spring 1932 that ZRS5 would be named *Macon*, a large city in the Georgia district of Carl Vinson, who was a veteran supporter of naval airships and facing a close primary contest. Others were played via the Hearst organization, which had so prominently featured the *Graf Zeppelin*'s transatlantic, global and polar flights. During early summer all papers in that broad news network featured stories about airships in the Navy and prospects for global commercial airship service – all buttressed with impressive pictures of *Akron* on her transcontinental flight. A Goodyear blimp undertook daily flights over the Capitol, with sightseeing for congressmen and their friends. Hunsaker's confidential report to Goodyear detailed the intensive programme of Goodyear lobbyists, including veteran Vissering who personally called on 200 congressmen, to round up the votes of supporters, 'friends' and hesitant doubters. Notable were political skirmishes to defeat several crippling amendments to the Bill. It finally passed in a full House roll-call in mid-June of 1932, though only by an uncomfortably close margin.[25]

While fully involved with developments in Washington and Friedrichshafen, Hunsaker and Litchfield also pursued the establishment of the Guggenheim Airship Institute at Akron, convinced that further effective naval and commercial airship development required stimulation from an organization where 'a few advanced thinkers might be put to work with benefit to the [airship] art'. With the participation of Harry Guggenheim's fortune, President Robert A. Millikan (California Institute of Technology) and the University of Akron, Hunsaker spent three years seeking to combine space at the new Akron airport, basic funding, and Cal Tech expertise in aeronautical engineering – into fostering the growth of naval airships and the promotion of IZT and PZT. The renowned German aeronautical expert, Theodore von Karman, accepted a joint appointment as professor at Cal Tech and director of the new Institute. These complicated negotiations came to final fruition in late June 1932 just after the House passed the Crosser Merchant Airship Bill, as the *Akron* completed her well-publicized transcontinental flight, as *Macon* was under construction, and as *Graf Zeppelin* was establishing regular commercial service to Brazil. Looking back, one sees this founding of the Guggenheim Airship Institute as the high-water mark of American airship prospects.[26]

Concurrently negotiations in the Senate moved less favourably than before. Here different procedural rules gave the Trippe interests new opportunities for tactical harassment. Again there were extended outside negotiations to make peace with PanAm. Then, unexpectedly, new problems arose with Senators favouring Labour who feared Trippe was threatening his pilots' union. By mid-May the Bill was finally on the Senate calendar. New difficulties arose from Senators seeking fiscal restraint. Thrice the Bill came up by calendar and thrice it failed on a tactical move to obtain Senate voice consent. By that time adjournment loomed for all politicians anxious to devote their energies to the upcoming national elections that featured Roosevelt vs. Hoover and an avalanche of Depression problems. However, there was still opportunity in the final, 'lame-duck' session to come, which had the same political structure as before. Hunsaker outlined a meticulous strategy for this session, anticipating Senate action by late December 1932, renewed House action in January 1933, and passage of a final joint Bill in February. Senatorial votes he tabulated at '40 sure and 20 that might be got', with 51 needed. Every influence with business and the media was exploited. Given all the drama of political warfare in the electoral campaign, it is remarkable that Hunsaker and his allies could schedule a formal Senate vote on the Joint Bill for 3 March 1933, the last day of the 72nd Congress. Just the day before, however, Senator Walsh of Montana suddenly died and the Senate adjourned in mourning respect, with no further provision for unfinished business. Much beset, Hunsaker and Goodyear faced a new year with a whole new legislative campaign. Heartened as they were by the christening of *Macon* on 11 March 1933 by Mrs Moffett and the panoply of airship celebration and publicity, they could still scarcely begin their new drive before mid-summer, when the most pressing tasks of the Roosevelt New Deal would have been authorized. But just a month after the missed Senate vote, in the early morning of 4 April 1933, the *Akron* and 73 men of her complement – including Admiral Moffett – were destroyed in her final fatal flight. That was the end for American commercial airship legislation.[27]

The day *Akron* crashed, Dr Hugo Eckener was in Berlin, testing the troubled political and financial waters for a delayed opening of the 1933 flight season to Brazil. Berlin was redolent of Nazi arrogance and anti-Semitism, all amplified by the vicious themes in radio and journalism directed by Dr Joseph Goebbels, the new Minister of Public Enlightenment and Propaganda. He opened a new era in public relations, where the need of the masses for political entertainment moved from the theatre to the streets and arenas for mass demonstrations of revolutionary nationalism for alleged social benefit. In Goebbels' own words:

> We are the signalmen of our time: we set the signals by which our thundering trains roll into the future ... We will answer worldwide propaganda against us with worldwide propaganda *for* us. We *know* what power propaganda wields and by what means and methods it is achieved. We learned this not from theorizing but by studying reality [Allied propaganda against Germany in 1914–18] ... Propaganda is best served by a few simple, emotional slogans and symbols. The masses best respond to old familiar impressions enhanced by new subtle variations.

That was where the zeppelin would play its part.[28]

Like Stalin, both Hitler and Goebbels used aviation for focused political effect. Planes flew in the election campaign of 1932 for maximum coverage and publicity, unheard of electioneering before that time in Germany. The zeppelin aura would also have been used, had Eckener agreed. As May 1933 approached, with its traditional workers' holiday, top Nazis debated what they could place in competition. Goebbels cut directly to the heart of the matter: 'Just leave the first of May to me. Man is a creature of habit ... With proper staging we can make a virtue of necessity and turn Marx's holiday into a demonstration of National Socialist conviction.'

And so it was done. The traditional socialist Labour Day was made over into a Nazi 'Day of National Work'. More than a million Berliners were brought into hastily built stands at Tempelhof airport – and the *Graf Zeppelin* was the major actor recruited for this political theatre. All existing labour unions were abolished; their membership (insofar as not Marxist or Jewish) was gathered into the new Nazi Labour Front (DAF).

Use of the airship for Nazi propaganda was only one aspect of Eckener's growing problems with the new Nazi state. As had been happening throughout German industry in the early 1930s, adherents of Hitler had been secretly infiltrating into the Zeppelin Company by creating 'cells' of the Nazi Works Organization (NSBO). Later integrated into the DAF, the NSBO was more than labour unions previously had been, seeking to gain influence by 'advising' management in order to 'improve' the entire business operation, ultimately to achieve political control there. The highest-ranking Storm Troop (SA) leader in Friedrichshafen had been with the Company since 1925 and left in 1934 for a higher post in that paramilitary organization. In fact, the Luftschiffbau had in its workforce most of the important local Nazis. About 1938 Eckener chose as his close office assistant a man who had been a student leader since 1929, but was personally loyal to the airshipman and to Eckener's singular zeppelin thrust within the large industrial conglomerate. With this local Nazi 'shield' Eckener held the aggressive Nazis within the Company at bay until war broke out. By that time the various subsidiaries had a majority of their business with the massive German rearmament thrust and Eckener was forced then to accept NSBO ideological intrusion into management decisions. Though NSBO cells were active on the prestigious German ocean liners, shadowing crews and passengers alike, apparently such intrusion did not occur on the great airships. They would be otherwise influenced by a later Nazi decision to deprive Eckener of control in supplanting the DELAG with a new service organization.[29]

After opening the 1933 flight year with the May Day show at Berlin, the airshipmen had further Nazi experiences. At month's end the Association of German Engineers, which had so favoured Count Zeppelin in 1896, staged its annual conference in the great hangar at Friedrichshafen that Eckener had denied to Hitler the year before. At this gala occasion the society's new young president mounted a swastika-draped podium in his Brown-Shirt uniform to pledge allegiance of the staid professionals to the new ideology. Next day the *Graf Zeppelin* left for Rome, where its enthusiastically acclaimed descent coincided with the earlier arrival that day of Goebbels on the first official celebration of Nazi–Fascist political togetherness. Radio and film publicity were enhanced by issues of colourful postage stamps for Italy and her colonies, featuring the airship over various classic Roman sites, and were all financial manna for Eckener's depleted coffers. And, political coincidence or not, the presence of the zeppelin over the Tiber gave psychic confirmation to the initial step of an emerging Rome–Berlin axis.[30]

By the summer of 1933, other unfavourable straws were blowing for the zeppelin in the increasing winds of political change. With great éclat Hermann Goering established the new Reich Air Ministry, allegedly a new home for Lufthansa and other civilian aviation but actually just camouflage for the still-secret growing Luftwaffe. All the zeppelin business of the old Transport Ministry went into the new bureau, but Eckener lost his major old ally Brandenburg, prematurely retired for political 'unreliability'. Also lost were Eckener's friends among the moderate Socialists, as the purged Reichstag became purely a Nazi publicity instrument. Eckener later recorded that about this time he heard rumours that the Gestapo had him under surveillance, and that he was saved from the concentration camp only by Hindenburg's protective intervention with Hitler. Eckener, who had been the toast of later Weimar Berlin, actually encountered Hitler personally only twice: first accidentally in the summer of 1933 at a lakeside cafe near Berchtesgaden, then formally in 1939 at the launching of the first Reich aircraft carrier, *Graf Zeppelin*. From 1933 onward, the Air Ministry provided a sufficient annual operating subsidy for the South American zeppelin service and began incremental construction aid for LZ129 by fostering 'voluntary' contributions from other industries or making direct loans for labour employment. Eckener paid his political price for these various benefits when he had to paint giant swastikas on zeppelin fins in accordance with the new Reich aerial identification law of 14 July 1933. And late that summer Goebbels chartered the *Graf Zeppelin* again, to overfly the Nuremberg celebration of the Nazi Party Day of Victory, staged on the broad Zeppelin Meadow where DELAG ships had called before the war.[31]

During 1933–5, airship service to Brazil grew famously from nine to sixteen annual round trips, with gains in paying passengers, mail and express freight. Fast Condor planes then carried these from Rio into all neighbouring nations; with a corresponding distribution of Latin American fliers to all Europe via Friedrichshafen. In early 1934, Lufthansa inaugurated its scheduled mail flights to Brazil, but since the flying boats did not have the range to fly nonstop across the South Atlantic, two seagoing ships equipped with catapults were stationed along the route. Landing on the water, the flying boats would be hauled aboard the support ship, refuelled and catapulted on their way. Before long, this service was integrated with the zeppelin service. Beneath seeming aviation harmony, however, zeppelin crewmen meeting Lufthansa personnel heard echoes of the enduring technological rivalry: 'Enjoy your pokey cruises while you can, fellas; the future belongs to our speedy craft!' In spring 1934, Brazil finally agreed to build the expensive Santa Cruz terminal, for in aviation politics she could now rival Argentina, as 'zeppelin' became a Latin American byword for punctual and reliable service between the continents. Still, as Rio was stimulated by increasing import–export trade with the now-reviving German economy, its Brazilian-German community reflected openly the political tensions repressed in the fatherland. The earlier enthusiastic, harmonious reception of zeppelin people was by 1935 marred with Nazi vs. anti-Nazi hostility, which Eckener found an increasing irritation in his continuing efforts to have the zeppelin symbolize the achievements and hopes of all Germans.[32]

As already noted, Eckener had long since learned of Gestapo 'interest' in him. He did not know, however, of other plans then under way to deprive him even further of his role as representative of German virtues at home and abroad. A document of unknown authorship, possibly arising from some ambitious clique in Himmler's power-hungry SS, was sent by secretive routes to top Nazi leadership. It extolled the fabulous heritage of Count Zeppelin and the great influence of his pre-war airships on public opinion at home and abroad. Now it was evident that no other nation could equal the great postwar magic of the zeppelin. France, Italy, and Britain had failed in their airship efforts. Thanks to German technological influence the American naval airships were superb, but their operation was faulty: *Akron* was down and *Macon* would inevitably follow. Germany alone had the expertise and experience to make a world-shaking success of the zeppelin in reality and propaganda. Two decisions were now required to ensure that continuing result. First, the Reich must devote full financial and administrative support to the venture. Second, it must be separated publicly from the unreliable person and control of Dr Hugo Eckener. To achieve both results it was necessary to separate the design and construction of zeppelins from their service operation, the latter passing to a new Reich organization, directed by reliable party members and focused on national and international Nazi propaganda. The still indispensable Eckener should function in an obscure advisory capacity, helping to train a new generation of loyal Nazi zeppelin captains and crews. The sooner the better, for the zeppelin mystique could only enhance the international image of Nazi Germany. This proposal would simmer in upper hierarchical levels for the next nine months.[33]

As the Nazis were pressing to make zeppelins a major carrier of future propaganda in Europe and the wider world, the French had already had quite enough of German political posturing with the zeppelin between northwestern Africa and South America. At home the new Nazi aggressiveness reinforced traditional Franco-German friction, while French citizens peppered Paris with protests about aggravated 'spying' airship overflights. Military and political authorities in the government pressed to exclude the zeppelin completely, but air officials were constrained by imminent negotiations with Berlin about expanded French flights over Germany to their Slavic allies in eastern Europe. Aéropostale collapsed in bankruptcy scandal in May 1934. The new government-sponsored carrier, Air France, needed those mid-European overflights and urged collaboration with Berlin. Meanwhile, the new company tried hard to restore lost prestige and influence in South America, pitting Argentina against Brazil with widespread promises of a fast new service to Buenos Aires with new planes. Eckener countered with a special zeppelin flight to Argentina, just as the promised new French air service faltered disastrously. From all over the southern hemisphere, French diplomats showered the Foreign Ministry with doleful accounts of impressive zeppelin-Condor successes from the Amazon to the River Plate and of a precipitous decline in French prestige. What could France do?[34]

In mid-January, French Air Attaché Poincaré in Berlin responded with a detailed report on the prodigious growth of German civil aviation since the Nazi rise to power. Given the strong pressure of Lufthansa in Europe, he focused on the three international routes most sensitive to political manipulation: Germany to Canton or Shanghai, Berlin to Brazil, and Germany to the United States. Based on research previously reported and on in-depth talks with General Milch of the Air Ministry, Wronsky of Lufthansa, and Eckener, Attaché Poincaré saw France seriously threatened in political prestige and international commerce by the German advance. Notably he focused on the imminent arrival of two new super-zeppelins further to impress Latin America and totally recast northwest Europe's passenger traffic with New York. Obdurate French resistance to inevitable German requests for zeppelin flights over central and northern France would be no creative response for Paris. France must move with the times, undertaking a crash financial and technological programme of development in aircraft and facilities: fast new service to Indo-China via the Middle East and India; reinvigorated Air France to South America; and realization at long, long last of North Atlantic flights in cooperation with Britain and

America. Only thus could France begin to win back her fading international aviation prestige, while not impeding the zeppelins in their impressive flights to Rio and New York. Poincaré's advice focused only on civil aviation. He apparently had no inkling that two months later Hitler would suddenly launch a small but fully operative Luftwaffe.[35]

As the fateful memorandum of the secretive clique was slowly working its way through the Nazi bureaucracy, fortune was smiling again at Friedrichshafen. LZ129 was on the way to completion, the DELAG was approaching its most profitable year of the Depression, and the *Graf Zeppelin* had become a steadily recurring symbol of growing Brazilian–German economic and political partnership. The DELAG celebrated its millionth postwar kilometre in flight with a Christmas trip to Rio, laden with a cargo of fresh fragrant Yuletide trees and all varieties of Nuremberg holiday delicacies. Early in 1935 occurred a plebiscite in the Saar Basin, predetermined in the Versailles Treaty in 1920. Here 90 per cent of the Saarlanders voted for reunion with Germany. The vibrant nationalistic campaign for approval vividly recalled the visit of the *Graf Zeppelin* in June 1933, where Eckener verified the role of his ship as a beacon of German association with blood brothers living abroad. But the Saar, he had then emphasized, was not 'abroad', but a vital element of Germany proper, momentarily separated from the homeland by hostile politics. This flight was a manipulated prelude to the Nazi celebration of an alleged 'triumph over the crime of Versailles'.[36]

As the zeppelin began its 1935 season of 16 crossings to Brazil, it was now emblazoned with bold swastikas on *both* sides of its vertical fins. Until President von Hindenburg died in August 1934, the Nazis had played a deceptive game of symbol manipulation, always displaying the old imperial colours black-white-red (that had persisted as commercial colours of the Weimar Republic) together with the upstart swastika, thus misleading millions of Germans into thinking of the 'national resurgence' of 1933 as a revival of Imperial German conservative values. As of late 1934, however, the dualism of colours and symbolism vanished; henceforth, it was only the new Nazi emblem. Old zeppeliners like Eckener, Pruss and von Schiller had lived uneasily with that symbol manipulation. Now the loss of traditional colours from their airship was just a foretaste of worse yet to come. Following closely upon Goering's triumphant shock of revealing an operational Luftwaffe in mid-March 1935, came his visit to Friedrichshafen at the end of the month. Here he personally presided at promulgating the essence of the 1934 secret memorandum on future zeppelin develop-

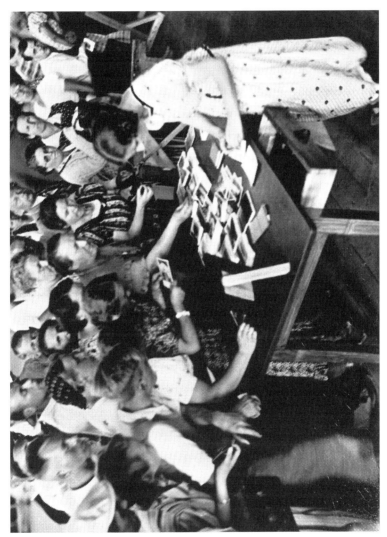

Funds for the Zeppelin cause. Zeppelin postcard sales, Friedrichshafen hangar

ment. The DELAG was abolished and a new zeppelin transport company was established under Air Ministry control composed jointly of Lufthansa interests, residual DELAG assets and the two zeppelins. The historic Zeppelin Company's monopoly of airship construction was assured for the future under Eckener's leadership, but he lost all control of zeppelin flying, unless periodically invited to participate by the Luft Hansa-dominated Deutsche Zeppelin Reederei (DZR). Eckener was 'kicked upstairs' to a participating administrative role, together with the more Nazi-favoured Lehmann. The basic purpose of the change was to isolate Eckener in provincial Württemberg, just as Berlin had done with Count Zeppelin in 1890. Like the Old Aeronaut, however, Eckener did not accept this professional and political rustication; and like the Old Aeronaut, he resolved to make himself heard and felt in his continuing efforts to make the zeppelin a prime instrument of worldwide commerce. Here, of course, his qualifications and experience made him indispensable for the German zeppelin future. And so for the next five years Eckener and the Nazis worked in a harness of hostility tempered by mutual necessity of each for the other.

Thus closed the most promising half-decade in Eckener's airship endeavours: commercial service moving smoothly to Brazil and realistic anticipation of opening flights to America with a new generation of super-zeppelins – all combined with the Nazi theft of his political endeavour on behalf of the German nation and loss of the heart of his enterprise to the new swastika-waving gang in Berlin.

Goodyear planned a great rally at the Airdock for the christening of the *Macon* on 11 March 1933. The Moffetts and other notables arrived, together with a large naval band. But only a few thousand Akronites and visitors were present, given a bitterly cold day in the unheated hangar and the grim impact of the American banking system having been shut down nationwide just a week before. Admiral Moffett spoke briefly and hopefully of more intensified naval airship use and of resurrecting the Merchant Airship Bill in Congress. It was a brave show for Litchfield and Hunsaker, but they knew that the Airdock would be empty for the near future.[37] *Macon* emerged from hangar tests six weeks later and after several trial flights was formally commissioned as a proper naval ship in late June. After long, repetitive further flight trials, notably to work the tricky trapeze aircraft into airship operations, *Macon* finally left Akron in mid-October for assignment with the Pacific Fleet and for stationing at newly-built Moffett Field near San Francisco. On this occasion Admiral King, now naval chief of BuAer, sent letters to Rear Admiral John Halligan (Commander Aircraft, Battle Force) and Admiral Daniel F. Sellers, CINCUS, urging proper use and respect for the dirigible:

> This [1934] is to be a critical year for the airship. We have only one airship. We must not be reckless, but if airships are to justify themselves, the *Macon* has got to show more than she has shown. ... This letter is a personal plea for (a) wider operation of the *Macon* directly with the Fleet and on additional problems which might be framed to suit her special characteristics; (b) for a square deal all around for the *Macon* during this critical year, so that at its conclusion when we come to total up the ledger, no one may say that she has not had a fair test.[38]

It was an open-handed but futile plea.

Meanwhile, other events were impacting deliberations and work at Akron. Returning to his alternative railroad activities, Vissering helped Goodyear contract with the New Haven Railroad to build an ultramodern, streamlined, three-car articulated light-metal passenger train in the soon-to-be-vacant Airdock. In the summer of 1933, just as the Navy began to place one or two naval airshipmen on almost every German zeppelin flight now in regular service to Brazil, Lufthansa began its trials with Dornier flying boats on the same route. These aircraft were expedited by mid-ocean refuelling stops at specially-modified service ships, which then catapulted the aircraft onward. The Lindberghs made another memorable transoceanic survey flight, this time eastward across the North Atlantic circle route in Trippe's initial exploratory step to establish PanAm's air service from the United States to Britain. In July, flying boats came centre stage on the same track, in reverse, when Fascist Air Commander Italo Balbo led his flight from Rome to the World's Fair in Chicago with a squadron of 20 military amphibious planes. *Macon* and other aircraft greeted him at Chicago on 15 July and four days later again in New York. Not to be outdone, Eckener then planned another zeppelin flight to America, also to the World's Fair, as soon as *Macon* had left the Airdock at Akron free. This flight would produce several unanticipated political consequences.[39]

The first effect emanated from the White House and precipitated an unpublicized German-American diplomatic flap. More than ever, Eckener needed good philatelic income from this flight and routinely contracted with the Post Office Department for a special American stamp to be featured together with another commemorative German issue. When this news reached President Roosevelt in September before the flight, he forbade the American stamp, not as an anti-Nazi gesture but because he had earlier resisted strong pressure from Italian-American groups thus to commemorate Balbo's spectacular flight. Even-handed though this decision appeared to Roosevelt, himself a well-known philatelist, the State Department argued that revoking the Post Office decision already taken, and used by Eckener himself to generate the German stamp issuance, would complicate the tension already evident in a diplomatic context strained by widespread unfavourable American public reaction to Nazi concentration camps and anti-Semitic outrages. With some difficulty Roosevelt's decision was reversed, but the event left a scar on the President's psyche, possibly awakening memories of Goodyear's refusal to rescue him in his ill-starred venture with Schütte airships in 1925 and certainly not boding well for his later reactions to matters about German or American airships.[40]

The second political effect came with the *Graf Zeppelin*'s last America flight in 1933. En route from Rio to Akron, the ship stopped at Miami. Crowds of many thousands swarmed to the field. For the first time Americans saw the huge swastikas emblazoned on the right sides of the vertical stabilizers, the left sides still showing the Weimar commercial colours. When Eckener was repeatedly asked why he was displaying the ugly symbol, he responded curtly that it was the law, new Nazi aircraft identifications valid since the previous July. Two German-American pro-Nazi honorary consuls tried officiously to politicize the visit at Miami and were directly overruled by Vissering, who was there to facilitate public relations. The consuls sent complaints to their Washington embassy that 'Jews' were disrupting their efforts to give 'the new Germany' a positive identity. International Nazi political manipulation of the zeppelin had begun.[41]

Next day the airship landed amidst huge crowds at the new Akron airport. For the only time in history its offices for passports, immigration and customs demonstrated an anticipated future in international commercial aviation. On to Chicago, where the welcome was less fulsome. Threats of sabotage moved von Meister of AZT to seek protection of the Cook County Sheriff. He responded with such a tight cordon of deputies that none but passengers bound for Akron could even approach the zeppelin. It remained a scant half-hour, but residents of the Windy City still had had a magnificent view of the ship as Eckener flew it around a broad circuit, carefully counter-clockwise so that Americans would mostly see the old German colours and not the swastikas. Eckener remained a day to tour the World's Fair and meet with six thousand guests of twelve different German-American organizations. The German Consul there later reported that there had been organizational tiffs between the various sponsoring clubs, not to mention some 'Jewish trouble-makers', but that Ambassador Luther and Dr Eckener had carried the day and given much credibility to the recently established 'Friends of the New Germany'. That was hardly Eckener's purpose; he later wrote:

> Always, up to now, the *Graf Zeppelin* had symbolized international friendship, good will and commerce. Now, with the cursed swastika on its tail, it's been perverted to a vehicle for Goebbels and that damned Ministry of Propaganda. Everything we worked for is being subverted and destroyed.

Three years would pass before the next zeppelin appeared in America. But in spite of admiration for Eckener, and in spite of the renewed impact of amazement and wonder that the next giant airship would stimulate, for many Americans the curse of the swastika would now fly with all zeppelins.[42]

But there was still the naval airship *Macon* to attract patriotic attention. Once arrived at her new west-coast base in early November 1933, she began serious flying with the Navy. Responding quite literally to instructions that she be 'employed to the fullest extent possible in fleet exercises, so that her military value could be determined', Admiral Sellers used the ship in essentially tactical situations, so that she was 'shot down' seven times, once even by battleship anti-aircraft guns. In April 1934, *Macon* flew east for Caribbean manoeuvres. En route over the Rockies, she encountered heavy turbulence that damaged one of her tail fins. Accordingly, it was decided that each one of the four control-area structures required reinforcement, 'to be accomplished from time to time, as opportunity offers, in order not to interfere with operating schedules'. Her captain understandably favoured his ship in subsequent exercises and left early for Moffett Field to begin reconstruction there. Promptly Admiral Sellers fired off a report that damned *Macon*'s performance with faint praise but judged overall that 'the airship has failed to demonstrate its usefulness as a unit of the fleet'. Admiral King countered with a more balanced evaluation, but views of most senior officers were reinforced that the huge expense of airships was not justified by such meagre results in fleet performance. Structurally and operationally the days of the *Macon* were numbered.[43]

American contacts with foreign airship activities continued. As of June 1934, two Goodyear engineers began three years of flying with the German zeppelins in preparation for Akron's still-anticipated transatlantic operations. Coincidentally, the Soviet Amtorg business-technical offices in New York contacted Litchfield for permission to visit Akron and discuss matters of airship construction. When Goodyear declined, there was a further request. Hunsaker suggested meeting with some of the half-dozen Soviet airship engineers from Nobile's enterprise who were coming to study at MIT, but apparently nothing ever came of this contact. Meanwhile, Goodyear was reassigning its most essential airship designers and builders to reserve positions in other parts of its enterprise, while the Airdock resounded with echoes of the new train in construction.[44]

In July 1934 *Macon*'s captain was relieved by Lieutenant Commander Wiley, the only surviving officer of the *Akron*. With new drive and purpose he remoulded the function of the aerial mother ship. The scout planes now played the major role in reconnaissance, while the *Macon*, hidden beyond the horizon, served as carrier, radio relay station and command centre. Soon after his arrival Wiley staged a spectacular airship event that put the *Macon* back on the front pages of newspapers. With fleet permission for a 'protracted flight to sea', he flew far south of Moffett Field to intercept a cruiser carrying President Roosevelt and staff from Panama to a conference in Hawaii. At noon on 19 July, the Washingtonians were surprised to find themselves buzzed by small fighter craft 1500 miles at sea. Shortly thereafter, *Macon* appeared from over the horizon to reclaim her planes and drop souvenirs of the occasion. Roosevelt sent Wiley a personal 'well done!', but carrier commander Reeves, now in charge of the fleet, sent a furious protest at this 'misapplied initiative'. In subsequent exercises *Macon* was still occasionally 'shot down', but Wiley's innovative tactics brought new respect for airship possibilities with the fleet. Between exercises, three of the four fins were fully restructured. Only the top fin remained for strengthening as plans were developed to fly *Macon* out to Hawaii in spring 1935 for Fleet Problem XVI, which would place her in the western Pacific at long, long last to perform the kind of scouting for which the new naval airships had been destined. But on her return from an intermediate exercise off Lower California, *Macon* was almost home when she was struck by a violent off-shore gust that ruptured the stern structure of the airship and caused its destruction within a half-hour. Nearly all personnel survived, but the American naval rigid airship programme of fifteen years was lost forever.[44]

German and American airship developments moved in disparate parallelism between 1931 and 1935. At the beginning, Eckener's team was planning the most successful zeppelin year ever. At the same time, airship *Los Angeles* at long last began service with the fleet and Akron's Airdock hummed with activity. Four years later Eckener was losing control of his superb venture and the second Goodyear airship was lost at sea. Those in government whom Eckener had often been able to manipulate favourably in 1929–31 were now gone and he was defenceless against the Nazi capture of the zeppelin aura for its own different uses. Similarly, the long positive Republican relationships of Goodyear dissolved in a national political upheaval that brought vast new changes and a President disdainful of Goodyear and open to favour PanAm. Akron's noble aerial construct became tainted by fears for its safety, while its slow speed and huge expense made it an easy prey to the more agile and less costly flying boats. In addition, for all his naval prestige, technical expertise and scrupulously proper lobbying, Jerome Hunsaker was losing effectiveness in countering the inscrutable lobbying and radical business manipulations of Juan Trippe as he manoeuvred to command transoceanic aerial service. In late March 1935, as Eckener bitterly accepted his new Faustian semi-cooperation with the Nazis, and as Hunsaker took cover at Akron to await his chances with the new German zeppelin enterprise, Juan Trippe received Washington's assent to make revocable leases on the islands of Midway, Wake and Guam – in cooperation with the US Navy. PZT's airship hopes for the Pacific gave way to PanAm's opening trial flights along the chain of islands to the Far East. But the future across the North Atlantic – with no comparable chain of islands – was still open to competition between airship and flying boats. The issue would be decided in the next three years.

7
Airship Wonder Captured by Nazi Ideology, 1935–40

Between 1935 and 1939 *der Zeppelin* was rapidly transformed as an image away from Eckener's vision of German airships as heralds of technological triumph over the ignominy of Versailles and for international reconciliation and commerce. It now rapidly became an aggressive advertisement for Nazi racist superiority. At home and abroad the zeppelin was commandeered to perform at ideological ceremonies like the Nuremberg *Parteitag* and their echoes among Germans in Brazil. Crews from the *Graf Zeppelin* marched in May Day celebrations at Rio, staged by party cadres of Germans Abroad (*Auslandsdeutsche*), with groups of Brazilian officialdom in attendance. Not so in the United States. Here Berlin alleged that the notorious German-American Bund was only an organization of American citizens, though secretly it got directives and funding from Nazi sources. The zeppelin was still using American Naval terminal facilities and was thus strictly closed to civilian Bund activities. But the *Hindenburg* in 1936–7 regularly flew over areas with large Bund membership, demonstrably cheered in Bund media and local celebrations. Within the Reich, and for broader Germanic consumption, occurred a growing surge of articles and books on the zeppelin's place in German tradition and society. One author could speculate that zeppelins *must* have been effective in the war: how otherwise to explain the vengeful prohibitions of Versailles and the subsequent restrictions on export of American helium? New works appeared praising the zeppelin heroes over England. The Old Count's first pre-war captain celebrated the 'Men of Manzell' who had made airship construction and flight possible, from triumph to humiliation and defeat – and now [1936] reborn with Nazi vigour, an almost mystical reminiscence through suffering to redemption. German tourism burgeoned with Nazi 'Strength through Joy' mass travel, honouring trips to Friedrichshafen and Frankfurt city and airport (with new international zeppelin flight facilities). Frankfurt itself was advertised as 'again a *German* city', freed of its former Catholic and Jewish perversion, illustrated in 1938 with a full-page picture of 'the recently-completed last great passenger airship, the LZ130 *Graf Zeppelin II*, sister ship to the Hindenburg, swastikas blazing on her fins'. Less and less these circumstances saw self-motivated German individuals responding to airship wonder; increasingly there were now masses directed and controlled in their zeppelin enthusiasm towards achieving specific ideological responses.[1]

1936 became the stellar year for transatlantic airship travel and propaganda. The *Graf Zeppelin* continued flying to Brazil, but was ageing as an experimental forerunner for airship travel. She needed successors: larger, faster and preferably helium-borne. Shortage of funds and delays in experimentation to place smaller hydrogen cells within larger helium ballonettes delayed completion of the new LZ129 *Hindenburg* until early 1936. Then, late in March, both ships were chartered by the Propaganda Ministry for a three-day cruise, criss-crossing Germany to drop election leaflets and trumpet Nazi slogans in advocacy of a national plebiscite to approve Hitler's bold reoccupation of the demilitarized Rhineland. On departure from Friedrichshafen, Captain Lehmann of the *Hindenburg* risked capricious winds on take-off from the hangar and damaged the lower vertical fin. Eckener, whom DZR failed to appoint to the flight, bellowed at him: 'How dare you risk the ship for this excremental flight [*Scheissfahrt*]!' This blast was promptly reported to Goebbels, who forthwith reacted to rid the Reich of Eckener's anti-Nazi irritations. At his next daily press conference Goebbels decreed: 'Dr Eckener has alienated himself from the German people. In future his name shall no longer be mentioned in news reports, nor may his picture be further printed.' Immediately upon completion of the election propaganda cruise, the *Hindenburg* set off on her maiden flight to Brazil. Goebbels' decree reached Eckener en route. He conferred at once with Commander Scott E. Peck, aboard as US naval observer, about possible political emigration to America. Once in Rio, however, Eckener did not seek the American Embassy there; instead he spoke at the Rio German Club, where he confirmed the veracity of Goebbels' denunciation and then went on to express his regret 'at the tensions and divisions that the local Nazi organization was causing within the whole German colony at Rio'. On his return to Germany, Eckener conferred with Goering, who agreed to consult Hitler about the ban – for his own Air Ministry propaganda depended

212

The *Graf Zeppelin* flies over the *Hindenburg* at the commencement of the Plebiscite Flight, 26–29 March 1936

on frequent manipulation of Eckener's image. Various sources confirm that a veritable chorus of German voices implored Nazi notables to rescind the ban and restore Eckener with his zeppelin to publicity favour. It was soon done, but Eckener was now a marked man in Gestapo quarters.[2]

Internationally these events had further ominous implications. Hitler's audacious thrust into the demilitarized Rhineland zone violated the Locarno Treaties of 1925 and gave Europe its worst war scare since 1919. Now France and Britain both forbade zeppelin overflights, emergencies excepted, and the zeppelins had to take expensive detours down the Rhine and through the English Channel to the Americas. In Switzerland, too, there was growing resentment of the swastikas overhead. Public opinion that had for years welcomed the German airships now turned against them, notably when, in spite of official Swiss warning, the zeppelin overflew military areas. German and non-German newsmen exchanged recriminations but the zeppelins flew right on.[3]

In the Americas the arrival of the new *Hindenburg* rejuvenated the old public enthusiasm for airship wonder and transoceanic travel. With three times the number of passengers as the old *Graf*, she also cruised in more luxury and comfort (including smoking aboard!) than any existing flying boat or other shorter range aircraft. At Rio, the super-zeppelin arrived at the new Santa Cruz airship terminal with sumptuous aircraft and passenger facilities newly provided by the Brazilian state. Pleas came to the DZR offices at Rio for overflights of various Brazilian-German cities, but official responses indicated that the new ship would hold strictly to her commercial schedules, apart from one regional Brazilian detour to celebrate the twentieth Atlantic crossing of the new dirigible. From Washington the embassy informed Berlin that reports of the *Hindenburg* dominated American international news in the first week of May. Indeed, Americans rushed to rooftops and the streets to see the new triumph of German technology. New also to Americans were the prominent multicoloured Olympic rings that Goebbels had ordered and paid to have emblazoned amidships on the *Hindenburg* in a further propaganda thrust of intermixing images and symbols for Nazi political effect. Within Germany the new zeppelin appeared at the opening of the Olympic Games, another propaganda coup celebrated worldwide by radio and newsreel. Later she overflew the Nuremberg *Zeppelinfeld* to exalt the annual *Parteitag*, amidst military and paramilitary parading, where Hitler openly signalized the great natural resources of the Ukraine for possible future

German advantage. The men of zeppelin flying, however, concentrated on making their transatlantic service regular, reliable and profitable. At summer's end, Eckener and Goodyear-Zeppelin staged a memorable airship cruise for 80 American businessmen, publicists and naval leaders over the colourful autumn foliage of New England to anticipate the opening of DZR service in 1937 together with the newly formed American Zeppelin Transport Company (AZT), using two new zep-

The *Hindenburg* over Berlin during the 1936 Olympic Games

pelins, and with intimations of another duo of larger ships to come. It appeared that the great postwar commercial airship expectations were finally being fully realized.[4]

But winged aircraft were about to overtake the airship. On the North Atlantic, Lufthansa had been intermittently catapulting planes with mails from German express liners since 1929. From 1934 onward, Lufthansa planes were being flown to Brazil with intermediate refuelling stops at catapult ships midway in the South Atlantic, a service that was shared with Air France from 1935 onward. As of late summer 1936, a large new catapult ship was stationed by Lufthansa for experimental flights across the North Atlantic. France also began trial flights with a large flying boat similar to the Do-X in 1936, which made nine round trips before war broke out in 1939. Most notable, of course, was Juan Trippe's success with PanAm transpacific flight. Though prideful of his first achievement, full flight to Manila by December 1935, his major focus was always on the north transatlantic enterprise, which was most promising commercially. He never took his eyes off his competitors. Since 1932 he had required steady reporting from his Rio agency on Eckener's progress with zeppelins to Brazil, as he also received reports from Hunsaker on IZT and PZT. By 1935, British tardiness in technological development and delays in flight experimentation irritated him and his PanAm board no end. His initial agreements with Imperial Airways in 1930, to insure there would be no British flights before PanAm was ready, became an impediment when Trippe was now experimentally ready and then was held up by British delays in aircraft development and on permits and leases in England, Bermuda and Canada. Trippe was a vigilant guest on the colourful VIP airship flight of early October 1936. A week later he was en route with PanAm's first flight to China, terminating at Macau when Hong Kong would not greet him. Thence he went on around the world by scheduled aircraft, including the *Hindenburg* to Brazil – a pioneering global trip by commercial aircraft. Already he could resolutely face the future. At midyear of 1936 he had ordered six Boeing 314 flying boats, *each* carrying almost as many passengers as the *Hindenburg*, due for initial delivery in late 1937. By spring 1938, it could be head-to-head, PanAm vs. DZR-AZT.[5]

But in November 1936, however, much promise was still seen with the airship. The board of DZR met at the Berlin Air Ministry to evaluate results of its first full year of operation. The facts were impressive. Passengers and express mail to Brazil had nearly doubled from 1935. Fantastic were the North Atlantic statistics: a thousand passengers, tons of mail and cargo, and unparalleled public enthusiasm on all three continents – altogether at the margin of profitability. Great were the prospects for 1937, when LZ130 would join the team, with passenger capacity enlarged by 40 per cent in both zeppelins. Orders were favoured for the even larger new LZ131–132. Under what auspices would the new ships fly? It was open to competition: AZT hoped for a ship under American charter; a Dutch consortium of shipping lines and KLM desired airships for its contemplated new service from America to Java, with intermediate stops in Spain and India; General Milch at the Air Ministry reserved LZ130 for German needs. Amidst all these favourable prospects Counsellor Willy Fisch, familiar with zeppelin matters since 1922, cautioned that helium must be sought, to which Captain Lehmann sharply commented, 'but then our profitability goes bust ...'. It would appear in retrospect that German hubris was inviting comeuppance.[6]

Already the operational criteria for zeppelins were changing. In 1975 Captain von Schiller recalled his long service with airships and commented: 'With business now dominant in our enterprise, there was new pressure on our conduct during 1935–37, speeding up our operations and adhering more closely to schedules.' In January 1937, AZT Vice-president von Meister sent Captain Lehmann a long detailed memorandum, indicating that the joint DZR-AZT service to open in May must come to terms with a basic new operational fact: the novelty and excitement of transatlantic airship travel had worn off and they must now face up to stiff competition from transatlantic express liners, from whose expensive first class many future airship passengers would most likely come. Such American and European clients were accustomed to impeccable service and comfort, he reasoned, which the airships must also supply. A cascade of suggestions followed, including upgrading the primitive landing facilities at Lakehurst, Americanizing creature comforts aboard, diversifying cuisine, and less rudely securing passenger cigarette lighters and matches when boarding. Especially noteworthy was his observation of a new air-travel phenomenon: that *boredom* during a 60-hour non-stop flight required creative innovations for passenger diversion and entertainment. It was all a farsighted and sobering anticipation of competitive air travel in transition from flight experimentation to business operation.[7]

In early May 1937, the *Hindenburg* left Germany on its first (and only) scheduled flight under joint German-American commercial auspices. Her passage over New York evoked continued American airship enthusiasm:

From windows, rooftops, sidewalks, fire escapes and points of vantage they viewed the giant airliner ... Traffic was impeded in some sections of the city as throngs choked thoroughfares and drivers stopped their automobiles to gaze skyward as the ship, its motors roaring and swastikas gleaming, passed over the city.

Delayed eight hours en route to Lakehurst by North-Atlantic storms, she arrived on 6 May 1937 in the late afternoon to find her destination beset by waning thunderclouds and forecasts for a new electrical front due before midnight. Observant of his schedule, Captain Pruss sandwiched his hydrogen-filled zeppelin between two slowly moving electrically charged weather disturbances. He sought a quick release of passengers and mails and speedy embarkation of a sold-out return flight before the next storm arrived. An unanticipated coursing of spontaneous electrical discharge along a new and more flammable outer cover, ignited impure hydrogen (probably residual from valving gas to achieve equilibrium for landing) and produced the greatest disaster hitherto known in commercial aviation. Thirty-six passengers and crew were lost, including airship pioneer Lehmann.

It was not a technological failure. It was an avoidable accident resulting from business operational dictates. With the tremendous worldwide publicity given the event by press, radio and news-film, the vibrant horror of the conflagration quite overcame the still-prevalent wonder of the airship. Henceforth only helium-borne craft could survive in public estimation. By early September the US Congress passed legislation making American helium open for export to lift airships worldwide. Meanwhile, AZT offices produced voluminous statistical evidence of airship technical vitality and commercial feasibility, even with more expensive and operationally limiting helium. It was bolstered with unconvincing public opinion polls – a new media phenomenon – showing a nice majority of continued acceptance of the attractive airships. Von Meister and Goodyear worked overtime to facilitate acquiring helium for the still-functioning DZR-AZT enterprise. At the year's end the first transatlantic trip for LZ130 was scheduled for late April 1938.[8]

In Germany, the catastrophe of the *Hindenburg* became a zeppelin event of national significance. Unlike the largely spontaneous public response to Count Zeppelin's loss of LZ4 at Echterdingen in 1908, however, Nazi propaganda centrally manipulated the event to maximum political advantage. The German victims were celebrated like fallen heroes from the battlefield. Full scenarios of military music

and marching storm-troop cadres, together with official party declama-
tions, intruded upon traditional religious funeral services. This political
theatrical celebration was not the only example of official domination.
When, like 1908, a grass-roots movement of individual public contributions for zeppelin reconstruction developed, there was a prompt
official response: such activity was expressly forbidden, on the excuse
that the ship had been fully insured. Actually, the Nazi system would
not tolerate any public reaction outside party sponsorship and control.
Though photographs of some phases in the accident were published in
the press, the much more shocking film sequence was ignored and
never seen in Germany until years after the war. Goering mobilized Air
Ministry publicity in resounding praise for zeppelins past, present and
future, including a commemorative medal inscribed *Nun erst recht!*
([Airships] now for sure!). And in late 1938, Eckener personally met
Hitler a second time, now officially on the dais at the ceremonial
launching of Germany's first naval aircraft carrier, the *Graf Zeppelin*. In
peace and war the airship image was still trumps in Germany.[9]

The adjustments in zeppelin activity during the year after the
Lakehurst accident required a pause in South American service and the
expensive conversion of LZ130 to flight with helium. Though the crew
of the 'lucky' *Graf Zeppelin* voted confidently to continue flying to
Brazil and advance German bookings exceeded capacity, Eckener
forbade further service until the causes of the recent accident were fully
understood. Actually, it was a welcome occasion to retire the veteran
Graf to a new museum at Frankfurt, where great crowds came to see the
revealed secrets of its structure and its memorable past. Otherwise, all
effort was focused on converting LZ130 to service with helium: cutting
a ton of weight from its cathedral structure; making technical adjustments to handle and conserve the expensive inert gas in flight; and
creating a new supplementary system to contain, transport and periodically purify American helium. Despite all that effort, it was still necessary to reduce the passenger and cargo capacity by half, a grim
verification of Lehmann's earlier comment about profitability. But
business was no longer the basic reason for flaunting the zeppelin
image worldwide: it was the visible prowess of German technology in
the service of Nazi ideology that mattered.[10]

The negative American counterpart to the increasing Nazi colour-
ation of the zeppelin image crested during 1938. Five years earlier, criticism had begun of the Nazi suppression of Weimar democracy, soon
to be overtaken by rapidly increasing repugnance at mounting German
anti-Semitism. Hearty Nazi efforts to emphasize friendly German hos-

pitality at the Olympic Games failed to offset the negatives of German remilitarization in 1935 and the violations of the Locarno Treaties in 1936. Then came the hostile impact of the German-Italo-Japanese Anti-Comintern Pact of late 1936, soon followed by Nazi intervention in the Spanish Civil War in 1937. The gradually rising tide of American anti-Nazism was not yet enough to counteract the still-surviving American popular enthusiasm for airships and revulsion at the hydrogen flames of the *Hindenburg* disaster, which together produced the helium export legislation of later 1937. American naval airship adherents were in no sense pro-Nazi. With their devotion to the airship technological cause in service of American defence, however, naval airshipmen clung to whatever support and advantage might accrue to their deteriorating fortunes from German airship developments. Goodyear-Zeppelin was, of course, intimately involved in continuing consultation with its junior partner at Friedrichshafen. Litchfield had invested over five million dollars to establish his airship construction and operating business during the previous fifteen years. It was an enormous commitment for his mid-sized enterprise and would not be abandoned as long as the Germans demonstrated such technological vitality. Thus Rosendahl, as Commandant at Lakehurst, was intimately concerned to maintain the bare bones of naval airship operations, actively with the small naval non-rigids and passively in the expectation of further German rigid flights. And at Goodyear, Hunsaker worked closely with von Meister on all aspects of helium procurement and development of German helium facilities – all the while still hoping to charter one of the next new zeppelins for service with AZT and eventually again to build airships at Akron. It was a strange twilight in which bright American airship hopes tried to survive in a darkening political scene.[11]

Circumstances became bizarre as 1938 unfolded. Early in February, Hitler asserted his control of the German Army, supplanting the dominant old conservative *Reichswehr* leadership with younger and more adventurous pro-Nazi officers of the new *Wehrmacht*. Similarly, Nazi von Ribbentrop replaced the staid traditional executives at the Foreign Office. In mid-March Germany invaded and annexed Austria. At Friedrichshafen all Germans, including airshipmen, cheered this 'return' of the *Ostmark* to the Reich, while Goodyear's representative there followed Hunsaker's lead to equip and instruct the zeppeliners in the use of helium. In Washington, zealous Congressmen Dickstein and Dies intermittently pursued their investigations of alleged un-American activities, notably those of Goebbels' propaganda and the German-

American Bund. Goodyear encountered increasing unfriendliness in Congress and among administration officials as they tried to assist reactivation of naval rigid airship construction. In mid-April, just as helium was about to be shipped to Germany, America informed Berlin that export of the inert gas was again forbidden, lest it be of aid to further German military ventures. Eckener promptly arrived in Washington for consultation with Interior Secretary Ickes to protest the decision. Ickes argued that zeppelins might be used militarily; Eckener countered that wartime experience had proved the rigids totally ineffective for war; neither conceived that the new zeppelin might conduct pre-war electronic reconnaissance. Quite probably Ickes fronted for Roosevelt's growing anti-Nazi vexation, though Goodyear's man in Friedrichshafen was convinced that PanAm and the British were instrumental in the prohibition. In July, Germany celebrated the centennial of Count Zeppelin's birth at the dedication of a new airship museum at Friedrichshafen, with Rosendahl as an honoured guest of the much-propagandized occasion. That same month the zeppelin image came boldly again to American attention. The prestigious magazine of American business culture, *Fortune*, published a long, superbly illustrated analysis of the skyward rivalries shaping up for the North Atlantic. Outstanding was a sequence of colour conceptions of the new flying boats visualized by Boeing, Douglas, Consolidated and Sikorsky. Most dramatic, however, was the broad oversized colour foldout labelled: THE LZ-130 IS GERMANY'S BID [!]. Meanwhile Lufthansa was in the midst of 26 North-Atlantic trial flights with two intermediate catapult motherships. Then, prophetically, just as *Fortune* was on the newsstands, a four-engine Focke-Wulf Condor airplane made the first non-stop winged flight from Berlin to New York in twenty-five hours – with early refuelling for prompt return to the Reich. The pioneering airship was now due for relegation to a museum of transatlantic flight.[12]

During later 1938 and 1939, circumstances other than transatlantic travel determined the flights of the *Hindenburg* sistership LZ130, built almost entirely with Nazi government subsidy. With little official participation during the mounting Czech crisis, Eckener christened the last airship again as *Graf Zeppelin* in mid-September 1938. His words were an updated echo of his earlier convictions:

> I wish this ship to carry forth the honour of German technology to all the world as a symbol of unshakable German will, to gain for the German people the place in the world to which they are entitled. To the German people and their leader! Sieg Heil!

Eckener had not become a Nazi, but he had resolved to maintain the technological heritage of Count Zeppelin through thick and thin, beyond the current Nazi madness towards continuation in some unknown post-Nazi era. Thus he had become a coactive *Wehrwirtschaftsführer* (defence-economic leader), in a Zeppelin Company now heavily involved with military production, and thus he had finally yielded to participation of the Nazi works council in the decision-making within his business. With test flights of LZ130 in the offing in August 1938, the Luftwaffe intruded upon the zeppelin enterprise to convert the commercial airship for military electronic surveillance of non-German radio broadcasting. Here efforts were astir to improve German aviation ground-to-air communication towards more sophisticated plane-to-plane communication. Luftwaffe Air Signals Branch was anxious to discover how far Germany's likely opponents had progressed in their own signals development. From the beginning, LZ130 flew with several dozen Luftwaffe signalmen in mufti, placed at two dozen measurement consoles in the broad transverse zeppelin dining-room to monitor non-German wireless wavelengths and data over a broad frequency spectrum. It produced a series of remarkable airship voyages and fine training for a new generation of younger airshipmen, but commercial operation was not the purpose of these flights.[13]

Luftwaffe operations of LZ130 for electronic surveillance began systematically in the late spring of 1939. Roundabout routes were taken on various flights to different German regions, generally proximate to foreign frontiers, thus providing the aerial eavesdroppers with ample opportunity to intercept foreign radio transmissions along border areas. The main target of this activity, however, soon became the nascent British radar system. Lufthansa commercial pilots had discovered mysterious clusters of tall masts arising along the southern and eastern British coasts. Here the zeppelin flew leisurely up and down off eastern England and Scotland to seek radar signals and make visual observations. For German purposes, however, these flights were unproductive, the surveillance team reporting only heavy 'static' and 'interference', including the intrusion of Germany's other ionospheric tests. Thus the Reich would launch World War II unaware of developing British radar which would later help turn the tide of the air war over Britain in favour of the Royal Air Force.[14]

The electronic reconnaissance flights of LZ130 required political camouflage and sophisticated propaganda deception. To these ends most flights were paced with developing international events and military espionage needs by orchestrated internal German propaganda. As the Sudeten Crisis of 1938 neared its climax the new zeppelin flew proximate with the southern Czech border to a resounding public welcome as it overflew recently-annexed Vienna. Conveying its might and majesty, LZ130 confirmed political assurance and generated confidence that all was well in Greater Germany. The notorious Munich Agreement required Czech loss of the Sudetenland and its three million inhabitants. Here again a plebiscite was staged to validate the opinion of the newly acquired population. And again a zeppelin flew over the 'liberated' lands to greet Hitler and his motorized cavalcade at Reichenberg, as loudspeaker military music blared forth from the airship and thousands of leaflets were again dropped urging all the Sudeten folk to approve their annexation to the Reich. During the following summer of 1939, as pre-war tensions tightened, the zeppelin made that series of borderland flights supposedly en route to Sunday 'Flying Days'. Here, huge crowds were drawn to politically orchestrated events that emphasized the new power of the Nazi state. The landing fields, decorated with swastika flags and reverberating to the rhythms of military bands, gave occasion for various paramilitary units to sing, march and manoeuvre in anticipation of the zeppelin landing. Once arrived, the ship was further glorified by speeches of welcome and political harangue to emphasize the political determination and resplendent might of revitalized Greater Germany. It was all grand political theatre and deflection from the secret military purpose of the flights. Above all, it was a total change in the behaviour of zeppelin crowds. Formerly they had gathered voluntarily to participate in a great aerial event: eager, good-natured and individually enjoying the zeppelin experience. In retrospect, these zeppelin crowds of 1939, untouched by the horrific filmed memory of the Lakehurst conflagration, were marshalled and subject to emotional drill – a monstrous re-staging of Pavlov's behavioural experiments with dogs, where now the zeppelin was the bell that induced the salivary flow of impassioned devotion to the National Socialist Germany.[15]

Meanwhile, the skyward rivalry of airship and flying boat reached its climax in the summer of 1939. As the war-clouds gathered over Europe, work with LZ131 was halted at Friedrichshafen, but Anglo-American aviation finally introduced the mature transatlantic service that would burgeon during the developing century. As British mail planes began flying the North Atlantic Circle route, PanAm opened with service directly across to the Azores and on to west European port cities. An initial test flight of the Boeing 314 flying boat left for Europe on the twelfth anniversary of Lindbergh's momentous flight to Paris. By late June, scheduled service was opened with 35 passengers and 12 crew per flight. Thus, after eleven years of Trippe's labyrinthine manoeuvring around the airships and his secret deals with the British, the first flying boats began service over the North Atlantic, while the last zeppelin probed the secrets of the enigmatic ether and by its continuing wonder in Germany hyperbolized the nation for war.[16]

American efforts with airships ground to a halt in the last year of peace. With the refusal of helium for Germany all plans for transatlantic airship service under joint DZR-AZT auspices were abandoned. As LZ130 was rapidly restored to hydrogen lift, Goodyear's man in Friedrichshafen encountered rising aversion from factory personnel and local officials. With the installation of Luftwaffe gear for electronic surveillance, he was excluded from customary hangar access and denied participation in test flights of the last zeppelin. His departure from Germany in late autumn just preceded Hunsaker's resignation from Goodyear-Zeppelin at the end of the year, to restore his professional career at MIT and give other aviation advice to the Navy. His decade of energetic work for commercial airship development was stillborn, his projects exceeded in operational planning and business sagacity only by the comparably highly successful career of Eckener. With the equally stillborn venture of AZT, Willy von Meister also turned to an alternative business career, developing blueprint duplication of business records. Both men left behind a much-reduced cadre of designers at Goodyear-Zeppelin who set aside their designs for more capacious commercial airships and now switched to further development of non-rigids for other naval uses and for potentialities in aerial commercial advertising. And the giant Airdock at Akron began to accommodate other technological ventures related to America's belated aerial rearmament.[17]

A small minority of American naval proponents continued their efforts to keep rigid airships alive for long-distance naval scouting. Favourable action by the House Committee on Naval Affairs in 1938 resulted, with Goodyear participation, in designs for a new training airship a bit larger than the scrapped *Los Angeles*. When Roosevelt learned of these developing plans, he intervened to insist upon a much smaller and quite impractical ship. Herein he was probably influenced to favour a Metalclad-type ship, with whose builder he had in 1936 conversationally referred sarcastically to 'that rubber company in Akron' – which had in 1925–6 failed to rescue him from his own ill-starred business venture with Schütte-designed airships. Subsequent efforts to meet the President's bias produced only the design of a rigid airship dwarf. Another naval study, requested of Admiral King and Captain Fulton in 1939–40, urged renewed continuation of naval rigid airship experimentation; but with war aflame in Europe and smouldering in the Far East, the proposal was turned down. Fulton voluntarily retired in 1940, leaving only Commander Rosendahl to carry the torch for naval rigid airships, which he would relight once again in 1946–8.[18]

As the 'phony war' of 1939–40 loitered on the European scene, LZ130 was emptied of her hydrogen gas cells and hung from the rafters of her great Frankfurt hangar. Rumours were rife for her suggested wartime use: carrying copper and manganese from Russia to support the Nazi war machine; a long-distance propaganda flight or trans-Siberian air service to Tokyo; and in March 1940 possibilities of a final trip of succour for embattled German forces at Narvik, much as LZ59 had been sent out in 1917 to aid the harried forces of German General Lettow-Vorbeck in East Africa. By then, however, the decision to eradicate the zeppelin terminal at Frankfurt airport was already under way. Climbing around the stripped structure of LZ130 in early March 1940, Goering (with a large retinue of high aviation brass) indulged in the folksy chatter that had endeared him to the German public:

> Na, that thing's for the birds! ... One match and the whole contraption will go up in flames! ... Go ahead, take a picture [of Goering in the zeppelin], it'll have future scarcity value!

General Milch sought to soften the blow for distraught airshipmen there: 'Look, fellows, be sensible. We need the space to regroup our fighter squadrons. After the war we'll gear up again [with airships]; you can depend on it'. But after the war there remained only the ruins of bombed out Friedrichshafen, where the zeppelin hangar had been converted to assemble V-2 rockets. And Eckener himself, under French occupational indictment for alleged conspiracy as a Nazi 'defence-economic leader', was embroiled with the Friedrichshafen city authorities over their decision to liquidate the Zeppelin Foundation in conformity with the Old Count's will, which stipulated that the company assets could go to meet city charitable needs if ever there was no further prospect of zeppelin development. Thus the god of war, to whose service the Count had initially dedicated the purpose of his remarkable invention, presided at the destruction of his aerial enterprise.[19]

Successful wartime endeavour in America, however, gave Litchfield at Akron a final opportunity to keep his rigid airship hopes alive.

Though Goodyear-Zeppelin was formally liquidated in late 1940 (by reason of its poor business prospects and now-suspect German association), Arnstein and remnants of his design cadre produced a proposal in 1943 for a hospital airship to carry 248 casualties and requisite emergency medical facilities in a craft 50 per cent larger than the *Macon*. By the end of the war Litchfield was pressing government aviation authorities to re-examine all aspects of commercial airship use. In late 1946, now-retired Vice Admiral Rosendahl became Goodyear's 'Aeronautical Consultant' in Wall Street and Washington. Here he tried to revitalize a faded generation of naval and business associations to assist Goodyear Aircraft's president Knowles and lobbying staff in resurrecting Hunsaker's lost airship legislation of 1930–3. While Goodyear worked the first Republican Congress in sixteen years, Rosendahl (even manipulating the brief postwar reappearance of Eckener in Akron and Washington) had little success in rousing media attention. Indeed, Goodyear's own publicity efforts were feeble and misbegotten. Its major argument, buttressed by varied plans of palatial passenger airship configurations derived from the wartime hospital airship concept, rested entirely on an overwrought argument of commercial airship superiority over the flying boat – just as flying boats had disappeared from transoceanic service now supplied by standard four-engine aircraft that had matured during the war. With such ineptness in playing the card of residual airship wonder, Goodyear's efforts languished in public unresponsiveness and congressional inattention for nearly two years. Finally, a puny remnant of the endeavour got congressional approval. A bill was passed in mid-1948, authorizing the Maritime Commission to study the effectiveness of airships in transoceanic commerce, only to fall victim to a presidential 'pocket veto'. Here evaporated America's once-vibrant public enthusiasm for naval and commercial airships – first with a bang, then with a whimper.[20]

Thus both in Germany (with alarming governmental manipulation and infatuated public acclaim) and in America (with official and political rejection plus failing public resonance) the wonder of the airship was finally wasted in ignoble Nazi manipulation and in American naval ineptness and ultimate business incompetence. Happily, however, the best memories of airship wonder, and of the men who sought its realization in beneficial enterprise, have lived on to engage the creative imagination of generations to come.

Conclusion

During the summer of 1999, television viewers in America were being solicited to purchase products of a major Japanese automobile producer with an unusual advertisement. Done not in brilliant colours, but restricted to basic black and white, it showed a sleek new silver sedan cruising down a black highway against grey and white tones of background mountains and skies. After a moment the camera lifted to the grey sky above, now dominated by the glistening silver image of a magnificent airship gliding along in majestic silence, inspiring awe and imparting its values of comfort, luxury and superiority. Thus sixty years of repeated television views of the crashing *Hindenburg* have still not destroyed the sense of immediate psychic response or nostalgia to the wonder of the airship. The days of those aviation rivalries have long since passed, but the airship image still attracts attention by its qualities of stimulating the human sense of incongruity and amazement.

The airship-dominated skyward rivalries of the half-century between the appearance of the first French military non-rigid in 1885 and the last military electronic surveillance flight of LZ130 in 1939 had a wide variety of manifestations. First came the technological contests between various types of military airships, followed by rivalries between lighter-than- and heavier-than-air craft. Soon appeared the promise and first realities of commercial aircraft, with airships having initially an apparently unbeatable technological advantage for transoceanic flight. Then developed a new version of competition between airships and airplanes for naval reconnaissance. Finally came the fading of airship promise over oceans, as flying boats closed in with rapid technological improvement. These different varieties of skyward rivalry were soon compounded and inflated by the early readiness of astute political personalities to manipulate the well-observed psychic attractiveness of airships for diversion to their own particular political purposes and objectives as long as airships were publicly seen as reliable, useful and potentially profitable.

The psychic response stimulated by air vehicles was a recognized popular phenomenon ever since the French brothers Montgolfier made their first balloon ascents in 1783. It persisted in the country-fair popularity of ever greater and more daring balloon spectacles into the mid-nineteenth century. Beginning with the wars of the 1860s came their serious use in artillery spotting and local terrain reconnaissance. Establishment of the Prussian Airship Battalion in 1884 for further development of tethered balloon observation was soon followed by French development of elongated *dirigible* balloons, the first real airships. This invention prompted Count Zeppelin's ideas for a rigid airship from 1887 onward and the introduction of international aviation rivalry into competing French and German militarism. For the next twenty years non- and semi-rigid airships developed slowly in several European military forces, generating some public attention. Meanwhile, scant notice was taken of the Count's several accident-prone ascents in provincial south Germany. Only in 1908 did public enthusiasm burst forth during Zeppelin's Swiss and Rhineland flights, culminating in the spectacular destruction of his airship at the peak of its public triumph. The almost instantaneous national crowds marked a massive surge in public psychic response to the awe, wonder and stimulating incongruity of the huge rigid airship moving spectacularly through the skies. This response quickly moved into German popular fantasies about aerial warfare, notably echoed in Britain, with its accompanying anxiety about German naval rivalry. With these circumstances the stage was set for international technological competition, militaristic rivalries and the intervention of political manipulation.

The political context of the initial intra-German technological airship rivalry featured the arrogance of the Prussian Airship Battalion versus the tenacious determination of the thwarted Württemberg General. Here the Count was fatefully held at bay for eighteen years until his spectacular successes of 1908. Sensing the remarkable upsurge of enthusiasm among the great apolitical majority of Germans, the Kaiser swung into the mainstream of popularity for the Count and his airship to overcome an Imperial disaster in public relations resulting from his *Daily Telegraph* interview. Previous committee, hierarchical and court politics were swept aside and the first zeppelins were thrust upon a reluctant German Army by revised Imperial favour. With this battle hardly won, the Count faced a new technological competitor in gifted engineer Johann Schütte, who forthwith also vied for armament contracts. The Old Aeronaut resisted the new evident improvements until disaster struck his first two airships for the German Navy. At this point in 1913, naval engineers became a powerful silent partner in zeppelin-building, and with the coming of the war they pressed effectively to combine the best of both rigid construction types in German wartime airships. Clearly, however, the Count was the victor with his widespread personal popularity and the earlier multiplication of his airships in short passenger flights. Together, he and the Kaiser were the first politically successful manipulators of airship technology: the Count to restore his maligned honour and to give his nation a superior weapon; the Kaiser to bolster his schizoid conception of popularity in a modernizing industrial country. And together they gave Imperial Germany a misleading image as the greatest aviation power of the world in 1914. Airship wonder, barely daunted by several German commercial and military accidents, held the excitement of aviation enthusiasts worldwide.

During World War I, zeppelins appeared initially to have military superiority, but rapidly they revealed their fatal weaknesses. Now the rivalry with airplanes began in earnest and by late 1918 the last zeppelin bombing raid was a culminating military defeat. Their image survived very differently among the warring powers. In Germany, wartime censorship heralded the heroism of German airshipmen and concealed the appalling record of zeppelin losses. Among Allied nations the initially successful civilian bombing raids caused much psychic disturbance that never fully left either British or French popular awareness in the postwar generation. A third type of awareness emerged curiously in professional naval circles in the sense of rigid airships as crucially important for naval reconnaissance. No doubt this conviction derived from some British explanations for their failure to achieve a decisive destructive victory over the German fleet at Jutland in 1916, allegedly because zeppelin scouts had made a German escape possible. Thus was born a myth of zeppelin superiority in reconnaissance that promptly produced a crash programme of British naval airship construction. The resulting craft arrived too late to affect the war and failed to survive in the postwar Royal Navy, but this brief British airship endeavour had a profound impact upon American strategic naval thinking for two decades. Thus the rigid airship remained in German minds as a popular icon of German superiority unimpaired by its concealed record of military failure. In England public sentiment never lost its revulsion against this instrument of death from the skies, unaffected by momentary naval initiative for developing airships to help rule the seas. In America, however, major naval circles perceived the airship as an indispensable instrument for reconnaissance out over the far Pacific in a likely conflict with Japan. Despite these passing specialized naval considerations, the airship had failed in its wartime service, already overshadowed by the airplane in effective tactical combat. What remained was a remarkably contradictory image of airship wonder and promise: horror weapon in wartime still giving the only likely expectation for transoceanic flight in peace.

Between 1919 and 1925, skyward rivalries reflected that dual image. In technological terms everthing seemed to favour the airship over planes, especially when R34 crossed the Atlantic non-stop in 1919, with 30 tons burden, while planes barely could complete non-stop London–Paris transits with six passengers. British naval circles gave up airships after already ordering the new R38, torn between military controversy and discomfort with the new RAF. Internationally, the Allies denied Germany all air power, though America's brash young power-seeking General Mitchell briefly bolstered Eckener's reawakening enterprise with a surprise illegal order of a military zeppelin. This Army aviation thrust challenged the American Navy, already sensitive to its inconspicuous performance during the war. By 1921 presidential authority reserved the rigid airship exclusively for Navy use; all the while Mitchell's planes were sinking outdated tethered battleships in highly publicized bombing runs. But the Navy's reply was already in process. Fulton, Hunsaker and naval engineers were building ZR1 and awaiting delivery of newly-purchased R38 from Britain. Meanwhile, Germany's bid of 1919 for limited domestic zeppelin service was nipped in the bud and her few remaining dirigibles were delivered to the Allies. Her zeppelin future seemed doomed, though remnant staffs with Eckener and Schütte turned their wartime expertise to planning for international commerce. Comparable projects also came from less expert British engineers and entrepreneurs, spread futuristically in staid books and popular journals. Here Burney shaped his first plans for an empire-wide commercial airship network. It all came to a sudden halt with the crash of R38, in process of delivery to America.

Henceforth the skyward rivalries took a new turn. Empire airship schemes were altered in a new technological competition, whereby British aviation design expertise challenged the allegedly backward zeppelin skill that was seen as the cause for the crash of R38, replicated from earlier downed German airships. The American Navy took another tack. Favouring the quality of German experience, it negotiated with the Allies to have an airship built by Eckener. Now American naval interest clashed with European policy to destroy German zeppelin expertise. Britain felt the loss of a potential American market for future airships; France was adamant to destroy all zeppelin enterprise; even Japan objected. The result was a new zeppelin of limited size and restricted function. Thus flawed by political manipulation, it would be withheld from fleet service until 1931, by which time its scouting potentialities would be overrun by the practical achievements of rapidly maturing naval carrier aviation. But these still unresolved naval aviation circumstances left opportunities wide open to manipulate the enthusiasm of the vast American apolitical majority. In that interim, power-holding Moffett continually paraded both airships before the public in stunning appearances that belatedly stole most of Mitchell's anti-Navy thunder – until ZR1 crashed in September 1925 and provoked a final flare-up of Mitchell's demagoguery against the Navy. His subsequent Army court martial closed that phase of skyward rivalry. Then airship competition and its political manipulation moved into the international commercial sphere. Unrestrained public enthusiasm for all aviation progress, no matter what accidents or heroic loss of life, did not allow four dirigible accidents in four different nations seriously to lessen airship wonder and its anticipated benefits for all mankind.

Between 1925 and 1930 the new international aviation rivalries appeared in four ways on a worldwide scale. Ever-present was the rapidly improving technological competence of winged aircraft. Increasingly planes narrowed the competitive gap with airships as they overcame earlier limitations of capacity, range and speed. And in transoceanic commerce, flying boats began gradually catching up to airship promise and achievement. Among airship entrepreneurs in three nations different aspects of contention appeared. First, Germany achieved a remarkable early revision of the hated Versailles Treaty that permitted her re-entry into commercial aviation: Luft Hansa with winged craft and Eckener with his zeppelins both emerged to compete with aircraft of the Allies, now politically at odds with each other over aviation matters. Both German aviation groups and their enthusiasts capitalized on themes of German political triumph through technological superiority, and the zeppelin swept the field in arousing the emotions of tens of millions in the Reich and abroad. Second, Britain undertook her ambitious Imperial Airship Scheme, a bold venture soon vitiated by internecine technological competition, which played off capitalist Burney against socialist Aviation Minister Thomson – a contest that power-holding Thomson seemed to be winning hands down in 1929–30, until its culminating disaster. Finally, there was the wearying stumble of the ever-delayed American naval airship programme, which had its positive aspects in Hunsaker's work with Goodyear-Zeppelin to adapt the naval dirigible for international commerce. Great crowds in Germany and America greeted every zeppelin appearance, and even the British, with their wartime zeppelin negativism, responded somewhat favourably to Thomson's continual manipulation of airship technology as a creative socialist success and Empire ornament. Worldwide public enthusiasm for airships as symbols of progress, dream-fulfilment and power was unabated until the crash of British R101. More than any of the other four previously publicized airship losses, this event (with its toll of notable personalities) had a profound negative impact upon popular airship enthusiasm. Henceforth every individual or mass reaction to airships and airship news was likely to be tinged with negativism: Was it safe? Could it survive adverse weather? Airship wonder had to accommodate to the apparent inevitability of one step back for every two steps forward.

Between 1931 and 1935 the international airship rivalry was reduced to two nations. In the broad background of general aviation competition, winged aircraft worldwide broke through technological barriers to achieve passenger appeal, favourable loads and operational reliability. Smaller flying boats established winged success along the coastal margins of continents; even German and French transoceanic winged monsters made their deficit-ridden debuts. All the economic woes of the Depression did not curb the development of commercial aviation with winged craft – of course with massive government subsidies. But for the vastly more expensive airships the Depression was crippling. With time of the essence in the technological contest, the first commercially practical zeppelin was delayed five years until airborne. First hampered in construction for three penurious years, the zeppelin enterprise was then 'rescued' by the belated financial support and insolent political perversion of the new Nazi regime. This upstart power-usurper tried to realize the kind of political success in airship manipulation that two other dictatorial regimes failed to achieve: Mussolini's sterile political venture to use Nobile's polar flights to embellish Italian fascism and Stalin's marginal efforts with bogus airship propaganda in his broader thrust of using aviation to proclaim the political superiority of Russian Communism. On the American naval scene, the rigid airship failed in practical use. It was beaten in deployment by carrier-borne winged aircraft, criticized for its huge expense and made strategically obsolete by a fundamental shift in war planning for a conflict with Japan. The operational failures of the two rigid naval airships only confirmed other more fundamental reasons for the demise of American naval airships. The projected commercial versions of these naval craft were left in limbo with Hunsaker's planning at Goodyear-Zeppelin, quite dependent now on the future of Nazi German zeppelin developments. America's promise for airship reliability with the use of non-flammable helium was proved no safeguard against the forces of nature in the skies. Wonder for airships was now increasingly shaken by doubts about the ability of engineers to build craft strong and fast enough to overcome adverse weather and of operators skilful enough to recognize airborne dangers and respond quickly enough to overcome them.

During 1935–9 Eckener and the Nazi government were mutually hostile associates as the only remaining airship contestants in the rivalry for transoceanic commerce and national prestige. Increasingly Goebbels' propaganda manipulated the zeppelins at home and abroad for pointed political emphases. The spectacular 1936 zeppelin flight season was a last momentary triumph for the skyships, as no effective competitor appeared on the North Atlantic and PanAm had barely got under way across the Pacific. Once again the airship aroused wide public wonder and amazement, while Goodyear-Zeppelin engineers and American naval airshipmen regularly flew along with the Germans for instruction to keep their operational expertise alert. Power-holders and power-seekers outside Germany, however, withdrew from manipulation of the newest skyship image, given its potential hydrogen hazard and dubious Nazi political association. A last effort to advance all international airship flight with American helium after the *Hindenburg* crash foundered with Hitler's grasp of Austria in 1938. A new *Graf Zeppelin II* ascended to arouse fervid enthusiasm at the Nazi Party Day celebration later that year and to affirm seizure of the Czech Sudetenland before year's end. During 1939 the new propaganda instrument did yeoman duty at weekends all summer long, as crowds marched and cheered with zeppelin ardour – while on weekdays the Luftwaffe used the ship for electronic espionage in preparation for war. And in that summer at long last the first PanAm and British flying boats began their transatlantic service. In spring 1940 the last two zeppelins were scrapped and their hangars destroyed – ultimate victims of the god of war for whose service they had first been conceived fifty years before.

Thus the sense of airship wonder was aroused, nourished and finally thwarted by indisputable practical realities. Some echoes continue as individual responses of psychic incongruity to the perception of occasional small airships overhead or as nostalgia for the comfortable zeppelins of yesteryear, or even as local excitement for cargolifters as yet untested. But the era of great airship wonder worldwide remains enshrined in psychic history as a unique phenomenon of the first half of the twentieth century.

Together with the widespread attention that airships attracted in their technological, military–naval and commercial rivalries, the rigid airships had three other kinds of significant influence in the world at large between 1900 and 1940. First was their role in beneficially fostering, or negatively influencing, the relationships between peoples and nations worldwide. Second was their unique appeal to the expertise and emotions of engineers in construction and operation of rigid dirigibles, notably in Germany, Britain and America, with echoes in Italy and the Soviet Union. Third was their role in producing a unique set of individual personalities, who used these impressive constructs for their proper functions or manipulated them for ulterior political purposes. Altogether these three kinds of circumstances produced an unusual set of happenings that gave international aviation in those years its unique character.

In foreign relationships among peoples and nations the rigid airship functioned foremost in ways of individual and group psychological acceptance or reaction. Basic was the impressive incongruity of this seemingly massive object in the skies weightlessly contesting with the forces of nature. Second were the aspects of its ubiquity – its everywhereness in contrast to the limited routes of ships, trains and road vehicles – and the unexpectedness of its fascinating appearances. Third was its element of harbouring dread, either in its death-dealing role of wartime or, more recently, in its potentialities for accident or for sudden self-destruction. Given these mixed qualities, the airship still had enormous popular persuasiveness, perceived as the impressive product of national genius or ideology; and thus it played its role as an admired agent of a nation's foreign policies or as the physical and ideological threat of a troublesome neighbour. Each nation had its own identity here, either resulting from its actual international behaviour or from emotionally altered perceptions of sister nations. Germany, above all, had the dominant identity with airships, first in war, then in peaceful postwar reconciliation, finally as agent of ideological intimidation.

Britain's major effort to develop airships as symbols of a still-powerful Empire was anticipated and welcome in her far-flung dominions, but had negative impacts on her Middle Eastern and French-Canadian subjects, not to mention likely hostility in India, had Lord Thomson's ill-starred voyage succeeded. For France the Zeppelin was the worst of Germanic threat personified, whether in war, in seeming postwar military menace or in actual postwar commercial threat to her political prestige in the Middle East and South America. Italian and Soviet dictatorship both played the airship card in internal propaganda and notions to enhance their political images abroad; both withdrew after notable failure or transfer of their propaganda effort to more readily manageable winged aircraft. America alone continued the airship as an element of its naval-political posturing: initially effective in gaining prestige, then obscured by delays and a vibrant carrier-aviation success, ultimately rejected in practice and strategic planning. Its anticipated commercial derivative, meant to dominate the Atlantic and Pacific, never ascended to strengthen America's prestige abroad; indeed, its final dependence on Nazi German resources had little redeeming quality in public perception. All the other lesser nations and peoples revelled in their recurring wonder about the airship overhead, though curiously detached from its ultimate success or failure. Thus the rigid airship in twenty interwar years carried its varied messages of national genius, political prestige and reawakening threat.

Turning to engineers and operators, let us note an unusual commentary. In 1948, British cultural historian Arnold Toynbee completed his multi-part study of the origins, survival and failure of twenty-four civilizations in all the history of mankind. Basic, though not exclusive, to his sophisticated multi-causal analysis was his observed interaction of challenge as the vital spark to human endeavour and its varied responses. Some early civilizations (arctic and subtropical) remained stunted by their overpowering environmental circumstances; a few (Western, Sinaic and Indic) have met their challenges successfully; all the rest have fallen by the wayside in their failure to develop effective responses to challenges too serious or too numerous in their course of passage through time. This pattern of comprehension is suggestive for an evaluation of the airship in the skyward rivalries of the twentieth century, notably in relation to airship engineers, fliers and entrepreneurs.

Engineers of all kinds were challenged by the rapid development of all aviation after 1890, but airship technology stimulated the minds of some of their most imaginative and creative members. In all aviation there was need to solve problems of lift, power, structural strength, capacity and endurance. In winged craft, lift and power were crucially linked and dominated all other factors. In airships, however, lift was independent of power; its proper development dominated all other factors: taming the various properties of gases; building massive structures light and strong enough to make use of the gas effective; and developing instruments of dirigibility and power effective enough to facilitate rapidity of change in the face of unfavourable weather. To devise, instrumentalize and integrate these varied elements in a successful aerial vehicle were the challenges that absorbed the energies of a generation of airship engineers.

As occurred with the various civilizations that Toynbee studied, challenge and response in airship engineering came not as a single conclusive event but as a sequence of developments. Count Zeppelin's career was a characteristic mix of trial engineering episodes with an ultimately successful technological response to the challenge of his personal humiliation at Prussian hands. Despite his interim failure to respond to the engineering challenge of Schütte, or to Colsman's press to found the DELAG, his accomplishment stands, at least to 1940, as the major breakthrough for all lighter-than-air craft. Schütte scored with his decisive engineering innovations but succumbed to his obdurate insistence on plywood construction for his ships until it was too late. Eckener became a self-educated engineering innovator, out of wartime service as instructor of naval airship crews, on frequent trial flights with his students and with hands-on communication with Friedrichshafen about crucial engineering and operational improvements. His major response to challenges came directly after the war: converting the wartime zeppelin to peaceful commerce; saving the airship works in cat-and-mouse negotiations with his former enemies; and seeking to combine broad meteorological intelligence with other measures for flight safety. His unsuccessful response to the hazard of hydrogen was less a personal failure than defeat by other unmanageable factors. As engineers, all three of course depended on the expertise of men like Kober, Dürr and Kruckenberg, but theirs was the innovative pioneering that gave rigid airships their great impact on the first generation of worldwide aviation.

British airship engineers experienced an unusual sequence of challenge-response circumstances. Responding to a misperceived challenge from German naval airships in 1916–18, they then first encountered the wonder of vast cathedral-like dirigible structures and the zest to propel them through the skies. They responded by taking what they could from German technological accomplishment. Except for Wallis's more innovative R80, they were four years behind in a developing state of the art. Their efforts to respond successfully within the parameters of zeppelin design culminated short of fulfilment in the crash of R38. The next response to that challenge of failure produced two further shortcomings by way of the Imperial Airship Scheme. First there was the decision for an engineering competition, sensible at first glance but concealing hidden springs of compensating for previous inadequacy with excessive experimental ambition for one enterprise and generating corresponding mild disdain for the other. Thus developed a kind of engineering arrogance, seen in the inability of the best minds in each team to consult and cooperate with the other for mutual benefit of the entire project. As Wallis and his team moved mostly straight forward with some innovation but limited resources, the Richmond team with government largess was impaired by lavish research in diverse avenues of engineering innovation, by distracting interim testing of different airship parts and by managerial deficiency in bringing it all together in a fully tested whole. A second shortcoming was the unfortunate association of political ideology with engineering and operational endeavour, which forced the Richmond team to public performance for high Imperial ambition with a less than fully tested aircraft – a situation already tragically comprehended by a few of the engineers, fliers and passengers on that final flight. With the imperfect response of one of the engineering teams and their focused political direction to Imperial aspiration, the whole venture was lost for Britain and had a sobering impact worldwide in illuminating the untamed hazard of flight with hydrogen.

American airship engineering was relatively free from the kinds of challenges that had confronted their German and British colleagues. The original Navy design team (Truscott, Burgess, Hunsaker) could move more deliberately in 1919–21 than had the British earlier in designing a naval airship. As they projected ZR1, similarly taking wisdom from downed zeppelin data, they also studied the British at work on R38 that was becoming ZR2. Theirs was some foreboding at too much British faith in theoretical design without commensurate operational experience. With the loss of R38, they took the lessons of that failure fully to redesign and strengthen their own ship. Subsequently, with Fulton at Friedrichshafen to observe the building of ZR3, some wisdom of German zeppelin experience entered into the completion of ZR1. These were not dramatic challenges but paced learning from others' circumstances. Following the loss of ZR1 in 1925, naval engineers Fulton and Settle carefully monitored the melding of German and American design and construction at the hands of Goodyear's Arnstein and his American-German staff. Their adversaries were the frustrating politics of naval and Washington institutional decisions. Galling was the two-year additional delay occasioned by the arrival of competing designs from Schütte and a variety of less-qualified American and foreign design contestants between 1927 and 1929. None of these delays, nor the fatal operational confrontations with extreme weather in 1933 and 1935, could be remedied by any prompt engineering intervention. The supreme challenge, that of winged aircraft to airships, so clearly evident and defined in the American Navy by 1930, was not open to resolution by Akron's engineers. It was a matter of technological Darwinian survival of the fittest, not just worse or better engineering. For the rest of that decade American airship technology, by way of Hunsaker's commercial planning at Goodyear-Zeppelin, had to suffer the blows of naval misfortune and subsequently to rely on Eckener's bold operational initiative with the *Hindenburg* ships – and their fatal hydrogen flaw. In response to that challenge the Americans moved quickly to make helium available at long last, but now for commercial airships unlikely to attract or carry enough passengers to produce business profits.

The technological and operational dilemmas of the rigid airship were outlined in 1988 by author Hans G. Knäusel in his study, *Blind Alley in the Sky*.[1] All the innovations of new technology and safe helium, he argued, still could not likely produce a reliably manageable and profitable vehicle for goods or passenger service. The great conundrum still remains technologically: how to develop metals light and strong enough to construct an airship hull durable in extreme weather, together with engines light and powerful enough to move the ship quickly through the skies? Once this solution was given, there was the management conundrum: how to be assured of skilled leadership and personnel attendant throughout the vast airship structure to recognize and deal promptly with rapid changes in the characteristics of lift that were constantly affected by changes in temperature, humidity, and altitude? Given that effective understanding in handling the delicate interrelationships of gas and ballast by a trained chain of command using reliable and distant machinery, how then to relate all that complicated technological intermixture with the power of weather buffeting the great structure as it moved through the sky? And finally: given some miraculous solution for the foregoing myriad of difficulties, once several dozen commercial airships were in operation, and more to

come (as one *DZR* official, fulfilling a programme of zeppelin development approved in principle by Goering and aligned with the Air
Minister's overall 1936 *Vierjahresplan*, foresaw in 1936 for the next
decade with hydrogen), was there enough helium left on earth to continue lifting so many skyships and to replenish their supply?

From the early 1880s onward all lighter-than-air engineers wrestled
with all the foregoing questions except the last. Their varied responses
in different circumstances were mostly to the basic challenge of getting
their ships into the air, moving them towards military or commercial
objectives and wrestling with all the varied moods of weather. Theirs
was practical schooling, learning from their failures as they went along,
as was happening with airplanes as well – though little airplane accidents were not as costly in human lives, machines and publicity as
were airships. Until the later 1920s both kinds of aircraft were still
often seen by their fliers and the public as instruments of heroic personal adventures, quite acceptable in the context of untamed natural
and technological hazards. Before 1932, when the Guggenheim
Institute at Akron became the first organization for systematic
advanced research in lighter-than-air understanding, engineers were
mostly involved in an intelligent process of trial-and-error learning by
doing, more sophisticated in some places than others. Little nourished
by much fundamental theoretical wisdom, airship engineers were
increasingly harassed by the challenge to their ventures from the
designers and operators of more nimble and more rapidly developing
winged craft. As they developed and flew their enormous and expensive experiments in the sky, they tended to become (as a professional
guild) aggressively convinced of the future of their conceptions and
also defensive of their partial unit successes and overall operational
limitations or failures. At best, notably with the Zeppelin Company in
Germany, with the Wallis team at Howden, and at Goodyear-Zeppelin,
their technological creativity was expressed with careful engineering
expertise and caution at every step. Some others buttressed themselves
with self-justifying and self-enhancing defensive postures. Here
evolved a fraternity of experts still excited by the fantastic engineering
dimensions of their design and construction challenges, yet increasingly subject to the assurance and protectiveness of the group itself.
This phenomenon seemed to offer confidence and pride in the face of
threatening forces. Initially it was resistance to the derogation of
service engineers as a guild in the three major navies – men seen as
indispensable technicians but careerwise inferior to line officers. Then,
as planes rapidly developed, so did the ribald jesting or outright hostil-

ity of Luft Hansa fliers vs. Zeppeliners, of RAF pilots vs. British airshipmen, and of American carrier personnel vs. the late-coming airshipmen
with their 'rubber cows' and 'helium heads'. And in Britain these
factors were compounded by a notable third, the rivalries of 'practical'
men in management and decision-making at the Air Ministry and
Treasury (with their Oxbridge education and social networks) vs. the
'boffins', the engineers from technical schools, with their 'tradesmen'
identities and implied social inferiority. It all came together in an engineering career world of fantastic appeal, hard work, and ultimately a
production of heartbreaking failed viability.

As for the outstanding leaders in airship development, how did each
of them draw the final balance of challenge and response in his career
with the skyward rivalries? Until the Zeppelin family archives are
opened to research we will not know the Count's final evaluation of
his momentous invention during the war years of 1914–17. For now,
suffice it to indicate that he probably felt that his government had
failed to use the zeppelins to best advantage and that he did shift his
construction emphasis to four-engine Gotha bombers to achieve the
victories that had eluded the airships. Schütte struggled until 1929 to
realize the full promise of his notable contributions to airship design,
frustrated during the war by his fatal distraction into plywood construction and subsequent inability to achieve effective metal alternatives. Wallis moved in just a decade from the perfection of R80 to the
positive realization of R100, then to leave airships altogether in design
of the Wellington bomber and the remarkable dam-busting weapon of
1944 – only to succumb to postwar subsonic transport competition.
Lord Thomson fell victim to his political strategies in oversight of the
Imperial Airship Scheme together with support of Socialist party ideals.
Admiral Moffett, who helped all naval airmen achieve recognized
status within the service and developed carrier aviation, gave his life in
the conviction that airships must prove themselves in effective operations. Fulton, Hunsaker and Arnstein made a useful transition out of
airships into the world of postwar aviation and to the frontiers of aerospace. Rosendahl, popularly the best-known American airshipman,
played a final role in determined organized lobbying in Washington in
1946–8 to revive Merchant Airship legislation. His non-success there
confirmed his lifelong conviction that political animosities doomed
the airship in war and peace. The ultimate international airship personality, Hugo Eckener, at the apogee of his career in 1931, fell victim
to the Faustian circumstance of Nazi financial rescue of his enterprise
while seizing the zeppelin image to promote its racist imperialism. He

remains a tragic figure in 1944, his factory converted to the assembly of V-2 rockets – done partly with concentration-camp prisoners. To the end it was his belief that Count Zeppelin's noble enterprise must be preserved to survive into a post-Nazi era, which it has, in the present booming industries of Friedrichshafen and the rebirth of a small zeppelin of new technology.

In various respects, the rigid airships were tokens of the men and the nations that tried to build and fly them. Their wonder stimulated great anticipation for the future, as major leaders and governments developed and employed them. They seemed strong and were proud; yet, they were also at the constant threat of winds no less shifting and unpredictable than those that buffeted the political ventures of their human political counterparts. Vacillating between peace and war, they never fully succeeded in either. Much like their creators, they were both instruments of political manipulation and victims of politics. Their fleeting triumphs and ultimate descent into practical oblivion were mirrored in the lives of many who championed their cause. And rigidity, their very claim to superiority, failed to guarantee their survival – a fact well worth pondering, even for their nostalgic enthusiasts of today and tomorrow.

Notes

Introduction: Technology and the Human Psyche

1. Quoted in Charlotte Schönbeck, 'Technik und Politik', *Kultur und Technik*. *Zeitschrift des Deutschen Museums*, 1/1989, p. 22.
2. *New York Times*, 12 Sept. 1923, p. 1.
3. Ibid., 3 Oct. 1923, p. 1.
4. Ibid., 16 Oct. 1924, p. 24.
5. For these general principles see S. Howard Bartley, *Principles of Perception*, 2nd edn (New York: Harper & Row, 1969), pp. 3–14.
6. Abraham H. Maslow, *Towards a Psychology of Being* (New York: Van Nostrand, 1962), p. 70.
7. See ibid., pp. 82–5.
8. *New York Times*, 7 May 1937, p. 19.
9. See Henry Cord Meyer, *Airshipmen, Businessmen, and Politics, 1890–1940* (Washington and London: Smithsonian Institution Press, 1991), p. 199.
10. Quoted in Barry Countryman, *R100 in Canada* (Erin, Ont.: Boston Mills Press, 1982), p. 92.
11. Hugo Eckener, untitled, undated MS, probably an address of later 1930, Schorn Archive, Friedrichshafen, p. 1.
12. Douglas H. Robinson, 'The Rigid Airship – The Dream and the Reality', *Bouyant Flight*, XXI (1974), 4.
13. See F. H. Allport, *Theories of Perception and the Concept of Structure* (New York: Wiley, 1955), passim.
14. Thus Gustav Le Bon, *The Crowd* ... (London: E. Benn, 1952), pp. 129–40.
15. Peter G. Masefield, author's note in MS. fragment, Catch the Sunlight; letter to Henry Cord Meyer, 22 April 1975.
16. Jim Murray, *Los Angeles Times*, Sports Section, 22 March 1974, III, p. 1.
17. *New York Times*, 3 Oct. 1923, p. 1.
18. Ibid., 16 Oct. 1924, p. 3.
19. J. S. Bruner and L. Postman, 'On the Perception of Incongruity: A Paradigm', in D. C. Beardslee and M. Wertheimer, *Readings in Perception* (Princeton, NJ: Princeton University Press, 1958), pp. 660–1.
20. Letter, Peter Loewenberg to H. C. Meyer, 13 March 1974.
21. Robinson, 'Rigid Airship', p. 4.
22. *Inside the Third Reich. Memoirs*, R. and C. Winston trans. (New York: Macmillan, 1970), p. 6.
23. In general see Douglas H. Robinson, *The Zeppelin in Combat ... 1912–1918*, 3rd edn (London: G. T. Foulis, 1971).
24. See Meyer, *Airshipmen*, p. 170.
25. J. Gordon Liddy, *Will. The Autobiography of J. Gordon Liddy* (New York: St. Martin's Press, 1980), pp. 1–2, 12–14. Note also the film *Two-Minute Warning* (1975), wherein the Goodyear blimp is used as an instrument of international assassination and makes a visually terrifying sudden appear-

ance very low over the edge of a football stadium filled with intended victims.

26. See Robert Darnton, *Mesmerism and the End of the Enlightenment in France* (Cambridge, MA: Harvard University Press, 1968), pp. 20–3.

27. Thus Gordon W. Allport, ed., *Cultural Groups and Human Relations*; ... (Freeport, NY: Books for Libraries Press, 1970); Elias Canetti, Carol Stewart, trans., *Crowds and Power* (New York: Viking Press, 1962); William McDougall, *The Group Mind*, ... (New York and London: G. P. Putnam's Sons, 1920); George F. Rudé, *The Crowd in History*: ... (New York: Wiley, 1964); Sam Wright, *Crowds and Riots; A Study in Social Organization* (Beverly Hills, CA: Sage Publications, 1978).

28. Paul Ditzell, 'The Day Los Angeles Had Zeppelin Fever', *Westways*, XLI (1969), 2.

29. Letter, Elias Canetti to H. C. Meyer, 5 May 1975.

30. Meyer, *Airshipmen*, pp. 94–6; Countryman, *R100 in Canada*, p. 92.

31. Meyer, *Airshipmen*, pp. 80–120, passim.

32. See T. H. G. Ward, 'The Psychological Relationship Between Man and Aircraft', *British Journal of Medical Psychology*, XXIV (1951), 283–90.

33. E. A. Johnston, 'Richmond of the R101', *The Dirigible*, No. 4, Oct.–Dec. 1990, p. 2.

34. Quoted in E. F. Spanner, *This Airship Business* (London: Williams & Norgate, 1927), p. 39.

35. In general see Erich Strauss, *The Ruling Servants. Bureaucracy in Russia, France, – and Britain?* (New York: Frederick A. Praeger, 1961).

36. *Science and Government* (Cambridge, MA: Harvard University Press, 1961), pp. 31–2, 56–63.

37. Robert A. Dahl, *Modern Political Analysis* (Englewood Cliffs, NJ: Prentice-Hall, 1963), pp. 55–71.

Chapter 1: Imperial German Precedents, 1890–1918

1. For this focus on Count Zeppelin see Henry Cord Meyer, *Airshipmen, Businessmen, and Politics, 1890–1940* (Washington and London: Smithsonian Institution Press, 1991), pp. 21–52.

2. On Count Zeppelin's political disaster of 1890 see Robinson, *Giants*, pp. 11–13 and Henry Cord Meyer, *Count Zeppelin. A Psychological Portrait* (Auckland, NZ: Lighter-than-Air Institute, 1998).The two best general studies of airship development available in English are Guy Hartcup, *The Achievement of the Airship* (London: David & Charles, 1974) and Douglas H. Robinson, *Giants in the Sky. A History of the Rigid Airship* (Seattle: University of Washington Press, 1973). The most recent, detailed and authoritative analysis of German and other lighter-than-air craft is Dorothea Haaland et al. *Die deutsche Luftfahrt. Leichter als Luft-Ballone und Luftschiffe* (Bonn: Bernard & Graefe Verlag, 1997).

3. Most important is Hugo Eckener, *Graf Zeppelin. Sein Leben nach eigenen Aufzeichnungen und persönlichen Erinnerungen* (Stuttgart: J. G. Cotta'sche Buchhandlung Nachfolger, 1938). Of all rigid airship authors to date, only Eckener had access to the voluminous archives of the Brandenstein-

Zeppelin family, with its many hundred pages of Count Zeppelin's diaries from 1859 to 1917. See pp. 100–3.

4. Basic for Germany is Luftwaffe Militärgeschichtliches Forschungsamt, eds, *Die Militärluftfahrt bis zum Beginn des Krieges 1914*. 2nd edn, 3 vols (Frankfurt: Mittler & Sohn, 1965–6). See here 'Das Ballonwesen im deutschen Heere', I, 1–11.

5. Eckener, *Zeppelin*, pp. 108–17.

6. *Militärluftfahrt*, II, Doc. No. 11, pp. 13–14; in general see I, 28–33.

7. Ibid., II, Doc. No. 19, pp. 28–31.

8. Ibid., I, 11–16, 310–13. A superb study of German airships with magnificent illustrations that uses new insights based on the hitherto inaccessible Prussian military archives: Jürgen Eichler, *Luftschiffe und Luftschiffahrt* (Berlin: Brandenburgisches Verlagshaus, 1993). See pp. 19–30.

9. Hans G Knäusel, *LZ1. Der erste Zeppelin. Geschichte einer Idee, 1874–1908* (Bonn: Kirschbaum Verlag, 1985), pp. 55–76; also Carl Berg, *David Schwarz – Carl Berg – Graf Zeppelin* (Munich: Eigenverlag, 1926), passim, and Hans Rosenkranz, *Ferdinand Graf von Zeppelin* (Berlin: Ullstein Verlag, 1931), pp. 132–5.

10. Knäusel, *LZ1*, pp. 77–144. The quotation is from Eckener, *Zeppelin*, p. 142.

11. *Militärluftfahrt*, I, 39–43; II, Docs. No. 21,22,24, pp. 34–37, 40–1. On Zeppelin's efforts see Wolfgang Meighörner-Schardt, *Die Geschichte des Luftschiffs LZ2* (Friedrichshafen: Zeppelin Museum, 1991); Eichler *Luftschiffe*, pp. 30–40.

12. *Militärluftfahrt*, I, 43–47; Eichler, *Luftschiffe*, pp. 40–8; August von Parseval, *Graf Zeppelin und die deutsche Luftfahrt* (Berlin-Grunewald: H.Klemm, 1926), pp. 50–3; Eckener, *Zeppelin*, pp. 151–4; Rosenkranz, *Zeppelin*, pp. 144–5.

13. *Militärluftfahrt*, II, Doc. No. 26, pp. 46–8; Eichler, *Luftschiffe*, pp. 44–6.

14. *Militärluftfahrt*, I, 43–57, II, Docs. No. 27–30, pp. 63.

15. Eckener, *Zeppelin*, pp. 156–7; Karl Clausberg, *Zeppelin. Die Geschichte eines unwahrscheinlichen Erfolges* (Munich: Schirmer-Mosel, 1979), pp. 39–46. For full technical details of zeppelin construction and early trials up to 4 Aug. 1908, see Robinson, *Giants*, pp. 23–39.

16. *Schwäbischer Merkur*, no. 363, 6 Aug. 1908.

17. These phenomena are described and interpreted in great detail in Peter Fritzsche, *A Nation of Fliers. German Aviation and the Popular Imagination* (Cambridge, MA: Harvard University Press, 1992), pp. 1–12. For a detailed analysis of German press propaganda see Jeannine Zeising, 'Reich und Volk für Zeppelin: Die journalistische Vermarktung einer technologischen Entwicklung', in Wolfang Meighörner, ed., *Wissenschaftliches Jahrbuch 1998* (Friedrichshafen: Zeppelin Museum, 1998), pp. 67–120.

18. Theodor Heuss, *Erinnerungen, 1905–1933* (Tübingen: Rainer Wunderlich, 1963), p. 140.

19. For a fulsome detail on these events see Fritsche, *Nation of Fliers*, pp. 205–6.

20. See documents in Eichler, *Luftschiffe*, pp. 52–3; Eckener's vivid recollection of these events is recorded in Thor Nielsen, *Eckener. Ein Leben für den Zeppelin* (Munich: Kindler & Schirmer, 1954). pp. 192–3.

21. Fritzsche, *Nation of Fliers*, pp. 22–35; Nielson, *Eckener*, pp. 205–6.

22. See the account in Nielson, *Eckener*, pp. 205–6.

23. On characteristics of German big business note the seminal work of Thorstein Veblen, *Imperial Germany and the Industrial Revolution*, pb edn

(Ann Arbor, MI: Univ. of Michigan Press, 1966), pp. 174–211. For Luftschiffbau Zeppelin see *Das Werk Zeppelins. Eine Festgabe zum 75. Geburtstag* (Friedrichshafen, LBZ, 1913), Hans Hildebrandt, ed., *Zeppelin-Denkmal für das deutsche Volk* (Stuttgart: Germania Verlag, 1925) and Hans Knäusel, *Unternehmen Zeppelin – Geschichte eines Konzerns* (Bonn: Kirschbaum Verlag, 1994). Important on the social milieu of this business history is Elmar L. Kuhn, *Geschichte am See. 24 I. Industrialisierung in Oberschwaben und am Bodensee* (Friedrichshafen: Kreisarchiv Bodenseekreis, 1984). On technology see Heinrich Walle, 'Das Zeppelin Luftschiff als Schrittmacher militärischer und industrieller technologischer Entwicklung vom Ende des 19. Jahrhunderts bis zur Gegenwart', *Technikgeschichte*, 59 (1992), pp. 319–40.

24. On the German airplane industry see John Howard Morrow, *Building German Airpower 1909–1914* (Knoxville, TN: Univ. of Tennessee Press, 1976).

25. In general see Meyer, *Airshipmen*, pp. 53–79. The authoritative technological account is Johann Schütte, *Der Luftschiffbau Schütte-Lanz, 1909–1925* (Munich: Oldenburg, 1926); on his contact with the Count see p. 126. On business history see Dorothea Haaland, *Der Luftschiffbau Schütte-Lanz, Mannheim-Rheinau (1909–1925) …* (Mannheim: Institut für Landeskunde und Regionalforschung der Universität Mannheim, 1987), esp. pp. 70–94, 211–13.

26. Basic here is Alfred Colsman, *Luftschiff Voraus! Arbeit und Erleben am Werke Zeppelins* (Stuttgart: Deutsche Verlags-Anstalt, 1933).

27. Ibid., p. 112.

28. Ibid., pp. 99–118.

29. Rolf Italiaander, *Ein Deutscher Namens Eckener* (Konstanz: Verlag Friedr. Stadler, 1981), pp. 21–84.

30. Note psychologist Daniel Capon, *Technology and Perception* (Springfield, IL: 1971), pp. 21–617.

31. See Karl Clausberg's brilliant narrative and analysis, *Zeppelin. Die Geschichte eines unwahrscheinlichen Erfolges* (Munich: Schirmer-Mosel, 1979), pp. 92–127.

32. Basic here is the discussion and documentation in Eichler, *Luftschiffe*, pp. 100–18.

33. Again, see detailed discussion and documentation in Eichler, *Luftschiffe*, pp. 118–28. For Count Zeppelin's military armament programme see the article by Major Oscar Wilcke in Hildebrandt, *Zeppelin-Denkmal*, pp. 128–39.

34. See, for instance, *Zeitschrift für Luftschiffahrt und Physik der Atmosphäre* (1881 ff.); *Illustrierte Aeronautische Mitteilungen* (1905 ff.). On leading developments, notably at Berlin's Johannisthal airfield from 1909 onward, see Annemarie Lange, *Das wilhelminische Berlin. Zwischen Jahrhundertwende und Novemberrevolution* (Berlin: Dietz, 1967).

35. Clausberg, *Zeppelin*, pp. 129–37; Fritzsche, *Nation of Fliers*, pp. 36–42. Note the seminal work of Paul Scheerbart, *Die Entwicklung des Luftmilitarismus und die Auflösung der europäischen Land-Heere, Festungen, und Seeflotten* (1909). Editor Artur Brehmer in 1910 published a thoughtful collection of essays on all aspects of European life a hundred years hence: *Die Welt in Hundert Jahren* (Berlin: Verlagsanstalt Buntdruck, 1910) that intermixed

various insightful reflections on the future of science, medicine and social progress with visions of destructive aerial war in essays by Rudolf Martin and F. W. Brown. [Reprint edition, Hildesheim, Zürich, New York, Olms Presse, 1988], pp. 68–102.

36. Alfred Gollin, *The Impact of Air Power on the British People and Their Government, 1909–1914* (Stanford, CA: Stanford University Press, 1989), passim; F. W. Brown, 'Die Schlacht von Lowestoft', in Brehmer, *Welt in Hundert Jahren*, pp. 91–102. See *Daily Mail* [London], 11 July 1909, for Martin's article. Note also as typical of serious publications, 'The Next War – in the Air', *Pearson's Magazine*, July 1913, pp. 43–58, which combined sensible technological fact with fantasy depiction of aerial warfare.

37. See the superb detail and documentation in Eichler, *Luftschiffe*, pp. 129–34. Also *Militärluftfahrt*, I, 82–110 and Morrow, *German Air Power*, passim.

38. Eichler, *Luftschiffe*, pp. 135–37. Basic for the German naval airships is Douglas H. Robinson, *The Zeppelin in Combat* ... (London: G. T. Foulis, 1962); see pp. 18–31 on the early history of naval airships.

39. Colsman, *Luftschiff Voraus!*, pp. 147–52; Meyer, *Airshipmen*, pp. 99–100.

40. Robin Higham, *The British Rigid Airship, 1908–1931. A Study in Weapons Policy* (London: G. T. Foulis, 1961), pp. 69–70, 351–5.

41. Note Harden's articles in *Die Zukunft*, 64 (July–Sept. 1908), pp. 237–49; 69 (Oct.-Dec. 1909), pp. 96–9; 75 (April-June 1911), pp. 350–7; 85 (Oct.-Dec. 1913), pp. 137–46. In general see B. Uwe Weller, *Maximilian Harden und die 'Zukunft'* (Bremen: Schünemann Universitäts-Verlag, 1970). On the disaster see Eichler, *Luftschiffe*, pp. 165–71.

42. James W. Gerard, *My Four Years in Germany* (New York: Grosset & Dunlap, 1917), pp. 52–3.

43. For superb detail, including diagrammatic tables of military organization, see Eichler, *Luftschiffe*, pp. 147–51.

44. On this 'Air Panic of 1913', see Gollin, *Impact of Air Power*, pp. 230 ff. Note also Daniel Cohen, *The Great Airship Mystery* (New York: Dodd, Mead, 1981).

45. Telegram text in Zeppelin Museum Archiv, Friedrichshafen.

46. Quoted in Clausberg, *Zeppelin*, p. 136.

47. Oscar Wilcke, 'Persönliche Erinnerungen an Graf Zeppelin', in Hildebrandt, *Zeppelin-Denkmal*, Pt. I, p. 152.

48. Superb in every way on the first half of the war is Eichler, *Luftschiffe*, pp. 175–98. The full naval record was: 283 brief or intermediate scouting missions and 202 long-range bombing flights. Best sources in English are John R. Cuneo, *Winged Mars*, II. *The Air Weapon, 1914–1916* and Robinson, *Zeppelin in Combat*, for the Navy during the entire war. On British responses and perceptions note Sir Walter Raleigh and H. A. Jones, *The War in the Air*, 6 vols (Oxford: Clarendon Press, 1922–35), vols. II and V.

49. James W. Gerard, *My Four Years in Germany* (New York: Grosset & Dunlap, 1917), pp. 52–3.

50. Zeppelin und Reichskanzler, privately printed and distributed as a manuscript, 1916.

51. See George W. Haddow and Peter M. Gross, *The German Giants: The Story of the R-Planes, 1914–1919* (London: Putnam, 1962). On Zeppelin specifically see Hildebrandt, *Zeppelin-Denkmal*, pp. 156–65.

52. For succinct technological summaries see Hans. G. Knäusel, ed., *Zeppelin.
    Aufbruch ins 20. Jahrhundert* (Bonn: Kirschbaum Verlag, 1988), pp. 156–211.

Chapter 2: Zeppelins in International Politics, 1919–21

1. In general see John H. Morrow, Jr., *The Great War in the Air. Military Aviation
   from 1909 to 1921* (Washington, DC: Smithsonian Institution Press, 1993),
   pp. 349–77. On British airship No. 23 at Harwich, note Higham, *British Rigid
   Airship*, p. 132. For Allied efforts to control German military power see
   Barton Whalley, *Covert German Rearmament, 1919–1939. Deception and
   Misrepresentation* (Frederick, MD: University Publications of America, 1984).
   Airship controls are not featured here.
2. Colsman's daunting postwar task in reorganizing the Luftschiffbau Zeppelin
   is superbly analysed in Rolf Striedacher's MS study, Anpassungsprozesse im
   deutschen Luftschiffbau. Das Beispiel Zeppelin [1919–1925]. Also Colsman,
   Luftschiff Voraus!, pp. 207–35; Italiaander, *Eckener*, pp. 156–9; Meyer,
   Airshipmen, pp. 135–8.
3. Ernst A. Lehmann, *Auf Luftpatrouille und Weltfahrt* (Berlin: Wegweiser
   Verlag, 1936), p. 213; Colsman, *Luftschiff Voraus!*, pp. 227–30.
4. Pronouncement for in-house distribution and ultimate publicity by Baron
   von Gemmingen [June 1919]. Lufthansa Archiv, Köln-Deutz.
5. Lehmann, *Luftpatrouille*, pp. 212–15. Various records of Zeppelin Company
   board meetings, Jan.–May 1919; Papers of Garland Fulton, Naval Historical
   Foundation, Washington Navy Yard, Washington, DC; Zeppelin Museum
   Archiv, Friedrichshafen; and Lufthansa Archiv, Köln-Deutz.
6. In general see R. W. Rieber, ed., *Wilhelm Wundt and the Making of a Scientific
   Psychology* (New York: Plenum Press, 1980) and Herman K. Haeberlin, 'The
   Theoretical Foundations of Wundt's Folk Psychology', ibid., pp. 229–49.
7. Italiaander, *Eckener*, pp. 14–105; Meyer, *Airshipmen*, passim.
8. Peter Kleinheins, *LZ120 'Bodensee' and LZ121 'Nordstern'. Luftschiffe im
   Schatten des Versailler Vertrages* (Friedrichshafen: Zeppelin Museum, 1994);
   Italiaander, *Eckener*, pp. 185–6; Colsman, *Luftschiff Voraus!*, pp. 227–35;
   Nielsen, *Eckener*, p. 271; DELAG-HAPAG travel brochure, Sept. 1919; interviews with Captain Garland Fulton, Bala Cynwyd, PA, 5–10 Aug. 1974.
9. Morrow, *Great War*, pp. 353–5.
10. American airship writers have designated the abortive Hensley project as
    LZ125, but German experts designate it as LZ124. See Knäusel, *Zeppelin*,
    p. 208. Data on the Hensley negotiations are derived from notes taken by
    Richard K. Smith (author of the standard study of airships *Akron* and *Macon*)
    while on research in 1959. Hereafter cited as Smith Notes, author's file.
    Thus: National Archives, Washington DC, Record Group 18, boxes 1053
    and 23. File 452.4, 1 Aug. 1919 to 29 Sept. 1920.
11. A sequence of plans drawn up between 1919 and 1923 visualized ships in
    size from thirty to a hundred thousand cubic metres gas lift (*Bodensee* was
    30, *Graf Zeppelin*, 105), for forty to eighty passengers and with six to twelve
    engines. Plan folders at Lufthansa Archiv, Köln-Deutz. Some of the draw-
    ings were reproduced in Harry Vissering, *Zeppelin. The Story of a Great
    Achievement*, privately printed at Chicago in 1922.

12. Interviews with Captain Hans von Schiller, Tübingen, 7–8 July 1973 and 14–16 July 1975. Italiaander, *Eckener*, pp. 186–90; Lehmann, *Luftpatrouille*, p. 320; Kleinheins, *LZ120*, pp. 64–72; Emilio Herrera, *Flying. The Memoirs of a Spanish Aeronaut*, Elizabeth Ladd trans. (Albuquerque, NM: Univ. New Mexico Press, 1984), pp. 181–2.
13. Zeppelin Museum Archiv, Friedrichshafen. No. 04 0021, 11 Feb. 1920.
14. Interview of Richard K. Smith with William C. Young (Goodyear Corporation), 21 June 1959. Smith Notes, author's file. See also Meyer, *Airshipmen*, pp. 140–5.
15. Ibid., pp. 63–4.
16. Data from Knäusel, *Zeppelin*, pp. 189–203; interview with Captain Hans von Schiller, 7–8 July 1973. In addition, L37 was dismantled and shipped to Japan, but was never reassembled there.
17. Higham, *British Rigid Airship*, pp. 12–74, 83–108; Hartcup, *Airship*, pp. 85–91; Arthur J. Marder, *From the Dreadnought to Scapa Flow ... I. The Road to War, 1904–1914* (London: Oxford Univ. Press, 1961), pp. 336–41.
18. Higham, *British Rigid Airship*, pp. 74–82, 124–72; Hartcup, *Airship*, pp. 110–15; Geoffrey Chamberlain, *Airships – Cardington* (Lavenham, Suffolk: Terence Dalton, 1984), pp. 1–23, 42–72. Most recent is E. A. Johnston, *Airship Navigator: One Man's Part in the British Airship Tragedy, 1916–1930* (Stroud: Skyline Publishing, 1994). On non-rigids see Higham, *British Rigid Airship*, pp. 109–23 and George Meager, *My Airship Flights, 1915–1930* (London: William Kimber, 1970), pp. 11–123.
19. Quoted in Richard Hough, *Edward and Alexandra* (New York: St. Martin's Press, 1993), p. 335.
20. For technical details of British airships in this era see Peter W. Brooks, *Rigid Airships, 1893–1940* (Washington, DC: Smithsonian Institution Press, 1992), pp. 110–37.
21. Higham, *British Rigid Airship*, pp. 83–108; C. G. Grey, *A History of the Air Ministry* (London: Allen & Unwin, 1940), passim; H. Montgomery Hyde, *British Air Policy Between the Wars, 1918–1939* (London: Heinemann, 1976), pp. 59–89, 160–3.
22. For a very full discussion of the labyrinths in which these arguments occurred, see Higham, *British Rigid Airship*, pp. 149–72.
23. Again for great and fruitless detail see ibid., pp. 173–82; Hartcup, *Airship*, pp. 133–5; Chamberlain, *Cardington*, pp. 96–108; Robinson, *Giants*, pp. 162–4.
24. Higham, *British Rigid Airship*, pp. 175–80.
25. Ibid., pp. 179–80; Hartcup, *Airship*, p. 139.
26. *New York Times*, 7 July 1919, p. 12.
27. Higham, *British Rigid Airship*, pp. 182–8; Robinson, *Giants*, pp. 164–6; Samuel T. Moore, 'The Uneasy Visit of R34', *New Yorker*, 13 July 1957, pp. 62–70.
28. The feats and trials of British airshipmen are chronicled in Hartcup, *Airship*, pp. 143–7; Chamberlain, *Cardington*, pp. 83–95; and Robinson, *Giants*, pp. 166–9. Interview with Admiral Charles E. Rosendahl, 8 Aug. 1974.
29. The further labyrinths of government arguments and decisions about commercial airships are chronicled in Higham, *British Rigid Airship*, pp. 188–98. See H. B. Pratt, *Commercial Airships* (London: Thomas Nelson, 1920); George

Whale, *British Airships Past, Present, & Future* (London: John Lane, 1919), focuses on the past of British non-rigids and rigids, with just a few, highly optimistic, considerations of rigid airships in Britain's future. On the role of Vickers of Barrow, a major wartime airship constructor and advocate of its postwar commercial projects, see J. E. Morpurgo, *Barnes Wallis* (London: Longman, 1972), pp. 84–8.

30. Higham, *British Rigid Airship*, p. 213.
31. Suggestive here is the detailed analysis of psychological influences and stresses among groups making highly controversial or politically significant decisions, as discussed in Irving L. Janis, *Groupthink. Psychological Studies of Policy Decisions and Fiascoes*, 2nd rev. edn (Boston: Houghton Mifflin, 1983), pp. 7–13, 174–7, and Figure 10-1 on Theoretical Analysis of Groupthink – all of which relate to foreign policy decision-making, but might well serve better to understand group-engineering controversies and decisions.
32. On the saga of R38 see Higham, *British Rigid Airship*, pp. 203–29 and for the Americans, Douglas H. Robinson and Charles L. Keller, *'Up Ship'! U.S. Navy Rigid Airships, 1919–1935* (Annapolis, MD: Naval Institute Press, 1982), pp. 17–39.
33. C. P. Burgess, J. C. Hunsaker and S. Truscott, 'The Strength of Rigid Airships', *Journal of the Royal Aeronautical Society*, XXVII (1924), 422.
34. Hartcup, *Airship*, p. 148; Higham, *British Rigid Airship*, pp. 225–9.
35. Robinson, *Giants*, pp. 180–1.
36. Walter Wellman, 'Will the Americans Fly to the North Pole?' *McClure's*, 29 July 1907, pp. 229–45. Other articles appeared in the *Scientific American, Review of Reviews, World Today*, and *Living Age*.
37. Walter Wellman, 'A Thousand Miles by Airship over the Atlantic', *Hampton's* [magazine], Dec. 1910, pp. 733–45. Similar articles appeared in other periodicals like those cited above. Indicative of airship interest in America: *Reader's Guide to Periodical Literature*, vol. 2 (1905–09) had over eighty entries on airships, one-third about Count Zeppelin.
38. Melvin Vaniman, 'The Vaniman-Seiberling Transatlantic Expedition', *Scientific American*, vol. 105, 21 Oct. 1911, pp. 366–7. See further, ibid, vol. 107, 13 July 1912, pp. 22, 28–9. Volume 3 of the *Reader's Guide* (1910–14) carried another eighty entries on airships, three-fourths being rigid dirigibles and with major focus on Germany.
39. Lee Payne, *Lighter than Air. An Illustrated History of the Airship*, rev. edn (New York: Orion Books, 1991), pp. 39–50. Hugh Allen, *The House of Goodyear* (Cleveland, OH: Cordat & Gross, 1923), pp. 168–71.
40. Smith, *Airships*, pp. xix–xxii.
41. Interviews with Captain Garland Fulton, Bala Cynwyd, PA, 5–10 Aug. 1974. Basic is Jerome C. Hunsaker, MS The History of Naval Aviation, vol. VI. The Development of Naval Aircraft, Rigid Airships. Notes, pp. 1–11 (author's file). See also Robinson and Keller, *'Up Ship'!*, pp. 1–12; Archibald D. Turnbull and Clifford L. Lord, *History of United States Naval Aviation* (New Haven, CT: Yale University Press, 1949), pp. 80–120; Clark G. Reynolds, *Admiral John H. Towers. The Struggle for Naval Air Supremacy* (Annapolis, MD: Naval Institute Press, 1991), pp. 98–116; Robert G. Albion, *Makers of Naval Policy, 1798–1947* (Annapolis, MD: Naval Institute Press, 1980), pp. 364–75; excellent chronological commentary in R. W. King, ed., *Naval Engineering*

and American Sea Power (Baltimore MD: Nautical and Aviation Publishing Company of America, 1989), pp. 416–25.

42. In March 1919, Hunsaker happened to find Mitchell a fellow voyager on his return to America. Their shipboard conversations yielded an early warning signal for the Navy Department. See William E. Trimble, *Admiral William A. Moffett. Architect of Naval Aviation* (Washington, DC: Smithsonian Institution Press, 1993), p. 68. Alfred F. Hurley, *Billy Mitchell. Crusader for Air Power* (New York: Franklin Watts, 1964), passim. Robinson and Keller, *'Up Ship'!*, pp. 116–19.

43. The futuristic picture of a zeppelin raid on Washington appeared in early 1917 in widely-read *Life* magazine. See John A. Durant, ed., *Predictions. Pictorial Predictions from the Past* (New York: A. S. Barnes, 1956), p. 113. Data on the Hensley negotiations are derived from Smith Notes, author's file, on documentation in the National Archives, covering the period from 1 Aug. 1919 to 29 Sept. 1920, Record Group 18, boxes 1053 and 23, File 452.4. Robinson and Keller, *'Up Ship'!*, pp. 117–19. Quotation from 'The Airship 1904–1976', in Eugene M. Emme, ed., *Two Hundred Years of Flight in America*. AAS History Series, vol. I (San Diego, CA: Univelt, 1977).

44. Robinson and Keller, *'Up Ship'!*, p. 118.

45. Robert L. O'Connell, *Sacred Vessels. The Cult of the Battleship and the Rise of the U.S. Navy* (Boulder, CO: Westview Press, 1991), passim. Edward L. Beach, *The United States Navy: 200 Years* (New York: Henry Holt, 1986), pp. 420–48. Higham, *British Rigid Airship*, 'The Impact of Jutland and L33', pp. 149–72.

46. O'Connell, *Sacred Vessels*, p. 300.

47. The basic work here is Edward S. Miller, *War Plan Orange. The U.S. Strategy to Defeat Japan, 1897–1945* (Annapolis, MD: Naval Institute Press, 1991). Also Philip T. Rosen, 'The Treaty Navy, 1919–1937', in Kenneth J. Hagan, ed., *Interpretations of American Naval History, 1775–1984*, 2nd edn (Westport, CT: Greenwood Press, 1984), pp. 230–6.

48. Robinson and Keller, *'Up Ship'!*, pp. 7–16; Beach, *United States Navy*, passim; Albion, *Makers of Naval Policy*, passim; Richard C. Knott, *The American Flying Boat* (Annapolis, MD: Naval Institute Press, 1979), passim; Charles M. Melhorn, *Two-Block Fox. The Rise of the Aircraft Carrier, 1911–1929* (Annapolis, MD: Naval Institute Press, 1974), pp. 6–38.

49. On Moffett in general see Edward Arpee, *From Frigates to Flattops* (Chicago, IL: privately published, 1953) and the more recent and authoritative biography by William E. Trimble, cited above.

50. For American political institutions and processes between the wars see Ellis W. Hawley, *The Great War and the Search for a Modern Order. A History of the American People and their Institutions, 1917–1933* (New York: St. Martin's Press, 1979) and Robert K. Murray, *The Practice of Normalcy. Governmental Theory and Practise in the Harding-Coolidge Era* (New York: W. W. Norton, 1973).

51. Fundamental to an understanding of the US Navy in American politics is the superb study of Vincent Davis, *The Admirals Lobby* (Chapel Hill, NC: Univ. of North Carolina Press, 1967), of which pp. 3–156 cover the era from 1918 to 1941. Robinson and Keller, *'Up Ship'!*, pp. 10–12. On Moffett's political sagacity see Trimble, *Moffett*, pp. 4–9.

52. Robinson and Keller, '*Up Ship*'!, pp. 17–49; Higham, *British Rigid Airship*, pp. 203–29.
53. Robinson and Keller, '*Up Ship*'!, pp. 50–9.
54. Robert W. Love, Jr., *History of the U.S. Navy, 1775–1941* (Harrisburg, PA: Stackpole Books, 1991), pp. 538–9. Also General Mitchell's bestseller, *Our Air Force* (New York: E. P. Dutton, 1921), passim.
55. See Harry Vissering, *Zeppelin. the Story of a Great Achievement*. Chicago: priv. publ., 1922.
56. Quoted in Frank Friedel, *Franklin D. Roosevelt*. vol. 2: *The Ordeal* (Boston: Little, Brown, 1954), p. 149. James Roosevelt later commented on FDR's investments: 'Father and Louis Howe lost money in all sorts of schemes to make a fast million in bonds, oil wells, shipping, lobsters, almost anything you can think of.' *My Parents: A Differing View* (London: W. H. Allen, 1977), p. 123.
57. Meyer, *Airshipmen*, pp. 64–7; Smith Notes, author's file: notes on interviews with Vissering associates and notes from studies at the Franklin D. Roosevelt Library, Hyde Park, NY, Gr-14 Hardesty file and Gr-14 (AIC). Also Frederick S. Hardesty, *Key to the Development of the Super-Airship, Schütte-Lanz, Mannheim-Rheinau, Germany, 1909–1930*. New York: priv. publ., 1930.

Chapter 3: Zeppelin Reborn in America, 1922–24

1. Monthly reports of Zeppelin Company activities, Jan. 1922 to Sept. 1924, Zeppelin Museum Archiv, Friedrichshafen. Also Robinson and Keller, '*Up Ship*'!, pp. 118–19.
2. See Nielsen, *Eckener*, pp. 136–40, for a likely exaggerated account given by Eckener just before his death in 1954. On Eckener vs. Colsman see Meyer, *Airshipmen*, pp. 135–9. Eckener seldom, if ever, reported on events to Colsman's credit. Certainly their personalities clashed: two autocrats each seeking full control in their joined activity spheres, where Colsman tried to develop a modern, variegated consumer-oriented industry, while Eckener single-mindedly determined to realize the postwar commercial airship. Characteristic Eckener comments can be found in Italiaander, *Eckener*, pp. 177, 189, 201, 272–3. Heinz Steude gives Colsman his due in a recently published study, *Alfred Colsman, Generaldirektor und Mensch* (Friedrichshafen: priv. publ., 1993). For American views of the two men and their conflict, see Robinson and Keller, '*Up Ship*'!, pp. 119, 124–5.
3. For German glider enthusiasm the definitive English account is Fritzsche, *Nation of Fliers*, pp. 103–31.
4. Robinson and Keller, '*Up Ship*'!, pp. 120–36.
5. Letter, Garland Fulton to Jerome C. Hunsaker, 20 Oct. 1922. Fulton Papers. Naval Historical Center, Washington Navy Yard, Washington, DC.
6. On the 1921 contract with Spain see Zeppelin Museum Archiv, Friedrichshafen, Nr. 16/0466. Further in that archive is a 20-page folder of notes and clippings on these hopes and plans.
7. Morpurgo, *Wallis*, pp. 113–14. Note also the detailed report by Barnes Wallis of his visit to Friedrichshafen in late May 1923: Barnes Wallis Papers, Science Museum, London, File Correspondence 1918–24.

8. There is a thick folder of documents on the Spanish-Zeppelin matter at the Political Archive of the German Foreign Office. This file reflects the interminable and frustrating negotiations. By 1924 neither Madrid nor Seville (site for the proposed international air terminal) could produce the required funding, and by then Eckener was firmly focused on North American prospects – though the South American hope still lingered on.

9. Higham, *British Rigid Airship*, pp. 230–4, 243–7. Hartcup, *Airship*, pp. 17–1. For broader English aviation developments in Europe and overseas note Robin Higham, *Britain's Imperial Air Routes, 1918 to 1939* (Hamden, CT: Shoe String Press, 1960), passim.

10. See the laudatory biography of du Plessis written by his immediate older relative, a professor of French social history at a regional Catholic University: Jean du Plessis de Grenédan, *La Vie héroique de Jean du Plessis, Commandant du 'Dixmude', 1892–1923* (Paris: Plon-Nourrit, 1925). On his own work, consult Jean du Plessis de Grenédan, *Les grandes dirigeables dans la Paix et dans la Guerre*, 2 vols (Paris: Plon-Nourrit, 1925–6). Briefly see Robinson, *Giants*, pp. 344–9. Also Commandant de Brossart, *Lâchez tout!* (Paris, 1956) and *Icare* 46 (Été-automne, 1986), pp. 44–7. Some of du Plessis's essays of 1917 to 1922 are available in English translation; see F. D. Buckley and R. L. Buckley, Jean du Plessis de Grenédan, *The Rigid Airship in Peace and War* (privately printed, Moffett Field, CA, 1942). See also the important, most recent study of Nick le Neve Walmsley, *Dixmunde. The Airship and her Commander* ... (publ. for the Airship Heritage Trust, Hoveton St John, Norwich, 1999).

11. C. P. Burgess, J. C. Hunsaker and Starr Truscott, address quoted in Higham, *British Rigid Airship*, p. 226. The Germans were less charitable in their own assessment.

12. The best work on Thomson is Peter G. Masefield, *To Ride the Storm. The Story of Airship R101* (London: William Kimber, 1982). For other interpretations of Thomson's career see Higham, *British Rigid Airship*, pp. 251–9; Robinson, *Giants*, pp. 297, 305–14; Morpurgo, *Barnes Wallis*, pp. 169–83; and Meyer, *Airshipmen*, pp. 182–93.

13. Higham, *British Rigid Airship*, p. 258. On this period in general see Higham's more detailed analysis, ibid, pp. 246–59. Also note especially the searing technical attack of E. F. Spanner, *This Airship Business*, 1st edn (London: Williams & Northgate, 1927), especially 'Parliamentary Proceedings', pp. 315–61.

14. Robinson and Keller, '*Up Ship'!*, pp. 62–3. On helium in the British Empire see Higham, *British Rigid Airship*, pp. 374–6 and Barry Countryman, *Helium for Airships and Science. The Search in Canada, 1916–1936* (Toronto: priv. publ., 1992). German airshipmen were confounded by an insoluble dilemma. On the one hand, they were convinced they had learned how to operate safely with hydrogen; on the other, they designed the *Hindenburg* in the hope that the American export prohibition could be relaxed. Meyer, *Airshipmen*, pp. 201–14.

15. For a succinct general discussion of these issues see Love, *History of the U.S. Navy*, pp. 479–540.

16. *Current History*, June 1922, p. 413.

17. *New York Times*, 'Big Airship Line Planned for the U.S'., 10 Feb. 1923, p. 9;
    ibid, 12 Feb., p. 12.
18. *Literary Digest*, vol. 76 (24 March 1923), pp. 60–2.
19. For details of Schütte's failed enterprise in America, see Meyer, *Airshipmen*,
    pp. 63–77.
20. Record of meeting on 3 Nov. 1923 in Smith Notes, author's file, FDR
    Library, Hyde Park, NY, file Gr-14 (AIC) Min. of Mtgs.; Goodyear Archives,
    letter Vissering to Wilmer, 19 Nov. 1923, file 4. Aviation A 101A.
21. Various monthly reports, Zeppelin Company activities, Aug. 1922 to March
    1924, Zeppelin Museum Archiv, Friedrichshafen; various correspondence in
    Goodyear Archives, file 4. Aviation A-101 & A-122. Interviews: Richard K.
    Smith with Mrs Vissering, 4 July 1959 and with William C. Young of
    Goodyear Corporation, 21 June 1959. Smith Notes, author's file.
22. For scores of airship references see *Reader's Guide to Periodical Literature*, VI
    (1922–24), 23.
23. Details in Burke Davis, *The Billy Mitchell Affair* (New York: Random House,
    1957), pp. 151–7. About twenty years later, nineteen B-17 C/D and four
    Martin B-26 bombers, stranded at Midway en route to fallen Clark Field in
    the Philippines were pressed into service at the famous Battle of Midway.
    Here they flew fifty-five sorties against the oncoming Japanese Fleet and
    dropped nine tons of bombs on the invaders. They scored exactly one hit,
    slightly damaging a slow-moving oiler. *Proceedings of the U.S. Naval Institute*,
    Aug. 1995, p. 32.
24. Robinson and Keller, *'Up Ship'!*, pp. 71–82. For characteristic publicity see
    widely-read *Literary Digest*, 'Proposed Arctic Flight of "Shenandoah"' [with
    map], 29 Dec. 1923, pp. 12–13. Comments by Captain Ernst Lehmann to
    Goodyear president Paul W. Litchfield on Lehmann's visit to Washington,
    meeting major naval aeronautical men, 11–13 Jan. 1924. Goodyear
    Archives, 4. Aviation A-101. Note also Junius B. Ward, 'Seeing America from
    the "Shenandoah"', *National Geographic Magazine*, XLVII (1925), 1–47.
    Superb aerial photography and pictures of admiring crowds.
25. Robinson and Keller, *'Up Ship'!*, pp. 120–1.
26. Ibid., pp. 121–2.
27. Letter, Garland Fulton to Jerome C. Hunsaker, 22 July 1922. Fulton Papers.
    Naval Historical Center, Washington Navy Yard, Washington, DC.
28. Robinson and Keller, *'Up Ship'!*, pp. 122–38. Interviews with Captain
    Garland Fulton, Bala Cynwyd, PA, 5–10 Aug. 1974. Various correspondence
    of Fulton with Moffett and Hunsaker, 1922–4, Fulton Papers.
29. Fulton to Hunsaker, 14 March 1923. Fulton Papers.
30. Various communications to and from Fulton, Hunsaker, Moffett and others,
    together with copies of two personal letters of Major Frank M. Kennedy to
    General Patrick and Major Geiger, 22 July 1922 to 5 Aug. 1923. Fulton
    Papers. Robinson and Keller, *'Up Ship'!*, pp. 126–30. Burke, *Billy Mitchell
    Affair*, pp. 158–84.
31. A. Wittemann, *Die Amerikafahrt des Z. R. III* (Wiesbaden: Amsel-Verlag,
    1925), p. 98. See the meticulously detailed analysis of Eckener's and US
    naval propaganda in Zeising, 'Journalistische Vermarktung', pp. 131–66.
32. Correspondence of Lieutenant T. T. Patterson, USN with Garland Fulton,
    April-May 1924, Fulton Papers. Wittemann, *Z. R. III*, pp. 70–100. Robinson
    and Keller, *'Up Ship'!*, pp. 136–8.

33. *New York Times*, 16 Oct. 1924.
34. Eckener, *Im Zeppelin*, pp. 62–8.
35. Ibid., p. 404.
36. Robinson and Keller, *'Up Ship'!*, pp. 90–6, 140.
37. *New York Times*, 16 Oct. 1924.
38. Higham, *British Rigid Airship*, pp. 256–9.
39. In general see Hans G. Knäusel, *Zeppelin and the United States of America* (Friedrichshafen: Luftschiffbau Zeppelin, 1981).
40. On theoretical aspects note Leonard W. Doob, 'Perception and Propaganda', in *Propaganda: Its Psychology and Technique* (New York: Henry Holt, 1936), pp. 90–8.

Chapter 4: Airships in International Political Competition, 1924–28

1. Eckener, *Im Zeppelin*, pp. 82–94; Italiaander, *Eckener*, pp. 207–24; Meyer, *Airshipmen*, pp. 146–50; *New York Times*, 16 Oct. 1924.
2. Germany. Foreign Office. Politisches Archiv. Büro Reichsminister, 135/7. Akten betreffend Luftschiffahrt, I. Okt. 1923–Mai 1926. Sequence of telegrams from 14 Oct. 1924 to 12 Jan. 1925.
3. Meyer, *Airshipmen*, pp. 154–62; quotation from p. 161. On Aeroarctic in general see ibid., pp. 159–67 and Guillaume P. S. de Syon, The Socio-politics of Technology: The Zeppelin in Official and Popular Culture, 1900–1939. Diss. Boston University, 1994, pp. 56–118.
4. Meyer, *Airshipmen*, pp. 161–2.
5. Eckener, *Im Zeppelin*, p. 95.
6. German Minister at Prague to Berlin, 2 June 1925. Germany. Foreign Office. Politisches Archiv. II F-Luft 65/2.
7. Germany. Foreign Office. Politisches Archiv. Reichskanzlei, R 43 I, vol. 737, No. 5802.
8. Letter, Hugo Eckener to Hans Luther, 15 Aug. 1925. Ibid., No. 5907.
9. Letter to State President Bazille, 3 Aug. 1925. Württemberg Staatsarchiv, Staatsministerium No. 4636.
10. Hans Hildebrandt, ed., *Zeppelin-Denkmal für das deutsche Volk* (Stuttgart: Germania Verlag, 1925).
11. Telegram, Gustav Stresemann to Hugo Eckener, 24 Aug. 1925. Germany. Foreign Office. Politisches Archiv. IIF-Luft 65/2. Note Stresemann's precautionary tardiness in transmitting his congratulations – lest they be read at the jubilee!
12. Quoted in Morpurgo, *Wallis*, p. 122. On details of the Wallis design and patents see ibid., pp. 126–34.
13. See Wallis's adverse comment as quoted in Morpurgo, *Wallis*, p. 139. On details of the rivalry see ibid., pp. 137–43; also the one-sided text of N. S. Norway, *Slide Rule. The Autobiography of an Engineer* (New York: Morrow, 1959). These two works are subjects of controversy among specialists, some of whom consider Norway as motivated by a very personal antagonism and thus not altogether reliable witness and Morpurgo correspondingly biased. No such shadow darkens Barry Countryman's splendid study, *R100 in Canada* (Erin, Ont.: Boston Mills Press, 1982). Higham's *British Rigid Airship*

254 *Notes*

is the best source to put it all into a professional context. See also Hartcup, *Airship*, pp. 168–98.

14. Morpurgo, *Wallis*, pp. 143–50.
15. Higham, *British Rigid Airship*, pp. 260–7. Chamberlain, *Airships – Cardington*, pp. 111–22. London *Times*, 22 Aug. 1925.
16. Robinson and Keller, *'Up Ship'!*, pp. 97–104, 139–46.
17. Ibid., pp. 104 10. On the Dearborn mast and Henry Ford, see Meyer, *Airshipmen*, pp. 140–53.
18. As quoted in Robinson and Keller, *'Up Ship'!*, p. 110. Note also Gerald E. Wheeler, 'Mitchell, Moffett, and Air Power', *The Airpower Historian*, VIII (1961), 79–87.
19. Ibid., pp. 109–14; Davis, *Billy Mitchell Affair*, pp. 214–329.
20. Quoted in Robinson and Keller, *'Up Ship'!*, p. 114.
21. Ibid., pp. 111–15.
22. Alexander McKee, *Ice Crash* (New York: St. Martin's Press, 1979), pp. 21–44. Gertrude Nobile Stolp, *Bibliografia di Umberto Nobile* (Firenze: Leo S. Olschki Editore, 1984), pp. 89–93 on details of Nobile's airships.
23. On Mussolini, Italian fascism, and their political manipulation of technology, see Claudio G. Segré, *Italo Balbo. A Fascist Life* (Berkeley, CA: Univ. of California Press, 1987), pp. 174–266.
24. For a vivid and illustrated brief account see the text in Rick Archbold, *Hindenburg. An Illustrated History* [of all airships] (Toronto: Penguin Books Canada, 1994), pp. 74–8; McKee, *Ice Crash*, pp. 55–72; Umberto Nobile, *My Polar Flights* ... (London: Fredrick Muller, 1961), pp. 15–96; Umberto Nobile, *La verità in fondo al pozzo* (Milan: Arnoldo Mondadori, 1978), pp. 15–29.
25. See Benito Mussolini, 'L'imprese polare: il successo, il percorso, i resultati, Discorso al Senato il 18 maggio 1926', *Rivista Aeronautica*, 1926, Nr. 6, pp. 1–13; also McKee, *Ice Crash*, pp. 73–90.
26. Nobile, *Polar Flights*, pp. 99–111; McKee, *Ice Crash*, pp. 99–109; Nobile, *La verità*, pp. 30–52.
27. Nobile, *Polar Flights*, pp. 99–272; McKee, *Ice Crash*, pp. 93–306; Nobile, *La verità*, pp. 33–165.
28. Germany. Foreign Office. Politisches Archiv. Büro Reichsminister 173/4. RM 35 Luftfahrtwesen. 14 May 1926, Reich Transport Ministry to State Secretary Reichskanzlei, Pariser Luftfahrtverhandlungen, pp. 235–42. Württemberg Staatsarchiv, Stuttgart. Memo from Württemberg Ministry of Labour and Nutrition to Minister of State with draft of text from German Ministry of Transport on Supplementary Regulations on Execution of Arts. 177, 178 and 198 of Versailles Treaty [for new regulations on German commercial aviation] No. B.3225, 1 June 1926. Note how carefully language of these texts explains only supplementary regulations for carrying out Versailles Treaty provisions and *not* for any change thereof! Memoirs of Heinz M. Wronsky, 15 Jahre Luftfahrt, typescript, author's copy, pp. 5–18.
29. In the mid-1960s Claude Dornier wrote an intimate memoir of a hundred pages or so about his life and technological career. It was printed and distributed in a very restricted edition to his family and a chosen few professional intimates, wherein he recorded the event of 1925 that provided the funding for his Do-X project. The text is reproduced in Peter Pletschacher, *Grossflugschiff Dornier Do-X* (Oberhaching: Aviatik Verlag, 1997), pp. 11–13.

On German secret rearmament in Russia see R. H. Haigh et al., *German-Soviet Relations in the Weimar Era* (Totowa, NJ: Barnes & Noble, 1984) and Yuri Dyakov and Tatyana Bushuyeva, *The Red Army and the Wehrmacht. How the Soviets Militarized Germany, 1922–33* (Amherst, NY: Prometheus Books, 1995). Note Edward L. Homze, *Arming the Luftwaffe ... 1919–39* (Lincoln, NB: Univ. Nebraska Press, 1976), pp. 39, 65.

30. For lively details of conducting the *Spende* see Italiaander, *Ein Deutscher*, pp. 230–46. On the Scherl–Hugenberg connection and other intimate aspects see Nielsen, *Eckener* [German edn], pp. 315–34. For Tucholsky see G. Knüsel, 'Zeppeline und Zeppelinismus', *Magazin Trans. Luft und Raumfahrt* [East Berlin], I (1989), 93–4.

31. Dozens of documents from the Weimar archives attest to concerned argumentation among government departments and to measures for restricting collection activities of the *Spende*. See Germany. Bundesarchiv Koblenz. Reichskanzlei, R 43 1, vol. 737.

32. Meyer, *Airshipmen*, pp. 130–5.

33. *Gaceta de Madrid*, 15 Feb. 1927. Royal Decree authorizing the Company Colon to establish a line of airships between Seville and Buenos Aires. Nr. 46, pp. 972–6.

34. Argentina. Presidential Decree authorizing establishment of airmail service between Buenos Aires and Seville. 10 Oct. 1928. Translation in British Secretary for Foreign Affairs. AVIA 2/355. Also: Germany. Foreign Ministry. Politisches Archiv. Report of German Embassy at Rio de Janeiro, Nr. 3260/27, Aug. 16, 1927.

35. De Syon, Sociopolitics, pp. 89–119.

36. Meyer, *Airshipmen*, pp. 136–8.

37. Interview with Ernst N. Shaffer, Bonn-Röttgen, 20 July 1974. Shaffer had then indicated to Eckener that he would not use this part of the interview for his news story of 1928.

38. Hartcup, *Airship*, pp. 171, 176–9. Morpurgo, *Wallis*, pp. 138–44. Chamberlain, *Airships – Cardington*, pp. 111–15.

39. Higham, *British Rigid Airship*, pp. 267–8.

40. See David Beaty, *The Water Jump. The Story of Transatlantic Flight* (New York: Harper & Row, 1976), p. 110.

41. Ibid., pp. 268–70. British Air Ministry, *An Approach to a System of Imperial Air Communications* (London, 1926). Chamberlain, *Airships – Cardington*, pp. 122–3.

42. Higham, *British Rigid Airship*, pp. 270–2. E. F. Spanner, *This Airship Business* (London: Williams & Norgate, 1926). His subsequent works are listed in Higham, pp. 413–14.

43. C. B. Thomson, *Air Facts and Problems* (London: John Murray, 1927), pp. 14–15, 123–4.

44. Higham, *British Rigid Airship*, pp. 273–5. Barry Countryman, *R100 in Canada* (Toronto: Boston Mills Press, 1982), pp. 21–7.

45. Burney Proposal to Trippe, 3 April 1928, pp. 8–9. Copy of document from PAA archives, in author's file.

46. Robinson and Keller, *'Up Ship'!*, pp. 148, 228.

47. Higham, *British Rigid Airship*, pp. 274–7; Morpurgo, *Wallis*, pp. 150–2; Chamberlain, *Airship – Cardington*, pp. 111–25; Hartcup, *Airship*,

pp. 185–90; see his entire ch. 7 for a lucid presentation of the myriad engineering and construction problems of building all the German, British, and American airships between the wars.
48. Robinson & Keller, *'Up Ship'!*, pp. 139–62.
49. Love, *History US Navy*, pp. 543–9.
50. Smith, *Airships*, pp. 5–18.
51. Comment reported by F. W. von Meister to author, Peapack, NJ, 3 Aug. 1974. See Hugh Allen, *The Story of the Airship*, 7th edn (Akron, OH: Goodyear Tire & Rubber Company, 1931), pp. 49–51. Note Clifford W. Seibel, *Helium: Child of the Sun* (Lawrence, KS: Univ. Press of Kansas, 1969).
52. Detailed interview of Richard K. Smith with William C. Young, 21 June 1959. Smith Notes, author's files.
53. Smith, *Airships*, pp. 16–17.

Chapter 5: International Airship Hubris and Adversity, 1928–30

1. Ernst A. Lehmann, *Auf Luftpatrouille und Weltfahrt* (Berlin: Wegweiser Verlag, 1936), pp. 251–9. English version of this study is E. A. Lehmann and L. Adelt, *Zeppelin. The Story of Lighter-than-Air Craft* (London and New York: Longmans Green, 1937). On the trial flights see *Berliner Tagblatt*, 3–4 Oct. 1928 and Eckener, *Im Zeppelin*, pp. 110–13.
2. Ludwig Dettmann, *Mit dem Zeppelin nach Amerika. Das Wunder von Himmel und Ozean* (Berlin: Hobbing, 1929).
3. Details of the flight are vividly recounted in the *New York Times*, 14–18 Oct. 1928. For an intimate German account see Hugo Eckener, *Die Amerikafahrt des 'Graf Zeppelin'* (Berlin: Verlag August Scherl, 1928). A standard American study is J. Gordon Vaeth, *Graf Zeppelin. The Adventures of an Aerial Globetrotter* (New York: Harper, 1958).
4. *Der Angriff* [Berlin] 22 Oct. 1928. Also Anne Morrow Lindbergh, *Bring Me a Unicorn. Diaries and Letters, 1922–1928* (New York: Harcourt, Brace, Jovanovic, 1971), p. 191; *Literary Digest*, 27 Oct. 1928, pp. 13–15; London *Times*, editorial, 16 Oct. 1928.
5. For Brandenburg's career see David Irving, *The Rise and Fall of the Luftwaffe* (London: Weidenfeld & Nicolson, 1973), pp. 16–19, and Raymond H. Freydette, *The Sky is on Fire* (New York: Holt, Rinehart & Winston, 1966), pp. 236–39.
6. On Eckener's international fame see Italiaander, *Ein Deutscher*, p. 262–7.
7. Eckener to Württemberg State Ministry, 14 Nov. 1928. Hauptstaatsarchiv Württemberg. Stuttgart. No. 3399/28, F2/1.
8. As quoted in Neilsen, *Eckener*, p. 356. In general see Eckener, *Im Zeppelin*, pp. 177–206; Fred F. Blau and Cyril Deighton, *Die Orientfahrt, die Aegyptenfahrt des LZ 127 'Graf Zeppelin'* (Lorch, Württ.: German Philatelic Society, 1980).
9. Quotation by Alan McGregor in *Aramco World*, July-Aug. 1994, p. 8. See also John Duggan, 'The Orient Flight of the Graf Zeppelin. Britain Opposes Trip of Zeppelin to Egypt', *Zeppelin Study Group Newsletter*, XI (1996), No. 41, pp. 13–17.

10. Commentary on this failed flight is totally missing in Eckener's memoir of Zeppelin successes; see Vaeth, *Graf Zeppelin*, pp. 70–81. Captain Hans von Schiller is both detailed in his account and grateful for French aid at Cuers. See his *Zeppelin. Wegbereiter des Weltluftverkehrs* (Bad Godesberg: Kirschbaum Verlag, 1967), pp. 88–90. Quotation from Friedrich von Rabenau, *Seeckt. Aus seinem Leben, 1918–1936* (Leipzig, 1940), p. 644.

11. Eckener, *Im Zeppelin*, pp. 221–5. Details about these matters and all the journalistic activities of Hearst are found in the voluminous Carl von Wiegand Papers in the archives of the Hoover Institution, Stanford, California. On postal financing see Henry Cord Meyer, 'How Philatelists kept the Zeppelins Flying', *American Philatelist*, Sept. 1979, pp. 796–8.

12. Accounts of the global flight abound in Eckener, *Im Zeppelin*, pp. 221–81; Lehmann, *Auf Patrouille*, pp. 282–90; Vaeth, *Graf Zeppelin*, pp. 82–108; and in Charles E. Rosendahl, *'Up Ship'!* (New York: Dodd, Mead, 1931). Note also Max Geisenheyner, *Mit 'Graf Zeppelin' um die Welt* (Frankfurt, a. M.: Societätsdruckerei, 1929), p. 65 for quotation.

13. Hans G. Knäusel, *Zeppelin and the United States of America* (Friedrichshafen: Zeppelin Druckerei, 1981) and Rolf Italiaander, *Hugo Eckener. Ein Moderner Columbus* (Konstanz: Fr. Stadler, 1979).

14. On Schütte see Thor Nielsen, *The Zeppelin Story* (London: Allan Wingate, 1955), pp. 182–4. For Russia and Japan, note Eckener, *Im Zeppelin*, pp. 234–5, 250–9. On America and the global flight see Paul Ditzel, 'The Day Los Angeles Had Zeppelin Fever', *Westways*, vol. 61 (March 1969), pp. 2–5 and (April) pp. 24–6.

15. For text see Walter Zechlin, *Pressechef bei Ebert, Hindenburg und Kopf. Erlebnisse eines Pressechefs und Diplomaten* (Hanover: Schuhuter, 1956), p. 101.

16. On Akron as a new industrial city see Meyer, *Airshipmen*, pp. 93–5. Maurice Holland has a full portrait of Hunsaker in his *Architects of Aviation* (New York: Duell, Sloan & Pierce, 1951), pp. 7–25, no doubt to be superseded by William F. Trimble's full biography of Hunsaker, soon to be published: *Engineering the Air. A Biography of Jerome C. Hunsaker.* The city of Akron and Goodyear-Zeppelin also appear favourably in Smith, *Airships*, pp. 31–3. On the Goodyear Airdock see Norman Beasley, *Men Working. A Story of the Goodyear Tire and Rubber Company* (New York: Harper & Bros., 1931), pp. 269–72.

17. Charles E. Melhorn, *Two-block Fox. The Rise of the Aircraft Carrier, 1911–1929* (Annapolis, MD: Naval Institute Press, 1974), pp. 105–15; Trimble, *Moffett*, pp. 200–29.

18. Robinson and Keller, *'Up Ship'!*, pp. 162–66. *New York Times*, 10 May 1929. R. K. Smith's detailed record of a long interview with Goodyear executive William C. Young on 21 June 1959 illuminates these unpublicized manoeuvres to gain support of newly elected Hoover and maintain the favourable Republican support for Goodyear specifically and airships in general. Smith Notes, author's files.

19. Smith, *Airships*, pp. 31–3; Hugh Allen, *The Story of the Airship* (Akron, OH: Goodyear, 1931), pp. 21–31, 63–4, 68–70.

20. London *Daily Express*, 24 May 1928.

21. London *Evening Standard*, 23 Aug. 1928.

22. In general on technology and politics of British airships in this period see Higham, *British Rigid Airship*, pp. 260–99. Also *Illustrated London News*, 9 March 1929, pp. 381–5.

23. MacDonald quotation in Stephen J. Lee, *Aspects of British Political History, 1914–1995* (London and New York: Routledge, 1996), p. 98. In general see T. O. Lloyd, *Empire to Welfare State. English History 1906–1967* (London: Oxford Univ. Press, 1970), pp. 146–61.

24. London *Daily Mail*, 25 Sept. 1929.

25. London *Times*, 14 Oct. 1929.

26. Charles Dennistoun Burney, *The World, the Air, and the Future* (London: Alfred A. Knopf, 1929), pp. 5, 21.

27. For an early study of pronounced revisionist German geopolitical emphasis see Richard Hennig, *Weltluftverkehr und Weltluftpolitik* (Berlin: Zentral-Verlag, 1930), notably pp. 29–31 on competition between airship and flying boat and pp. 35–42 on worldwide aviation as a stimulus to political irritation.

28. On Colsman-Eckener see Meyer, *Airshipmen*, pp. 135–9. For Eckener's political activities consult Italiaander, *Ein Deutscher*, passim, and particularly notations by Paul Löbe, *Der Weg war Lang. Lebenserinnerungen* (Berlin-Grunewald: Argni-Verlag, 1965), pp. 138–43. For Dornier's great flying-boat see the profusely illustrated and very one-sided account in Peter Pletschacher, *Grossflugschiff Dornier Do-X* (Oberhaching: Aviatic Verlag, 1997).

29. On LZ128 see *New York Times* interview with Dr Ludwig Dürr, 28 Sept. 1930, Sect. 1X, p. 6 and *Gasbag Journal*, No. 37 (Sept. 1998), pp. 23–4; 'Honors to Dr. Hugo Eckener', *National Geographic Magazine*, LVII (June 1930), pp. 653–89; Meyer, *American Philatelist*, Sept. 1979, pp. 796–98; *General-Anzeiger* [Bonn], 6 April 1930; on Cardington visit see John Duggan, *England Flights of the 'Graf Zeppelin'*, (Ickenham, Middx: Zeppelin Study Group, 1998) and Masefield, *Storm*, pp. 199–202.

30. Vaeth, *Graf Zeppelin*, pp. 138–54; Robert M. Levine, *Pernambuco in the Brazilian Federation, 1889–1937* (Stanford, CA: Stanford Univ. Press, 1978), pp. 21–47.

31. On France and Brazil see Jean Gérard Fleury, *La Ligne de Mermoz, Guillament, Saint Exupéry et de leurs compagnons de l'époppé* (Paris: Gallimard, 1939); William A. M. Burden, *The Struggle for Airways in Latin America* (New York: Council on Foreign Relations, 1943), pp. 16–17.

32. Eckener, *Im Zeppelin*, pp. 122–3.

33. Dyakov and Bushuyeva, *Red Army and the Wehrmacht*, pp. 97–100, show Soviets as still thinking of the Zeppelin Company as an inherent part of Germany's armaments production. Ambassador Jean Herbette to Foreign Minister A. Briand, 11 Sept. 1930. Ministère des Affairs Étrangères. Archives-Zeppelin, 1930, No. 459.

34. On Hunsaker visit see his report of 13 Oct. 1930, reprinted in *Gasbag Journal*, no. 37 (Sept. 1998), pp. 23–6.

35. For data on American airship kitsch and toys, we are indebted to Charles M. Jacobs for his unpublished study of the American cultural and artifact enthusiasm, entitled Pop Goes the Zeppelin! As regards the Empire State zeppelin mooring mast, it was a bold prosperity-era publicity stunt. Eckener

found it far too hazardous at 1200 feet above the ground even to consider its use. Only one American non-rigid ever tried to moor, though faked photographs exist of either the *Los Angeles* or *Graf Zeppelin* seemingly thus secured above the canyons of Manhattan.

36. For detailed information on Hunsaker and Goodyear in this era we are especially grateful for assistance from Prof. William F. Trimble's studies in his forthcoming biography of Hunsaker. For full details on IZT and PZT see R. Kalabash Wordsmith (pseud.), 'Notes on the International Zeppelin Transport Co. (IZT) and the Pacific Zeppelin Transport Co. (PZT)', *Bouyant Flight*, vol. 39, nos. 4 and 5 (May-Aug. 1992).

37. Ibid, and J. J. Quinn, 'Airships to Fly the Pacific', *Western Flying*, Jan. 1930, pp. 102–4, with illustration of plans for projected accommodations.

38. On Trippe and the Air Mail Act of 1925 see Marilyn Bender and Selig Altschul, *The Chosen Instrument. Pan Am and Juan Trippe. The Rise and Fall of an American Entrepreneur* (New York: Simon & Schuster, 1982), pp. 65–77, 96–122.

39. Trimble, Hunsaker, ch. 8; *New York Times*, 17, 22 April 1930.

40. Robinson and Keller, *'Up Ship'!*, pp. 166–8.

41. Smith, *Airships*, pp. 33–5; personal files of C. H. Schildhauer for Dornier Company of America, Schildhauer to Repr. Charles L. McNary, 17 April 1930; also text of telegram to McNary, 21 April 1930. Interview, H. C. Meyer with C. H. Schildhauer, Owings Mills, MD, 16 Sept. 1975.

42. London *Times*, 15 Oct. 1930; other detailed accounts on 13, 16, 29 Oct. 1929. For Thomson's address in the House of Lords, ibid, 22 Oct. 1929. On Thomson's emphases on the need of careful experimentation with the airships, see Masefield, *Storm*, pp. 189–211 passim.

43. Ibid, p. 212–34.

44. Ibid, p. 218–19.

45. As reported in ibid, p. 232.

46. Masefield, *Storm*, pp. 212–34.

47. Basic is the superb book of Barry J. Countryman, *R100 in Canada* (Erin, Ont.: Boston Mills Press, 1982). On the flight itself see Captain George Meager, *My Airship Flights, 1915–1930* (London: William Kimber, 1970), pp. 183–224; Norway, *Slide Rule*, pp. 105–21; and Hartcup, *Airship*, pp. 208–15. On French Canada see France, Ministère des Affairs Étrangères, Série Allemagne, Aviation, 1930–1, report of French Consul General at Montreal to Foreign Minister Briand, 9 Oct. 1930. On Burney and Bennett see London *Times*, 13 Aug. 1930. See also the positive account, 'The Homecoming of R100', in *Aeroplane*, 20 Aug. 1930, XXXIX (1930), 453–4.

48. Masefield, *Storm*, pp. 255–6; Higham, *Rigid Airship*, pp. 305–6. On the British Post Office, see letter to Sir Sefton Brancker, 28 April 1930: London Post Office Archives, Post 33 2161 XVII. Note interesting imaginary account of British Post Office stamp plans for the airship flights: Henry Cord Meyer, 'A Postal Historian's Daydream', *Zeppelin Study Group Newsletter*, vol. 12, no. 44 (Sept. 1997), pp. 3–5.

49. Masefield, *Storm*, pp. 276–96.

50. Masefield, *Storm*, pp. 283–4; PRO, Air 5, 984, 2914, Bullock to Dowding, 13 Sept. 1930, enclosure of draft minute for Thomson.

51. Basil Collier, *The Airship. A History* (London: 1974), pp. 199–200. Note his biography, *Leader of the Few … Lord Dowding* (London, Jarrolds, 1957), passim.
52. Masefield, *Storm*, pp. 329–402; Chamberlain, *Airships – Cardington*, pp. 146–60.
53. Ibid, pp. 163–5; London *Times*, 13 Oct. 1930.
54. See the careful reconstruction in Masefield, *Storm*, pp. 421–37 and Chamberlain, *Airships – Cardington*, pp. 164–78.
55. Atherstone quotation from Masefield, *Storm*, p. 351; letter to Bibescu, p. 286.
56. On a more positive view of interteam consultation, see Hartcup, *Airship*, p. 179; Norway, *Slide Rule*, pp. 128–9.
57. Ibid, p. 121.
58. American business consultant Edward B. Cochran wrote firmly about Thomson's failure in basic principles of management to cross-check the conclusions and advice of his technical people. See *Gasbag Journal*, no. 38 (Dec. 1998), pp. 24–5.
59. Morpurgo, *Wallis*, pp. 181–2.
60. On India see Martin Gilbert, *Winston S. Churchill*, vol. V, *1922–1939* (London: Heinemann, 1976), pp. 367–93. For declining fortunes of the British airship venture after Oct. 1930, see Masefield, *Storm*, pp. 526–39 and Chamberlain, *Airships – Cardington*, pp. 179–207.

Chapter 6: A Buffeting for German and American Airships, 1931–35

1. Airship Sub-committee, Aeronautical Research, No. AS 22 (strictly confidential). Eckener to the Air Ministry, 2 Jan. 1931. Barnes Wallis Papers. Science Museum. London. Also: Response of Royal Airship Works, Cardington, 27 Feb. 1931. PRO Air-5. 1042. 2784.
2. Alan McGregor, 'Contrary Winds. Zeppelins Over the Middle East', *Aramco World*, vol. 45, no. 4 (July-Aug. 1994), pp. 15–17. On this flight Mr Gossage of the Royal Airship Works, Cardington, accompanied Booth and reported an in-flight conference with Eckener about future Anglo-German cooperation in airship development, 12 April 1931.
3. Vienna *Neue Freie Presse*, 12 & 13 July 1931; Rudolf Beier, 'Zeppelintag in Wien', *Flug* [Vienna], no. 7–8, June-July 1931, pp. 15–17.
4. In general, note Vaeth, *Zeppelin*, pp. 109–23; Eckener, *Zeppelin*, pp. 353–98. For scientific details see L. Kohl-Larsen, *Die Arktisfahrt des 'Graf Zeppelin'* (Berlin: Union Deutsche Verlagsgesellschaft, 1931) and the illuminating interpretations of Arthur Koestler [Ullstein correspondent on the flight], *Arrow in the Blue* (New York: Macmillan, 1952), pp. 215–45.
5. Italiaander, *Ein Deutscher*, pp. 278–9; on the Do-X and its various fortunes, in great pictorial detail, see Pletschacher, *Grossflugschiff Dornier Do-X*, passim.
6. Jean Gérard Fleury, *La ligne de Mermoz, Guillaument, Saint Exupéry et de leurs compagnons de l'épopée* (Paris: Gallimard, 1939), p. 219.

7. For the Franco-German zeppelin relationship see Meyer, *Airshipmen*, pp. 168–81. Note also the more recently published *Szenen einer Hassliebe – Zeppelin & Frankreich* (Friedrichshafen: Zeppelin Museum, 1998).
8. On political details see Italiaander, *Ein Deutscher*, pp. 279–99. For Eckener's own story see *Im Zeppelin*, pp. 439–53.
9. Eckener, *Im Zeppelin*, pp. 339–44; Lehmann, *Auf Luftpatrouille*, pp. 329–32. Note 'Die erste Zeppelin-Schnitzeljagd', *ADAC-Motorwelt*, 6 July 1932, p. 6. For South American flight experiences see Albert Sonntag, *Mit Graf Zeppelin und Kondorflugzeugen. Europa–Brasilien!* (Bonn, 1932).
10. On the interaction of Russian Communist ideology with science and technology, see Kendall E. Bailes, *Technology and Society under Lenin and Stalin. Origins of the Soviet Technical Intelligentsia, 1917–1941* (Princeton, NJ: Princeton Univ. Press, 1978).
11. Ibid, pp. 381–406.
12. Umberto Nobile, *My Five Years With Soviet Airships*, Frances Fleetwood trans. (Akron, OH: Lighter-Than-Air Society, 1987).
13. Ibid, pp. 49–54.
14. Ibid, pp. 73–75, 100–40. For Soviet aviation in the Stalinist era see L. L. Kerber, *Stalin's Aviation Gulag. A Memoir of Andrei Tupolev and the Purge Era* (Washington, DC: Smithsonian Institution Press, 1996).
15. Full details of these flights are given in Robinson and Keller, *'Up Ship'!*, pp. 168–74. The *New York Times* discussion of 25 Feb. 1931 is fully presented in Edward Arpee, *From Frigates to Flat-tops* (Chicago: priv. publ., 1953), pp. 205–7. For contemporary evaluation of airships in naval service, see C. E. Rosendahl, *Up Ship!* (New York: Dodd, Mead, 1931), pp. 246–78. Note R. G. Mayers, 'Have Naval Airships a Future?', paper given to Los Angeles Chamber of Commerce in 1934, reprinted in *Gasbag Journal*, no. 36, June 1998, pp. 19–22. On politics of airships after 1945, see John McPhee, 'Profiles (The Aeron-1)', *New Yorker*, 10 Feb. 1973, p. 52.
16. Hartcup, *Airship*, p. 178; E. J. King and W. M. Whitehill, *Fleet Admiral King. A Naval Record* (New York: W. W. Norton, 1952), pp. 220–1. Interview with Vice Admiral C. E. Rosendahl, Flag Point on the River, NJ, 8 Aug. 1974. Interview with Vice Admiral Scott E. Peck, Chula Vista, CA, 7 May 1978.
17. Albion, *Makers of Naval Policy*, pp. 364–75; Melhorn, *Two-block Fox*, pp. 106–15. Generally also note Clark G. Reynolds, *The Fast Carriers* (New York: McGraw-Hill, 1968), pp. 14–21; Trumbull and Lord, *History of U.S. Naval Aviation*; Davis *Admirals Lobby*; and O'Connell, *Sacred Vessels*.
18. Miller, *War Plan Orange*, pp. 122–79; Alan R. Millett and Williamson Murray, eds., *Military Innovation in the Interwar Period* (New York: Cambridge Univ. Press, 1996), pp. 210–21, 399–401; Michael Vlahos, *The Blue Sword. The Naval War College and the American Mission, 1919–1941* (Newport, RI: Naval War College Press, 1980), passim; John B. Hattendorf, et al., *Sailors and Scholars, Centennial History of the U.S. Naval War College* (Newport RI: Naval War College Press, 1984).
19. Smith, *Airships*, pp. 35–7.
20. On trapeze and scouting see illustrations and analysis in Smith, *Airships*, pp. iii–vii, 109–12.
21. Ibid. pp. 37–92.

22. Trippe was elected to the board of PZT on 12 May 1931. He thus received PZT's Report of the Annual Meeting of Stockholders and Directors, 1 July 1931 and subsequent reports until PZT expired. Data from files of PanAm, once located in the New York PanAm Building.
23. Bender and Altschul, *Chosen Instrument*, pp. 91–203; R. E. G. Davies, *Airlines of the United States Since 1914* (London: Putnam, 1972), pp. 210–39; Beaty, *Water Jump*, pp. 90–3.
24. J. C. Hunsaker, Merchant Airship Legislation, 1931–32. Confidential Report for IZT-PZT files, dated July 1932. University of Akron Archives, LTA Society Akron files, Box 5, folder 4, pp. 1–3; quotation from p. 3.
25. Ibid, pp. 4–14; Smith, *Airships*, p. 95.
26. See Trimble, Hunsaker, ch. 8.
27. Hunsaker, Confidential Report for IZT-PZT files, Akron files, pp. 15–27; Smith, *Airships*, pp. 77–92.
28. F. A. Krummacher, ed., Josef Goebbels: Das Dritte Reich und seine Propaganda. Recording. Ariola-Athena Platte 70,566KW (Gütersloh, 1964). See also Ernst K. Bramsted, *Goebbels and Nazi Propaganda, 1925–45* (East Lansing, MI: Michigan State University Press, 1965).
29. Interview with Mr Max Schorn, Friedrichshafen, 10 July 1975. For full details of the Nazis at the Zeppelin Company see articles by Barbara Waibel and Wolfgang Glaeser in *Zirkel, Zangen und Cellon. Arbeit am Luftschiff* (Friedrichshafen: Verlag Robert Gessler, 1999), pp. 27–54, 81–95.
30. Karl-Heinz Ludwig, *Technik und Ingenieure im Dritten Reich* (Düsseldorf: Droste, 1974), pp. 411–17.
31. Eckener, *Im Zeppelin*, pp. 453–60, 96–8; Italiaander, *Ein Deutscher*, pp. 309–20.
32. Eckener, *Im Zeppelin*, pp. 340–4; von Schiller, *Zeppelin*, pp. 107–10.
33. Germany. Bundesarchiv Koblenz. R43II/697b, 'Aussenpolitische Nachrichtensammelstelle Sonderbericht', May 1934. Italiaander, *Ein Deutscher*, states that German archivists were unable to clarify at which level of the party or the government this issuing group may have functioned. See p. 319.
34. Meyer, *Airshipmen*, pp. 174–8.
35. France. Ministère des Affairs Étrangères. Série Allemagne: Graf Zeppelin, 1934–35, Air Attaché Poincaré, Berlin, to French Air Minister, 16 Jan. 1935. On comparable German airplane developments see Joachim Wachtel, *The History of Lufthansa* (Cologne: Lufthansa German Airlines, 1975), pp. 37–75.
36. Klaus Holländer, 'Zeppeline an der Saar: Faszination und Propaganda', in Jürgen Bleibler et al, *Zeppeline an der Saar* (Walsheim: Verlag Europa, 1998), pp. 5–24.
37. Smith, *Airships*, p. 97.
38. Ibid, pp. 107–9.
39. Meyer, *Airshipmen*, pp. 110–12; Wachtel, *Lufthansa*, pp. 39–42; Segré, *Balbo*, pp. 230–43.
40. Brian C. Bauer, 'Baby Zeppelin Stamp was a Political Hot Potato', *Stamp Collector* [Magazine], 15 May 1993, pp. 8 ff.
41. Vaeth, *Graf Zeppelin*, pp. 155–61.
42. Ibid, pp. 160–3. *Akron Beacon Journal*, 24–25 Oct. 1933; *New York Times*, 27 Oct. 1933; report of Chicago Consul Jaeger to Berlin, 31 Oct. 1933.

Germany. Foreign Office, Politisches Archiv, Botschaft Washington 15/195, Zeppelin 331/4; Eckener, *Im Zeppelin*, pp. 469–75. Carefully detailed is Cheryl Ganz, 'The *Graf Zeppelin* and the Swastika: Conflicting Symbols at the 1933 Chicago World's Fair', *Proceedings of the 1995 National Aerospace Conference*, pp. 56–66.

43. Robinson and Keller, *'Up Ship'!*, pp. 186–9.
44. For full details of this Goodyear association with the German zeppelin flights, see Harold G. Dick and Douglas H. Robinson, *The Golden Age of the Great Passenger Airships* Graf Zeppelin & Hindenburg (Washington, DC: Smithsonian Institution Press, 1985), pp. 48–78, 11–37. On Goodyear & Amtorg, Goodyear Archives, 4. Aviation A 101c, G. P. Braito [Amtorg] to Litchfield, 25 April 1934 and Hunsaker to Litchfield, 18 June 1934.
45. Robinson and Keller, *'Up Ship'!*, pp. 189–92.

Chapter 7: Airship Wonder Captured by Nazi Ideology, 1935–40

1. *Schriften zu Deutschlands Erneuerung, Nr. 41 a/b, Unsere Zeppelin-Luftschiffe* by Erich Beier-Lindhardt, Breslau [1935]; Felix Lützkendorf, *Zeppeline über York* (Berlin: Franz Schneich Verlag, [1939]); Georg Hacker, *Die Männer von Manzell. Erinnerungen des ersten Zeppelinkapitäns* (Frankfurt, 1936); KdF. *Jahres-Urlaubsprogramm*. Gau München, Oberbayern, 1935, p. 28; *Jugend und Heimat* ... Heft 9, Jahrg. 18, Sept. 1937, p. 124.
2. Dick and Robinson, *Golden Age*, pp. 83–110. On the late-March election flight see ibid, pp. 108–10; note Lehmann's rhapsodic account in *Auf Luftpatrouille*, pp. 360–76; Eckener, *Im Zeppelin*, pp. 490–5; on official pronouncements and fall-out from the Goebbels denunciation of Eckener see documentation in the Brammer, Sänger and Oberheitmann Collections, German Bundesarchiv, Koblenz.
3. Swiss Federal Archives, Bern, Folio E27, No. 23330.
4. Dick and Robinson, *Golden Age*, pp. 111–38; detailed reports from German Embassy at Rio and Washington at Germany. Foreign Office. Politisches Archiv, folders DZR-Südamerika 1936 and 1937, plus DZR-Nordamerika 1936; *New York Times*, 5–9 May 1936. On the Olympic propaganda see Zeising, 'Journalistische Vermarktung', pp. 171–80.
5. Lufthansa *History*, pp. 39–59; Higham, *Imperial Air Routes*, pp. 182–202; interview with John C. Leslie, Vice-President, PanAm, New York, 12 Sept. 1975; Bender and Altschul, *Chosen Instrument*, pp. 244–66. The best general account of the emerging airplane in transoceanic flight is Richard K. Smith, 'The Intercontinental Airliner and the Essence of Airplane Performance, 1929–1939', *Technology and Culture*, XXIV (1983), 428 ff.
6. Sitzung vom 20. November 1938 betreffend Luftschiffragen. Reichsminister der Luftfahrt, LB 1, 2 Nr. 6048/36, Confidential. To the Foreign Office, 14 Dec. 1936. Germany. Foreign Office. Politisches Archiv.
7. Letter, F. W. von Meister to Captain Lehmann, 18 Jan. 1937. Zeppelin Museum Archiv.
8. *New York Times*, 7 May 1937; Archbold, *Hindenburg*, pp. 141–204; AZT Staff Memorandum, American Commercial Airships, 1 Aug. 1937, from archive of F. W. von Meister.

9. Meyer, *Airshipmen*, p. 214; recollection of Nazi funereal manipulation by Robert Moser, 'Als die Weltgeschichte für einen Tag nach Winzeln kam', *Schwäbische Zeitung*, 3 May 1997.
10. For full detail on the entire brief history of LZ130 see Manfred Bauer and John Duggan, *LZ130 'Graf Zeppelin' and the End of Commercial Airship Travel* (Friedrichshafen: Zeppelin-Museum, 1996); as seen by a contemporary American, note Dick and Robinson, *Golden Age*, pp. 151–60.
11. Ibid, pp. 161–3. Harry Bruno's PR firm reaped handsome rewards during the 1930s publicizing the zeppelins in the United States. During World War II, however, he seemed to recall various nefarious spying activities of the zeppelins. See his chapter, 'Rubber Cows and the Crooked Cross', in his *Wings Over America* (New York: R. M. McBride, 1942), pp. 272–88.
12. On the German–American helium controversy see Bauer and Duggan, *LZ130*, pp. 81–7; *New York Times*, 15–20 April, 7–21 May 1938. The Focke-Wulf Condor flight is covered in the *New York Times*, 10–14 Aug. 1938.
13. Bauer and Duggan, *LZ130*, pp. 104–6; see also Albert Sammt, *Mein Leben für den Zeppelin* (Wahlwies: Verlag Pestalozzi Kinderdorf, 1981), pp. 156–70.
14. Bauer and Duggan, *LZ130*, pp. 106–60; Meyer, *Airshipmen*, pp. 218–27.
15. Full details of zeppelin visits and public reception in Bauer and Duggan, *LZ130*, pp. 106–63; Meyer, *Airshipmen*, pp. 245–6.
16. Bender and Altschul, *Chosen Instrument*, pp. 288–93.
17. Dick and Robinson, *Golden Age*, pp. 168–71.
18. Smith, *Airships*, pp. 163–70.
19. Translation of excerpts taken from authenticated typed copies of correspondence about the future of the airship and of the protocol of Goering's visit to the Frankfurt zeppelin base on 1 March 1940, as studied by Meyer in 1979 in the airship history files of Alfred F. Weber at Karlsruhe, Germany. For revised, more detailed later statement of data see Bauer and Duggan, *LZ130*, pp. 176–80.
20. Rosendahl's activities as consultant are outlined in his incredibly detailed reports to Knowles at Goodyear Aircraft, 1946–8, now held in the airship history collection at the University of Akron. No record remains of Goodyear's lobbying activities in Washington in the same period, except for a single propaganda piece, [Goodyear Aircraft Corporation], *America Must be First in the Air* [Akron, 1947?], 27 pp. also at the University of Akron airship history collection.

Conclusion

1. Hans G. Knäusel, *Sackgasse am Himmel. Anmerkungen Zur Luftschiffahrt damals und heute* (Bonn: Kirschbaum Verlag, 1988).

Suggested Further Reading

Althoff, William F. *Skyships – A History of the Airship in the US Navy*. Shrewsbury: Airlife Publishing, 1990. A capable British account of American airships.

Bauer, Manfred and Duggan, John. *LZ130 'Graf Zeppelin' and the End of Commercial Airship Travel*. Friedrichshafen: Zeppelin Museum, 1996. Superb, authoritative account with excellent illustrations.

Beaubois, Henry. *Airships: An Illustrated History*. M. and A. Kelly, trans. London: Macdonald and Jane's, 1974. A spectacularly beautiful work on every aspect of lighter-than-air craft. Authoritative.

Brooks, Peter W. *Zeppelin: Rigid Airships, 1893–1940*. Washington, DC: Smithsonian Institution Press, 1992. Superbly illustrated, highly factual and authoritative work by an author with lifelong research in airships.

Chamberlain, Geoffrey. *Airships-Cardington. A History of Cardington Airship Station and Its Role in World Airship Development*. Lavenham, Suffolk: Terence Dalton, 1984. A standard work profusely illustrated.

Collier, Basil. *The Airship: A History*. London: Hart-Davis McGibbon, 1974. Useful.

Countryman, Barry. *R100 in Canada*. Erin, Ont.: Boston Mills Press, 1982. Authoritative work on the building of R100 at Howden, together with full account of the airship trip to Canada in July 1930. Profusely illustrated.

Cuneo, John R. *Winged Mars. I. The German Air Weapon, 1870–1914*. Harrisburg, PA: Military Service Publ. Co., 1942. Written before publication of the authoritative German Luftwaffe study of 1943, but still very competent in light of sources then available.

Deighton, Len. *Airshipwreck*. London: Jonathan Cape, 1978. Informed commentary and spectacular photographs of airship smash-ups.

Dick, Harold G. and Robinson, Douglas H. *The Golden Age of the Great Passenger Airships GRAF ZEPPELIN & HINDENBURG*. Washington DC and London: Smithsonian Institution Press, 1985. Dick was Goodyear representative in Friedrichshafen in 1936–8; Robinson was dean of American airship historians. Together they make this the standard work on the subject. Many illustrations and expert technical drawings. Translated crew manual of the German Zeppelin Transport Company, 1935–40.

Eckener, Hugo. *Count Zeppelin: The Man and His Work*. London: Massie Publication Company, 1938. English translation by Leigh Farrell of Eckener's standard German biography of the zeppelin inventor. A scarce work difficult to find.

Eckener, Hugo. *My Zeppelins*. London: Putnam, 1958. Douglas H. Robinson's translation, somewhat abridged, of Eckener's German memoir of 1949 reviewing his life as an airshipman.

Hardesty, Frederick S. *Key to the Development of the Super-Airship, Schütte-Lanz, Mannheim-Rheinau, Germany, 1909–1930*. New York: priv. publ., 1930. A one-sided compilation of documents and data by Johann Schütte's American lawyer.

Hartcup, Guy. *The Achievement of the Airship: A History of the Development of Rigid, Semi-rigid, and Non-rigid Airships.* London: David & Charles, 1974. Scholarly, detailed, readable. Illustrations and diagrams. The best of all the general books from England.

Higham, Robin. *The British Rigid Airship, 1908–1931: A Study in Weapons Policy.* London: G. T. Foulis, 1961. Detailed, scholarly, authoritative.

Jackson, Robert. *Airships in Peace and War.* London: Cassell, 1971. Useful.

Johnson, E. A. *Airship Navigator: One Man's Part in the British Airship Tragedy 1919–1930.* Stroud: Skyline Publishing, 1994. A sensitive analysis of the personalities involved in the R100 and R101, revealing crew member criticisms of Lord Thomson.

Knäusel, Hans G. *Zeppelin and the United States of America: An Important Episode in German–American Relations.* Friedrichshafen: Luftschiffbau Zeppelin, 1981. Very readable, useful compilation of text, documents, and illustrations.

Leasor, James. *The Millionth Chance.* New York: Reynal, 1957. Journalistic exaggeration of British politics and technology concerning R101.

Lehmann, Ernst A. *Zeppelin.* London: Longmans & Green, 1937. J. Dratler trans. Dramatic overview of the author's life as an airshipman, though not always factually reliable.

Litchfield, Paul W. and Allen, Hugh. *Why Has America No Rigid Airships?* Cleveland, Ohio: Corday & Gross, 1945. The last effort of Goodyear to capitalize on its construction experience to resurrect the rigid airship as a viable transport competitor with the flying boat or airplane.

Masefield, Sir Peter G. *To Ride the Storm: The Story of Airship R101.* London: William Kimber, 1982. The standard work, nicely illustrated.

Meyer, Henry Cord. *Airshipmen, Businessmen, and Politics, 1890–1940.* Washington DC and London: Smithsonian Institution Press, 1991. Pioneering study of the interaction of politics and business with airship endeavour in the western world.

Meyer, Henry Cord. *Count Zeppelin. A Psychological Portrait.* Auckland, NZ: Lighter-than-Air Institute, 1998. An intimate study of the Count's struggles with German political and military opponents to achieve his goal of lighter-than-air flight.

Morpurgo, J. E. *Barnes Wallis: A Biography.* London: Longman, 1972. Readable account of Sir Barnes's entire life and work, based on family papers and on materials from the Vickers archives subsequently destroyed. Basic for R100. Some illustrations.

Morrow, John Howard, Jr. *Building German Airpower, 1909–1914.* Knoxville: University of Tennessee Press, 1976. Nicely illustrated, basic study derived from German sources.

Neilsen, Thor. *The Zeppelin Story: The Life of Hugo Eckener.* P. Chambers trans. London: Allen Wingate, 1955. Journalist interacting with aged Eckener's somewhat flawed memory.

Nobile, General Umberto. *My Polar Flights.* London: Frederick Muller, 1961. Frances Fleetwood, trans. Understandably defensive account of the Italian airshipman's efforts with semi-rigid airships in the Arctic.

Nobile, General Umberto. *My Five Years with Soviet Airships.* Akron: Lighter-than-Air Society, 1987. The only reliable non-Russian source of information about Stalin's effort to manipulate airship technology for Communist Russian propaganda. See also the nicely illustrated article on this theme by Clive Foss, 'Russia's Romance with the Airship', *History Today*, December 1997, pp. 10–16.

Norway, Nevil Shute. *Slide Rule: The Autobiography of an Engineer*. New York: Morrow, 1959. Colourful though occasionally unreliable account of this engineer-novelist's life up to 1939. With Morpurgo and Countryman, a good source on building of R100, with personal antipathy towards R101 and those associated with her.

Payne, Lee. *Lighter Than Air: An Illustrated History of the Airship*. Revised edition. New York: Orion Books, 1991. Carefully researched with many illustrations.

Robinson, Douglas H. *Giants in the Sky: A History of the Rigid Airship*. Seattle: University of Washington Press, 1973. The standard work on the subject by America's best rigid airship historian. Readable and well illustrated. Indispensable statistical tables.

Robinson, Douglas H. *LZ129 The Hindenburg: Famous Aircraft Series*. New York: Arco Publishing, 1964. Authoritative account, fully illustrated. Translation of Hugo Eckener's LZ120 *Bodensee* flight manual appended.

Robinson, Douglas H. *The Zeppelin in Combat: A History of the German Naval Airship Division, 1912–1918*. Henley-on-Thames: G. T. Foulis, 1971. The standard book.

Robinson, Douglas H., and Keller, Charles L. *'Up Ship!': US Navy Rigid Airships, 1919–1935*. Annapolis, MD: Naval Institute Press, 1982. Another standard work, fully illustrated.

Rosendahl, Charles E. *'Up Ship!'*. New York: Dodd, Mead, 1931. America's best known airshipman writes enthusiastically about his profession.

Rosendahl, Charles E. *What About the Airship? The Challenge to the United States*. New York: Charles Scribner's Sons, 1939. A fervent plea to revive the airship for defence and commerce in America.

Smith, Richard K. *The Airships Akron and Macon: Flying Aircraft Carriers of the US Navy*. Annapolis, MD: US Naval Institute, 1965. The standard work, fully illustrated.

Toland, John. *Ships in the Sky: The Story of the Great Dirigibles*. New York: Henry Holt, 1957. Reads like a novel. For the disaster buff. Inevitable inaccuracies.

Vaeth, J. Gordon. *Graf Zeppelin: The Adventures of an Aerial Globetrotter*. New York: Harper, 1958. Written with assistance by F. W. (Willy) von Meister. Interesting and reliable, with appealing travel illustrations.

Lord Ventry and Kolesnik, Eugene M. *Airship Saga: The History of the Airship Seen Through the Eyes of the Men Who Developed and Built Them*. Poole, Dorset: Blandford Press, 1982. Nice documentary and reprint collection by one of Britain's venerable men of lighter-than-air enthusiasm.

Vissering, Harry. *Zeppelin: The Story of a Great Achievement*. Chicago: priv. publ., 1922. Rare book by the man who initiated German–American airship cooperation.

Whale, George. *British Airships: Past Present and Future*. London: Bodley Head, 1919. Well-illustrated account by an informed layman.

Index